The Life and Lies of Harry Morris

Daniel Gardner

Clink Street

Published by Clink Street Publishing 2024

Copyright © 2024

First edition.

The author asserts the moral right under the Copyright, Designs and Patents Act 1988 to be identified as the author of this work.

All rights reserved. No part of this publication may be reproduced, stored in a retrieval system or transmitted, in any form or by any means without the prior consent of the author, nor be otherwise circulated in any form of binding or cover other than that with which it is published and without a similar condition being imposed on the subsequent purchaser.

ISBN:
978-1-915785-35-0 - paperback
978-1-915785-36-7 - ebook

For Harry's daughters:
Susan, Belinda and Anabel

Contents

Preface

On my mantelpiece I have a square mahogany-framed photograph of my grandfather, Harry Morris, taken in the late 1950s I would guess. It is a close-up, cut off at the knee, of him sitting in a rattan wicker chair in front of what looks like a conservatory at Rowena Court, a seaside hotel in Kent. The glass building is probably the hotel's Solarium, and the unknown photographer is standing on its lawn, the Tea Garden.

Harry had bought Rowena Court to occupy his wife Betty while he stayed in London to enjoy the perks associated with being a 'well-known night-spot proprietor' and 'friend of the famous'.[1] By this stage they had lived apart for over a decade but it is not surprising to me, given his entire life was built on charm and evasion, that the estrangement and his continuous philandering had proved no impediment to his relaxing in her garden.

The image is of a good-looking man in his prime: Brylcreemed steel-grey hair parted to one side, sun on his forehead, Ray-Ban Aviators obscuring his eyes. He is wearing flannel trousers and a short-sleeved shirt which is clearly hand-made as its breast pocket is monogrammed. His hand is extended in the photograph, his wrist adorned with an eye-catching Omega: the sort of watch that signals affluence.

The impresario may have been at rest but the firm set of his jaw is an indication of the fighting qualities he must have possessed to succeed in such a cutthroat business. Below his sunglasses he certainly has a fleshy boxer's nose; he has landed and taken a few punches in his career and it has not been without

---

1   22 October 1963, Obituary, *Evening News & Star.*

stress. It is a black-and-white photograph but one can almost see the nicotine-staining on the forefinger and middle finger of his left hand.

As I look a little closer at the familiar face, however, I cannot decide whether the slightly pursed lips are a sign of toughness or simply annoyance at something or someone off-camera. It could have been his eldest daughter, Susan, with whom he had a very brittle relationship. She was studying at the Central School of Speech and Drama at the time – a career choice he might have viewed as whimsical given his whole life was an act.

In fact there is more of a riddle to the shot than appears at first glance. The initials 'HM' on his shirt pocket stand for 'Harry Morris' but that was not the name he was born with. He was already 30 by the time he legally adopted it. Like one of those convicted felons who ask a court for previous offences to be taken into consideration, in his deed poll he promised to stop using not one but two previous aliases: Harry Vigoda and Harry Cohen. Not something the judge heard every day I imagine. It is fortunate for Harry that one doesn't have to plump for a single birth date in a deed poll as he had at least three of those as well.

I never had the opportunity to question Harry on this muta-bility as he died on 22nd March 1963, 17 days before I was born.

Nevertheless 'HM' was always a presence in my life because my mother nursed a metempsychotic belief that I was somehow his reincarnation. Harry's immortal soul, corporally imprisoned on its never-ending journey, had been released by his death only to be almost immediately trapped again in my body. In her eyes that explained the strong familial resemblance which she invoked at whim. (Looking at the photograph I have to admit she had a point.) She also saw the juxtaposition of our anniversaries as a sort of cosmic baton-passing of Harry's drive and business acu-men. His death while she was still a teenager had robbed her of the chance of a life of ease and comfort. I would restore the family fortunes. That shaped a lot of the decisions she made on my behalf as I was growing up and some of those I have taken for myself as an adult.

That should have been enough to spark a dialogue with her about her father. Yet whenever I questioned my normally well-organised mother about him and his family, her answers were sketchy. She knew he had three siblings – Rose, Anne and Ben – and that his father may have been called Moshe but she didn't know the name of his mother. She knew Harry had an aunt in New York called Fannie because she had stayed with her in the 1950s. When pushed, Mum could dredge up the first names of a couple of cousins – David and Michael – but suspected there were others.

I suppose a more assiduous family memoirist would have spotted that Harry was the hinge between two worlds and challenged her equivocation, but I didn't. Neither she nor her sisters ever volunteered much about him; we were all complicit in his gradual fading from view until two things combined to shake me out of my complacency. First, my mother died, and with her, any opportunity to enlarge the record of her reminiscences. Second, I required major surgery to remove an adrenal tumour. In the course of this brush with mortality I realised that I was already older than Harry was when he punted his soul. If now wasn't the right time to find out about my semi-mythical maternal grandfather, when would be?

A liar needs a good memory, it is often said; Harry fibbed so much that the collective memory was all but lost. He did not 'weave a tangled web', so much as leave no web at all. He permitted his conjugal family to fraternise with his Jewish birth family for a grand total of three times in 25 years. He separated the hemispheres of his life to such an extent that they were unable to communicate with each other once he had gone.

We lie when we intend to deceive by providing information we believe to be untrue. Does that cover the withholding of information? Absolutely, if the questioning is specific enough. I'm sure Harry justified his evasions with the age-old excuse that he was simply telling the rubes what they wanted to hear or, perhaps more accurately, not telling them what they did not want to hear. Whether they were customers, colleagues or his own children he reasoned they would always prefer his congenial flim-flam to tricky truth.

The trouble is that in doing so he treated his daughters as no more than a means to an end. Harry might have viewed his lying as venial and small-scale but how could they not feel manipulated and regarded as something less than fully human in the sense that they didn't deserve the truth? Much of what could have enriched their experience – a family tree with hundreds of people across the planet – was withheld from them. The rupture is made all the more inexplicable because Harry carried on seeing his parents and siblings long after he had airbrushed them from his children's history.

I started researching Harry's biography to understand why he was so keen to ensure the two halves of his life never intersected. I wanted to see if he had any moral justification for his dissembling. He lived through an era when it was disadvantageous, even physically dangerous to be marked as a Jew. Did he worry about the safety of his wife and daughters? Was that why he was so rigid in his compartmentalising?

If I am honest I also savoured the fact-finding because, like the rest of the world, I have always enjoyed rags-to-riches tales. These models of individualism and social mobility met my need to believe that the seemingly irreversible rise in wealth inequality can be defied, if only by exceptional characters. The lowlier the beginnings, the greater the striving for wealth or power, the bigger the appeal to me. Harry was just such a self-made man.

When I started working in the City of London in the Thatcherite '80s, 'barrow boy' was a sort of lazy slur we brokers would use to describe traders; in Harry's case the epithet was a precise description of his first job. How he overcame such humble beginnings made his journey compelling to me. Even more so because of the suspicion of amorality that accompanied his ascent. Harry often played host to both gangland players and establishment figures in his clubs in the 1950s.

Like that other master of self-presentation, Jay Gatsby, Harry had first become rich by flouting the law to sell overpriced booze to thirsty Americans – not, like Gatsby, during Prohibition but during the Second World War. Before the war Harry had built up a moderately successful chain of greengrocers in South London. He was living above one of his shops in Putney High Street. At the end of hostilities he could flaunt a nightclub in Knightsbridge, a flat in Park Lane and a Georgian country house for Betty and his three daughters, complete with nanny and cook. He had swapped his grocer's van for a Rolls-Bentley. Sadly, and similarly to the antihero of Fitzgerald's novel, he and others around him would pay a price for all this material success.

My challenge was how to unpick a life consciously built on misdirection and deceit, winkling out the truth embedded in the few stories that he deigned to share with his daughters over the years. By his nature Harry left more ellipses than evidence so this book could never have been one of those objective, God's-eye-view biographies. Nor could it ever be impersonal given my proximity to the subject. The choices he made in his life, particularly with regard to his daughters, have shaped mine so I make no apologies about the personal pronoun making a repeated appearance in the book.

On my mother's death I became the keeper of the family record. The bulk of the collection is made up of her photograph albums, barren in earlier years, and her diaries, mostly unfilled in recent vintages. The gap in the pictorial record is frustrating. One early album offers blanks where its images should be, just dozens of white adhesive corner mounts with nothing in between. It must have been raided by my grandmother before it came into my mother's possession and the photographs are now lost. There cannot be many sadder sights in family genealogy.

Mum's chain of diaries includes five black oblong Conrad leatherette pocketbooks, each a tangible link between Harry and Mum's lives since the diaries come 'with the compliments of the Colony Restaurant, Berkeley Square, Mayfair 1657'. This was the venue where Harry hosted royalty and the stars of stage and screen, where he befriended 'the famous'. It was always the 'Colony Restaurant', not the 'Colony Club' – there was already one of those graced by such habitués of the Soho demi-monde as Francis Bacon and Lucian Freud. Harry didn't ever want to be confused with them.

The legends on the diaries promise 'Star Cabaret Nightly, Lunch, Dinner, Supper, Dancing, two famous bands and open from 8.30pm to 2.30am', although quite when lunch was served in these opening hours is not made clear. They are small enough to go into a suit pocket or handbag. Mum must have liked the small size because she also had a sixth Conrad pocket diary for 1963, brown this time and unbranded. It has a poignancy of its own because it is a permanent reminder that Harry had ceded control of the club the year before.

Aside from the diaries and albums there is a little stash of ephemera including a copy of Harry's entry in the Marine Register of Deaths at Sea, his will and a newspaper obituary.

Amongst the monochrome array, the artefacts in colour stand out. One is a postcard sent by Harry to Mum: a view of a harbour on Tinos depicted in those hyperreal 1960s Kodachrome colours. There is a banal message on the reverse: *This is where I joined the yacht from Athens on Weds – the islands are most interesting and the yacht is very comfortable and I am relaxing and enjoying it – hope you and Barry are well. Love Daddy.* It is not dated but must have been sent in 1962. Another is a folded airmail lettercard with a picture of a ship, the *Caronia*, on the front. It was sent to Mum by Harry from Honolulu in February 1963.

The postcard, the lettercard and an airmail letter sent from Hong Kong on the same cruise are the only surviving examples of Harry's slanted, intermittently cursive script. Famously, Shakespeare's handwriting is known to posterity from only six legal documents. Well, at least as far as our family archive is concerned, he managed to do twice as well as Harry.

Looking more closely at the snaps in Mum's albums that highlight her father, one, probably from 1950, is an action shot taken on Westgate Promenade in Kent. Mum and her younger sister, Anabel, are holding Harry's hands as the three of them walk towards the photographer. Betty stands to one side. They are all somewhat misattired for the seaside – the children in school skirts, Betty in a fur and Harry in a Prince of Wales suit and tie. It is the only picture of Mum and Anabel actually touching Harry.

There is one of the pair of them together on the day of Mum's marriage to Barry Gardner but it features possibly the most uncomfortable-looking Father of the Bride ever. The obligatory picture of the newly-weds and their respective parents had to be taken on the road outside the church because a last-minute attack of religious superstition meant Harry refused to give his daughter away in an Anglican service.

If we are short of family portraits and letters, we are doubly short of family possessions. How improbable is it that our inventory amounts to just two Christmas tree ornaments: a glass drop-shaped bauble and a fairy. It is clear that a man with such avidity and greed for life once possessed much more. A flattering profile in the populist daily newspaper, the *Sketch*, on New Year's Eve 1958, described Harry as a 'racehorse owner and art-lover, his collection of paintings includes works by Simon Saint-Jean and Charles Spencelayh'. The entry in Mum's diary for Sunday 12th May 1963 reads: *Went up to the flat to get the books, records and glasses etc. Got Mum's silver. Got some fabulous records. Mort Sahl etc.* Where did they all go? Were they all discarded by my mother as part of the 1960s mania to repudiate the past?

I may be condemned to make my imaginative leap without physical artefacts but I do at least have the stage set for Harry's life. If he is the leading actor in this drama, the cruise ship he frequently travelled in – the *Caronia* – is the backdrop. Harry spent over a year of his life on board this ship and he died on it. Nearly half of the archive's pictures are souvenirs of him on various cruises taken by the ship's photographer. They show Harry posing in front of some hapless islanders, Harry with a flower lei around his neck, Harry in black tie wielding a gavel in Master of Ceremonies mode. The ones of Harry in Bermuda shorts and even in fancy dress intrigue me. What was it about this ship, I wonder, that persuaded him to drop his guard and let himself be pictured at ease when he is so watchful in all the other post-war pictures? Communications being what they were then – airmail for cruise passengers had to be sent to port agents up to a week in advance of the ship's arrival – these voyages were much more of an escape than they would be now. That might be part of it but I think the rarefied world of this particular liner gave Harry the licence to peel off his many masks.

With a sort of scruple that might well have bemused Harry I want to make it clear that while the itinerary and characters of the Great World Cruise of 1963 are real, all of their thoughts and actions on board are imagined. This is particularly the case for Harry himself – I have conjured his presence into life on this final circumnavigation from just two letters and a death certificate. I admit that it is from such flimsy material that I stand behind his shoulder on the voyage and visit the places he visited. Nevertheless, attempting to make him flesh and blood again is the least I owe him after fishing him up from his watery grave.

So let us join Harry on the *Caronia* in New York Harbour on a frigid January afternoon in 1963 for the trip of his lifetime, taking advantage of the incaution the ship engenders in him to peer under the disguise and fill the void he bequeathed.

New York

Friday 25th January 1963

Liners buzz on embarkation days and never more so than on one that marks the start of a cruise around the world. The prospect of over three months of uninterrupted leisure stirs even the most jaded tourist.

Caronia's crew had spent the last three days cleaning furniture, buffing floors and polishing brass to create that crucial first impression for their exacting guests. Six hundred passengers were arriving in the late afternoon for the midnight sailing, not counting all the friends and relatives coming on board to wish the circumnavigators 'bon voyage'. Baggage and travellers and guests were being matched to staterooms where stewards, dispensing smiles and endless cups of tea, were making the whole entourage welcome.

Harry Morris, bundled up against the late-afternoon cold and leaning on the Sun Deck's rail, was standing apart from all the activity. He was looking down at the ice in the river: New York winters were not known for their balmy temperatures but this January it was ten degrees colder than normal. The ship's foredeck had a thin covering of snow criss-crossed with the footprints of some of the crew.

Caronia was too close to the Elevated Highway for Harry to fully appreciate the skyline's inverted parabola. He didn't need to see it all. He had been coming here for 35 years and was very familiar with the island's outline – the way the low-rise buildings of Chelsea and the Meatpacking District separated the midtown and downtown skyscrapers. He knew he would still be able to enjoy that magical moment when the city's lights came on. It was the most magnificent man-made stage ever lit: a daily performance that was free of charge.

Harry could afford to take a leisurely approach to the day. He had spent a couple of nights ashore at the Warwick during the changeover, but was now settled in his stateroom, the same one he had occupied since joining the *Caronia* three weeks earlier in Southampton. He had plenty of time before Mrs Vinnie O'Donnell, his mistress and near-constant companion of the last three years, came aboard.

Harry was in buoyant spirits at the prospect of the imminent reunion. Reconciliation might be a more accurate word. Their liaison had been under strain for some time and they had not parted under the best of terms. Vinnie had returned to the US a couple of months before Christmas on the pretext of catching up with her nieces and nephews, but neither of them were under any illusion about the real reason for her leaving. Understandably she had had no desire to witness Harry's recent ill health, reminding her, as it did, of her late husband's decline. Harry knew that his treatment had been an unwelcome distraction but it was now done with. If a Grand World Tour could not rekindle a relationship, what could?

In fact they had met a decade ago on an equivalent cruise. At the time his attraction had been visceral and immediate, and the small matter of her being married already was no deterrent to his pursuit. Harry went out of his way to seduce her. It did not take her very long to reciprocate his feelings. What had surprised them both was that the mutual craving, once consummated, had turned into a committed relationship that spanned the Atlantic and then had survived cohabitation in London. To outside eyes it may have been a self-serving partnership – his showbiz lifestyle for her covetable charms – but it worked.

The crossing from Southampton via the Bahamas had proved as recuperative as he had hoped. He had already swapped his hospital pallor for what his stateroom steward called a 'bronzie'. There was every prospect that his skin tan – and health – would continue to improve in the months ahead as the ship worked its usual magic.

He rehearsed the itinerary: down to Nassau, turning west through the Panama Canal to Acapulco, up the Mexican Riviera to the bright lights of California and then over to the hushed guitars and swaying palms of Honolulu, which was one of his favourite ports of call. Across the Pacific to Japan, Hong Kong, and Jesselton in unspoiled North Borneo – a first for him – and then the tropical paradise of Bali and the seething metropolises of Singapore, Bangkok and Colombo. Then round to Bombay, gateway to India, the Crown Colony of Aden on the tip of Arabia, the Suez Canal and the romantic Mediterranean in springtime before heading home with a host of memories of the whole wide wonderful world.

Harry wasn't sure how much time he spent in reverie. He would return to see the city lights later; it was time to complete his afternoon assignment, securing a prime table in the Balmoral Restaurant. Once booked, he and Vinnie would occupy it for the whole of the trip.

Although *Caronia*'s two main restaurants differed little in terms of size and decoration the cruising cognoscenti knew about the invisible demarcation line across Restaurant Deck on the North Atlantic service. When *Caronia* wasn't cruising, cabins forward and alongside the Balmoral were designated First Class, those aft or alongside the Sandringham, Cabin Class. Moreover, on cruises the shore excursion staff counted as passengers. They all sat in the Sandringham and Harry knew Vinnie had no wish to dine in the same room as them. Even though the ship was avowedly 'one-class' on its cruises, the Balmoral Restaurant was first amongst equals.

Vinnie wanted one of the two four-tables by the Balmoral's port-side entrance doors. These – along with two deuces, seating two each – were adjacent to the Restaurant Manager's desk, giving them a prized combination of privacy and proximity. Harry knew that there would be evenings when Vinnie wanted nothing more than a tête à tête, the subject matter being the antics and peccadilloes of their fellow passengers, so sharing a table was out of the question. Not sharing also meant that they could avoid the indignity of having to arrange 'swaps' when they wanted to host dinner. A spare couple of places at table were an unmistakable sign of status on board.

As it happened they would be hosting straight away. That evening before departure they were entertaining his eldest, Susan, who worked for a law firm on Madison Avenue and lived downtown, and Vinnie's younger brother, Merrill, a lighting consultant who was up in town for business.

Going back inside he walked down two flights to Main Deck, ignoring the photographers by the gangway capturing the moments of arrival. On embarkation day there was a constant stream of rich old biddies in their furs having their photos taken. A lifebelt bearing the legend '*Caronia*' had been carefully placed in the foreground. In due course the subjects would all be offered the opportunity to wire the snap to the offices of their local papers. No doubt it would be published under a headline like 'Kentuckian Leaves On World Cruise' to the amusement and secret envy of their fellow matrons.

Walking pointedly past the arrivals table set up outside the Purser's Office, Harry took the elevator down two further floors to the Restaurant Deck. The Balmoral was not immune to the ship-wide bustle: he could see waiters lifting blue hide chairs and slaloming around tables that had already been set with silverware and flower vases. The Head Waiter and the Chief Wine Steward, in their smart blue uniforms, were at their stations. The latter, somewhat absurdly given the time of day, was already wearing his huge silver chain around his neck.

Harry held strong views on how a restaurant should be run. If a guest proactively offered a gratuity it was a strong signal that they expected service beyond even customary levels of excellence. Harry made it a rule to tip early on the cruise, to stand out while his fellow diners stayed anonymous: creating an impression of confederacy and flamboyance that later tippers would have to pay far more to match.

Both the Head Waiter and the Chief Wine Steward acknowledged the folded wads of high-denomination dollar bills – the only currency accepted on board – as Harry handed them over. His mission was only partially accomplished. Now he would approach the Maître D', stationed in the Main Lounge in anticipation of exactly the sort of pre-emptive move Harry was executing, with a well-padded envelope of lucre.

Having secured the table, Harry took the elevator back up three floors to Promenade Deck. He had one ritual to undertake before heading to the Lounge – something he did at the start of each voyage on the *Caronia*. The elevator doors opened aft of the Cocktail Bar. A clock and gilded horses on a polished veneer panel stood above the entrance to the Main Lounge across the square opposite. A sign said the artwork was called 'Horses Released from Work', a sentiment Harry applauded inwardly, especially after all his health travails recently. He was ready to begin his holiday.

*

Harry loved New York: for its restless energy which mirrored his own and for the chance it offered to reinvent himself in a way that was so much harder to do in London.

The *Caronia* also held a special place in Harry's heart. He did not explain to his family why he spent so much time cruising on it: they could not have been expected to understand what the ship symbolised for him. It was more than just the prestige of being associated with a yacht full of millionaires. It was because of the first time he had travelled by ship to New York, also on a ship called the *Caronia*, when he was crew and had to be 'below decks' on arrival. Rubbing shoulders with fellow passengers on this particular liner mattered to Harry in a way that was very personal. He would never have dreamed of exposing the depth of his feelings about it to anybody.

The combination of the ship, the city – all *Caronia*'s world cruises started in New York – and the turn of the calendar made this an auspicious day. A moment of exquisite anticipation – of new horizons and better fortune.

Harry had lymphoma. He had learned to live with its symptoms – the bouts of tiredness, the night sweats and the way his neck sometimes swelled. In one way the diagnosis had even been good for him as it had meant that he had not become a heavy drinker: something of an advantage in his occupation as he had seen plenty of competitors descend into dependency. This last year, however, he had felt permanently fatigued.

Even my mother, who could be forgiven for being unobservant as at twenty years old she had just got married and was expecting her first child, noticed Harry's difficulties. Her diary on the 16th November 1962 has the simple entry: *Daddy unwell.* She made the same comment a week later after one of her regular dinners with him at his Park Lane flat.

Harry had been uncharacteristically open with his elder daughter. Mum received a letter dated 24th November from my aunt Susan: *I had a very nice letter from Daddy last week. He sounds very run down and upset that the deal with the Mirabelle did not come off.*[2] *He says he will be here on January 21st and then I think he is going on the Caronia world cruise, that should cheer him up a bit.*

In early December Mum saw him in a private room in St Mary's Hospital, Paddington. She wrote that he looked very unwell and apparently had a 'gland in the liver'.

By that stage he had paid for the world cruise, or more accurately Vinnie had. *Caronia* insisted that invoices were settled in US dollars three months before departure date. It made sense to avoid transferring Sterling even for someone as adept as Harry at navigating Britain's post-war financial regulations and exchange rate controls. The £/$ rate had been fixed at $2.80 per £1 for the last thirteen years, during which time Sterling had become increasingly uncompetitive. Vinnie had substantial funds in the US, Harry would pay her back with deposits he had lodged in

---

2   Celebrated French restaurant on Curzon Street, round the corner from the Colony.

New York to pay the talent agencies. Or at least that was the story he told her: he may have still been flash but he was no longer flush.

Without Vinnie there might not have been a grand voyage on which to accompany Harry. She is integral to our story; so who was this paramour turned temporary patroness?

Vinnie Lorraine O'Donnell née Pearson was about the same age as Harry. She had been born in a place called Spooner, a remote railway stop that had bred a tiny town amongst the pine forests and lakes of North-West Wisconsin. Generations of immigrants from Scandinavia seemed to find the landscape and the frigid temperatures to their liking. Their number included Andrew Pearson from Sweden and Mayme Martinson, whose family was originally from Norway. They married in about 1900 and Vinnie was the fourth of six children Mayme produced in the space of ten years.[3]

The constant gestations, or the climate, or a combination of the two, taxed Mayme's body to its limit. There might also have been complications from the birth of her sixth child, Merrill, in April 1911 for Mayme died the same year, aged 27 or 28.

Vinnie may have grown up in a frosty environment metaphorically as well as climatically for her father, a bank manager, remarried soon afterwards and stayed in Spooner. Perhaps it was Mayme's premature death or a generally repressed Lutheran childhood that explains the gay abandon with which Vinnie and her elder sister, Nina, pursued their lives as adults. Whatever the reason, something propelled Vinnie to follow Nina to New York soon after high school graduation.

Nina, who had modified her surname to Pierson, was making quite a splash by then as one of the chorus girls in the Ziegfeld Follies. Somewhat improbably, she had been talent-spotted while working as a schoolteacher in Minnesota. Florenz Ziegfeld signed her to a showgirl contract and she spent the mid-1920s in the

---

3 *www.findagrave.com* for all the anniversaries of the Pearson and Martinson families. Vinnie was born on the 27th September 1906.

revue on Broadway. Once she was established she brought her younger sister to live with her.

The sisters cut quite a swathe through New York's nightlife, especially the mercurial Nina who was a big-time socialite: the main qualifications for being a showgirl came down to beauty and availability. There is a possibility that Harry got to watch Nina in the Follies on his first trip to New York. Vinnie might have been sitting in the audience that night as well – an intoxicating thought – although both would have both been way out of his league in those days.

Contrary to the rumours of the time, Nina was probably never involved with Ziegfeld himself but her on-off romance with Tommy Manville, a much-married heir to an asbestos fortune, was fodder for the tabloids. So was the episode when she ran off to London to marry a French industrialist named Paul Leviton in 1934, only to divorce him in Mexico a year later.

Nina's behaviour became increasingly erratic. She eloped to Gretna Green with an upper-class black sheep going by the delightful name of Percy Ughtred St George Kirke: a union which appeared to last only one day. A few weeks later – at the age of 34 – Nina died suddenly from an embolism while staying at the Hotel George V in Paris. The gossip columns had her dying from an 'overdose of sleeping pills' and 'surrounded by a dozen champagne bottles'. This event allowed the papers to picture her as another in the line of Ziegfeldian tragic heroines, young starlets who had paid the ultimate price in their lust for fame.

Vinnie had caroused with her sister in London and Paris. If she had not been in the hotel when Nina died, she was there shortly afterwards. Nina's ashes were turned over to a Mrs Vinnie de Casasus of Mexico City. That was our Vinnie – her social life was hardly less hectic than her sister's. In 1938 she was already on her second marriage.

With four husbands, long-running affairs and no children, Vinnie was surely an attractive proposition. Her first husband was Kenneth Thornhill of New York about whom nothing other than his name survives. Her second was Mario de Casasus who might have been twelve years her senior – she seems to have had a taste for older men – and the son of a sometime Mexican Ambassador to the US. That would explain why she was in Mexico City in 1938 and also in 1945 because that is where she met Robert J. 'Bob' O'Donnell, a movie theatre magnate, her third husband. They married in New Orleans in July 1948 and it was his death in 1959 that made Vinnie Lorraine O'Donnell rich: rich enough to donate more than $1 million (nearly $10 million in 2022) to the Dallas Museum of Fine Arts in his memory and to pay for Harry's ticket on the *Caronia* when he asked her to.

Vinnie's nickname was 'Tootsie', which nods to promiscuity. Years later she liked Harry to use this familiar form in addressing her, something that indicates she was happy with its connotation throughout her life. How much of her chequered past she revealed to Harry can never be known. She would have witnessed some of his duplicity first hand so perhaps felt no compunction in redacting the less favourable aspects of her own backstory. In that sense they were well suited to each other.

Harry had been a support after Bob's death and offered Vinnie an entrée into London café society. She was no ingénue but needed Harry's Rolodex: at least at the start. Her own charisma eventually filled her diary, and Harry's poor health only stirred unwelcome memories of mortality. She took him at his word when he said he was well on the way to recovery but if that proved not to be the case, as a well-travelled escort she had little time for sentiment. There were plenty of other men, Brits and Americans alike, who could provide company and invitations to first nights, galas and showbiz parties.

*

Vinnie was on board for the set-piece dinner that Harry had organised with Merrill and Susan. The four had a cocktail in the Promenade Lounge and then walked down the Art Deco main staircase to the favoured table. The rule that *Caronia* cruise passengers had to dress for dinner was relaxed for embarkation night.

Even so, this meal had some ceremony. Vinnie and Susan would have been used to the 'show' Harry demanded around all his meals: the professional host in him was rarely not on duty. In his London flat that meant a roast dinner prepared by Torr, his man-servant, and carved at the table by Harry himself. If Torr was off, then the Dorchester Grill was the only acceptable alternative for Harry's guests. Fortunately, his requirements mirrored *Caronia's* own insistence on the highest standards of service. Two waiters had been standing at their station when they arrived. There were fresh blue flowers in a little silver vase and the table had been laid in crisp linen in the fashion it would be for the rest of the cruise.

The setting was reassuringly familiar to Harry: the decorative linoleum floor, the large mirrors standing in for windows, the limewood panels of rustic scenes intended to represent the cycle of the seasons.

Informal pre-embarkation supper it may have been, but they ate Cantaloupe melon, Turtle Soup with sherry, salmon for the fish course, and then beef. Susan and Merrill found room for a Coupe Neige des Alpes. Harry may have wanted to join them but didn't. Vinnie, ever watchful of his weight, insisted he eat nothing other than jelly for dessert. At least the presence of their guests meant she relaxed her usual demand that he eat his dessert standing up.

Harry was a master of appearance but on this occasion his burdens were visible. The contrast with Vinnie's younger brother, apparently in rude good health, might have been stark as even the normally self-preoccupied Susan noticed: *I didn't think Daddy looked at all well when he was here, he had a very nice dinner party on the* Caronia *the night they left. I was flirting with Mrs O.D.'s baby brother, who comes from Minnesota. He is very good looking but very dull, he looks about 50, very well preserved though, but what does that make her? He has a big house with a boat, and quite a large family, he asked me to go down and spend my vacation with them, actually it might be rather fun, I might just do that.*[4]

4   Morris, Susan. Letter to Mum, March 12, 1963.

At some time before 11.30pm the party broke up; Susan and Merrill headed off to join the friends, relatives and hundreds of other sightseers on the pier and Harry and Vinnie went to their cabins to dress warmly for the traditional send-off on deck.

The decks were icy so they had to watch their footing but they found a spot together on Promenade Deck, their pockets stuffed with streamers to make their contribution to the colourful cat's cradle of ribbons holding the ship to shore. In fact twelve lines from bow to stern held her in position on Pier 90. It was a much-repeated piece of theatre but never failed to mesmerise as first the gangways were taken away and then the huge mooring lines cast off in pairs – one bow, one stern – until only the landlines held the *Caronia* in place. Two of the burliest mates unhitched these in a final act of release. At three minutes past midnight the streamers broke as the ship – tugs fore and aft – slid from the quay and with barely a vibration turned to head south into the Hudson River. The crowds of people on shore frantically waved goodbye, the gap between the ship and them growing ever wider, and Harry got what he wanted – that smell of salt and fish and diesel that evoked the excitement he had felt on previous trips. Harry had rejoined his exclusive club. Three loud blasts from *Caronia*'s deep Typhon horns meant farewell for 92 days. First stop, Nassau, 900 miles to the south.

Harry and Vinnie lingered at the rail. It was a clear night. There was a new moon, which Harry thought appropriate as no celestial object was bright enough to compete with the million-watt glow from this city. Later, after Vinnie had claimed fatigue and left for her room, when the lights of Manhattan fell far behind, he looked up at the great spray of stars and was reminded of the pin lights behind the bandstand at the Colony.

He spared a thought for all those crew who wouldn't have got the chance to be on deck; just as he hadn't been able to all those years ago on his first voyage. He knew from experience that the departure would be the main talking point for all the guests the following morning.

Nassau

Saturday 26th January

Harry was not usually an early riser. He had spent the last two decades of his life entertaining into the small hours six nights out of seven, a working pattern which often made him somnolent during the day, particularly after lunch. In the three weeks he'd been at sea, however, he had acclimatised to the daily rhythm of the ship so he was awake when the General Landing Card, the *Ocean Times* and the passenger list were delivered in a bundle before breakfast.

The most prominent of these was the passenger list. It had been designed to convey its status as a key tool of social intercourse on board. Its cover was an overhead view of the ship and it was fastened together with a braided gold cord like a soldier's aiguillette.

Harry ignored the sections about the principal officers and the cruise staff and skipped the 'General Information for Passengers', which he was quite sure hadn't changed since leaving Southampton. Instead he worked his way through the alphabetised list of passengers looking for interesting domiciles or names he recognised.

He wanted to sparkle tonight at that enduring custom of the first day at sea: the Officers' Line, where the senior officers were presented to all the guests. If a lifetime of hosting in clubs and restaurants had taught him one thing it was that memorising names paid dividends. He would show Vinnie that he hadn't lost his ability to work a room.

The thought of Vinnie brought a sharp reminder that he was perusing the pamphlet on his own in his cabin. When she had advanced the price of the ticket she had insisted they take separate staterooms to give their relationship breathing room. She had picked one of the best suites on Main Deck with ample space for private parties while he was further aft in a twin-bedded room with single beds.

At least his berth was still on Main Deck. On a cruise, all of *Caronia*'s accommodation was designated First Class but nobody was fooled: in the cloistered hierarchy of on-board addresses, Main Deck was the *crème de la crème*. As if to reinforce the point, Vinnie had taken a second cabin on A Deck by the stairwell below her suite, simply for use as a walk-in closet.

Caronia had ten decks but other than the restaurants there was little reason to venture below Main. All the ship's thirteen public rooms – in the Arc Deco Ocean Liner style pioneered by the French before the war – were on Restaurant Deck or above.

Below it, the ship's interior subsided into ever-increasing alphabetical obscurity: B, C, D and the passenger-inaccessible E Deck. Nobody ever talked about the reasons to visit B Deck, such as a private conversation required in the Purser's Office or worse, a trip to the infirmaries – one for each sex – or the Operating Theatre.

In all his years on *Caronia* Harry had not once visited the gymnasium on D Deck. He knew of its reputation as probably the most claustrophobic place on the entire ship: a low-roofed metal box right on top of the propeller that effectively made it an echo chamber. That gave him ample excuse not to exercise.

He was confident that his physical fitness would soon be restored sufficiently to allow for deck games on Sports Deck. He could envisage whiling away mornings playing shuffleboard or quoits with Vinnie followed by a good lunch in the Verandah Café overlooking the terraced open-air lido below. Lunch would be slept off on one of the recliners on Sun Deck or worked off by pacing the boards on the part-open, part-covered Promenade Deck.

One ritual would certainly not change. Atmospheric conditions permitting, every evening at six o'clock, before changing for dinner, he would make a point of catching the news broadcast in the Smoking Room. With its deep armchairs and mock fireplace, the Smoking Room was typical of the intimate country-club atmosphere *Caronia* aimed for in its quieter public rooms. Increasingly Harry was drawn to these spaces rather than the Main Lounge or, God forbid, the irredeemably ersatz Raleigh Room which attempted to recreate a British pub afloat.

Dinner with or without invited guests would be followed by the Theatre, where the chairs were comfortable and the lights low enough to allow for surreptitious post-prandial naps. That would fuel the boilers for some late-night dancing to one of the house bands. The prospect was all very pleasing.

His thoughts were interrupted by an announcement on the Tannoy. All on board were requested to muster at their allotted stations for boat drill. It was a supposed highlight of the first morning in open sea but Harry had listened to enough recounting of the safety procedures and witnessed one too many lowerings of the lifeboats to bother. He ignored the steward's tap on the cabin door and turned back to the register of passengers; 90 percent of them appeared to be from the US or Canada. Though Harry, true to form, would never take information about provenance at face value.

*

The Officers Line, at the end of the first full day at sea, was all the encouragement the passengers needed to dress formally and it was what Harry had been looking forward to since waking. Who knew, the reception might prove as significant in his life as the corresponding occasion on *Caronia*'s World Cruise nine years earlier.

The 1954 cruise was the one Harry remembered most fondly. First, it had an unusual itinerary. *Caronia* spent the time it would have taken to circle the world criss-crossing the Pacific instead, enabling calls to otherwise inaccessible outposts like Easter Island

and the Pitcairns. It was also the first cruise to call at ports in Japan in more than fifteen years. On arrival, passengers received the sort of reception reserved for film stars and royalty. Second, Harry was travelling alone and women outnumbered men almost two to one. And third, it was when Harry first met Vinnie; and of course her husband Bob.

Bob O'Donnell was an archetypal American entrepreneur, the sort of man that Harry had learned to appreciate in his dealings with talent agents. Harry and he had much in common: a modest start in life had fuelled their ambition for wealth and success and both had chosen a similar route for advancement. They shared a passion for the entertainment business, an interest in good dressing and an addiction to nicotine. They were both charismatic extroverts who dropped showbiz names to each other in friendly rivalry. And Bob's attraction was only enhanced by the presence of the icily beautiful, immaculately dressed and coiffed Vinnie on his arm. Judging by all the on-board photographs of the three together, they became firm friends.

Bob was born fifteen years before Harry and Vinnie to Irish immigrants in Chicago, which was where he started working as a vaudeville theatre usher at the age of twelve. His knack for business must have been obvious because within eight years he was managing theatres and a booking agency on Broadway. In the year that Vinnie joined her sister in New York, Bob moved to Texas to manage the fledgling Majestic Theatre in Fort Worth for Karl Hoblitzelle, the owner of Interstate Amusements. Later that year he was made general manager for all the Majestic Theatres in Texas.

The Great Depression of the 1930s turned out to be his and Hoblitzelle's big break. They took advantage of the numerous movie theatre receiverships to expand Majestic and cobble together the Interstate Theatre Circuit. At its peak O'Donnell presided over more than 200 separate movie theatres scattered across the Midwest and was seen by Hollywood producers as the number one movie exhibitor in the United States.

O'Donnell made some pioneering moves – creating promotional gimmicks just the right side of state lottery laws to entice customers in, developing new Hispanic markets by contracting for Spanish language films made in Mexico and responding to the post-war population drift to the suburbs by building drive-ins and theatres outside the downtown area. He did not neglect regular business though, successfully finding tenants for the chain's commercial space and famously even ensuring a reliable supply of popcorn during World War Two. Nevertheless, the rise in television viewing would have been a worry on that cruise in 1954. Perhaps the strain of dealing with it was why he and Vinnie had elected for an extended period of rest and recuperation.

When it came to name-dropping, Bob had the whip hand over Harry. The comedian Bob Hope, no less, credited O'Donnell as the person who gave him his break into show business. As did the actor Audie Murphy. After Murphy returned to Texas in 1945, a decorated war hero and the subject of a cover story in *Life* magazine, it was Bob who suggested that he be interviewed on a regular Sunday Interstate Theatres broadcast called *Show Time*. He also got Murphy a couple of bit parts through Hollywood contacts which launched his career in action movies. It must have been through Bob that Vinnie met another Texan, the actress Joan Crawford. She and Vinnie would become the best of friends.

By all accounts Bob O'Donnell was a likeable and generous man, a leading light of the Dallas business community and one of the early movers in the Variety Club of America. But like her previous husband he was much older than Vinnie. Bob was vulnerable to cuckolding by a man like Harry regardless of his famous friends or good works.

*

Vinnie had already been to the hairdressers when he picked her up. She was wearing a silver metallic brocade evening gown that served to accentuate her naturally pale complexion. Harry noticed the admiring glances when he chaperoned her to the Lounge.

The receiving line was bookended by two of the most travelled people on the *Caronia*, the pair entrusted with the day-today experience of passengers: the Social Directress, Lorna Yost and the Cruise Director, Vaughan Rickard. Rickard would travel over 200,000 miles on the ship by the time he finished.

After a Master-of-Arms had announced each guest's name in full voice, Lorna set the pace for this social marathon, using a technique for propelling guests that Harry himself used in the club: speaking and simultaneously shaking and drawing the hand along. A thoughtful, motherly hostess, she was blessed with almost perfect recall for names and faces. In a gentle Southern drawl she effortlessly remembered the 1954 cruise to Harry and Vinnie when it was their turn to be presented.

She introduced the Captain – Geoffrey Marr – who was also a familiar face. He had been the Staff Captain on the 1954 cruise. Temporarily belying his nickname of 'Tatty' he looked resplendent in black tie and white mess jacket with four gold stripes on his shoulder and the ribbons of his Distinguished Service Cross and other decorations on his chest (he had been a Navigating Officer on the King George V when she sunk the Bismarck). He welcomed Harry in a softly spoken northern accent – he had been born in Yorkshire but had been at sea since the age of fourteen. Harry and Vinnie were handed on to the Staff Captain, also with four gold stripes on his shoulder; the Chief Engineer, the same number of stripes but with purple in between them; the Purser, three gold stripes with white between; the Chief Steward, three gold zig-zag stripes; and so on and so on, the line a hierarchical mix of dress uniforms and white dinner jackets. Despite himself, Harry paid particular attention to the Principal Medical Officer and Surgeon, Messrs Cuthbert and Winer, both of whom sported red (for blood?) between their three gold stripes.

The Cruise Director stood at the end of the line. Harry lingered a few moments longer than necessary with Vaughan Rickard, the courtesy one professional host pays another. Like Harry, Vaughan was naturally gregarious and skilled at bringing people from different backgrounds together. He knew how to circulate a room slowly, how not to get caught up in cliques and how to leave parties with a 'pay off' gesture, usually a comic anecdote from his time as an enlisted man or when he tried his hand at acting in New York. He was the sort of person – fun loving, loquacious, a moderate drinker – that Harry liked to be around.

The crowd made their way down to their restaurants. The main, round eight-seat table at the head of the Balmoral was the Captain's. On either side of the centre point were the Chief Engineer and Chief Medical Officer's tables. Vinnie looked chagrined. Harry surmised that it was because they had not been invited to the Captain's table on this most public of nights but he was secretly pleased he had been spared the inevitable interrogation this early on in the trip.

Harry, an aficionado of band music, rated Aidan McNally's on-board ensemble higher than Victor Manico's. Both housed the same musicians, rebranded from the Light Orchestra at teatime to the Dance Orchestra for late night. But McNally seemed to get more out of them. McNally might have been a jobbing band leader but with his five-piece band, the Aidanaires, he had actually cut a disc onshore. In Harry's view, both orchestras were infinitely preferable to the 'Wandering Minstrels' who plagued the cocktail hour and dinner in the restaurants. The only thing that could be said in their favour was that they had a lot of ground to cover, so auditory exposure was mercifully brief.

After dinner, back in the Main Lounge, he and Vinnie watched McNally and the Orchestra play for the resident dancing professionals, Anton and Janetta Morrow. Harry, proud of his dancing artistry, always made a point of taking to the floor, but this time he was not confident about managing much more than a slow waltz. So he largely sat out while Vinnie was accompanied by a seemingly endless stream of acquaintances from previous trips. He cheered himself up with the thought that even McNally's band would not have been good enough to join the Colony's roster.

Harry couldn't shake off the notion that history was about to repeat itself, the usurper usurped by a younger, fitter man. After all, he had moved quickly after sensing the opportunity in '54.

Vinnie had spent part of the summer in London and they had both joined *Caronia*'s Christmas cruise at the end of that year as singles, though Vinnie was still married to Bob.

This set a pattern of clandestine meetings that would last the rest of the decade. Bob died from lung cancer on 11th November 1959. Two days later Harry flew into New York and then on to Dallas. Bob had suffered a very short illness but even so Vinnie was ready: she sailed for England within the month and she and Harry went to Nice in January 1960. If she wore no widow's weeds for Bob, what could Harry expect?

Sunday 27th January

The first day out might well have lulled the cruising neophytes – the light oncoming breeze had made for a slight sea and low swell. If so, the second morning came as a rude awakening. The southerly gale was only classified as 'moderate' in nautical terms but it caused the liner to roll and pitch in a way that belied its 34,000 tonnes. It was not the sort of storm to get the crew scurrying to secure the deadlights over the portholes but it was enough to expose the *Caronia*'s characteristic corkscrew gait and induce widespread seasickness.

Harry, who had hardly set foot on land in over three weeks, wasn't affected by the lurching ship. A cup of morning bouillon on deck, as was his daily habit, had suppressed any queasiness on his part. Vinnie, however, while no sailing amateur, was confined to her suite.

Harry went along to commiserate and to admire the paintings Vinnie had brought to personalise her sitting room. She had also acquired a drinks cabinet from somewhere. He noted balefully that her bedroom had two double beds but they agreed again that while he was regaining his strength and she found her sea legs it was better for both that he slept in his stateroom.

Owing to the inclement weather much of the day's programme had been cancelled, so in the afternoon, at a temporary loss for something to do, Harry went to the matinee showing of the 'Sunday Classic', Anna Karenina. He wasn't much interested in seeing Greta Garbo in a historical drama but it was one way of spending the time.

Even on a day when the ship showed her malign side, Harry still loved her. The 'Green Goddess', named for her distinctive pale green hull, had always been special to him from the moment of her launch back in 1947.

Harry had seen the British Pathé footage at the time: the young Princess Elizabeth, sacrificing a bottle of champagne on the ship's bow, accompanied by Lieutenant Mountbatten, blond and dynamic, but already condemned to a lifetime of walking in public two steps behind his wife. Her cut-glass accent was no match for the infernal din and cloud of dust caused by the coiled chains fighting to slow the towering keel's descent into the water.

The black-and-white pictures captured *Caronia*'s yacht-like profile: her concave clipper bow, long, stepped fo'c'sle and single funnel and mast. For Harry it would have been a memorable sight in a drab period even without his connection to the ship's predecessor.

It would not be too long before *Caronia* earned the sobriquet 'The Millionaire's Yacht'. That suited Harry's self-image perfectly. For fifteen years *Caronia* had ruled the waves, and if she was now trading more on her reputation than any pretence at still being exceptional, in a sense that made man and ship even more suited. Harry was a nightclub owner in name only; the *Caronia* had been superseded by faster forms of transport. Nevertheless, sitting there in the largely deserted Theatre, Harry could not help but feel a deep sense of satisfaction at how far his drive and talent had taken him from his start in life.

*

Harry Morris was not the name my grandfather was born with. It wasn't even the second name to which he answered. Not until I came across the deed poll did I realise I was dealing with a nameshifter. At a stroke the possibility of a family hinterland was opened up by the admission of Harry having previous aliases.

The snippets he chose to share with his daughters would turn out to be dubious at best. He volunteered that he was the second eldest of four children, that his father was from Poland and his mother from the Black Sea port of Odessa. While he was coy about his parents' full names he did take pains to say that he had grown up in the Henley Buildings on the Boundary Estate in Shoreditch, attended Rochelle Street School and worked for a time on a barrow on the Old Kent Road.

By the time he was disclosing these verities he was a West End nightclub owner with an image to protect which might explain why there were so few facts in the first place. He was also living a double, or even triple, life: keeping his birth and conjugal families apart, living alone in London and enjoying the benefits that came with his nocturnal calling. By that stage his lying had become habitual.

His father, Moshe Wygoda, did indeed come from Poland but so did his mother, Chaya Ester. She was born in Goworowo, a small *shtetl* or village just a few miles from Moshe's birthplace, Różan, in East Central Poland. It stretches credulity to think Harry did not know his mother's birthplace. The misdirection seems inexplicable unless he thought Odessa sounded more exotic to his daughters. Moreover, Harry was older, not younger, than his sister, Rose. Telling his children that he was not the first-born again seems a gratuitous lie.

Commonly enough we seek to emulate the characteristics of those we admire but Harry possibly went a step further by commandeering the biographical details of contemporaries who took his fancy. The entertainment magnate, Louis Winogradsky, better known as Lew Grade did have parents who hailed from Odessa. Magpie-like, did Harry assume the same derivation? Another role model and later friend was the business tycoon, Sir Charles Clore. I don't think it's a coincidence that both these favoured individuals attended Rochelle School and at least one of them lived in the Henley Buildings.

In any event the fact that Harry never gave his girls the opportunity to interrogate their grandmother about either her beginnings or the birth order of her children is evidence of just how keen Harry was to compartmentalise his life.

On the face of it, these fragments weren't much to begin a search for Harry's roots but they would be enough to unravel some of his deviations. As it turns out, the most important piece of information that Harry condescended to reveal to his daughters was that his mother had a sister in New York called Fannie Marmelstein. In fact, Fannie was the only member of his family that he ever encouraged his girls to stay with. She must have passed Harry's snobbery test. Good for her but, for our purposes, her surname was the key to unlocking the family history.

Like a lot of other Polish families, much of what there is to know now can only be uncovered by working backwards from US immigration records. Because of those assiduous Ellis Island clerks, I knew that the surname to look for on Harry's maternal side was Sztern or Stern. I could also triangulate back to a place, courtesy of multiple records of entry: Goworowo, in the Lomza *gubernia* or province.

In most parts of modern-day Poland, vital registration was only introduced to facilitate conscription after Napoleon's attempt to invade Russia. Polish Jews were required to adopt surnames for the first time. Prior to this they simply used traditional patronymics, which is why it is nigh-on impossible to trace the average Polish Jewish family before the nineteenth century. I would only be able to wind the clock back a couple of generations but that would be enough to unearth clues about Harry's background.

Goworowo might have been ground zero as far as the family is concerned but I would have to look at records from neighbouring *shtetlach* like Różan, Ostrołęka or Ostrów Mazowiecka.[5] The Jewish communities in all of these settlements were closely interwoven by marriage and trade so the Sterns could have registered births, marriages and deaths in any of them. Even if they

---

5 The surviving nineteenth-century Jewish records from Ostrołęka and the other towns have been extracted and translated by Jewish Research Index – Poland.

had stayed put, at times, the smaller villages used the registers of nearby larger settlements – the earliest records that survive from Goworowo are kept in the register books of Ostrołęka, for instance. It was going to be quite a search.

The challenges quickly became evident on Harry's father's side. I had just two discrete pieces of information to go on. First, in the comprehensive register taken in Britain on the eve of the Second World War, Moshe stated that he had been born on 10th October 1877. Second, his *matzevot* or gravestone in Edmonton Cemetery follows Jewish tradition in that it bears his father's Hebrew name as well as his own. Moshe's masonry reads 'Moshe ben (son of) Abram'.

The surname Wygoda offered hope as well. It was almost certainly an occupational surname as the word means 'comfort' in Polish and was used to refer to hostelries and taverns. Keeping an inn was one of the few jobs open to Jews at that time. It seems that running restaurants was in Harry's blood. The surname's chief attribute, however, was its relative scarcity and concentration in towns in the Lomza province.[6] The place to look was undoubtedly Różan as there were more entries for the name Wygoda in Różan than for anywhere else in the region: 130 of them in a population of less than 2,000 in 1900.

Alas, in an all-too-common experience for Polish families, the records covering Moshe and Abram's time in Różan are lost. Innumerable gaps in the archive have been caused by fire, flooding, simple negligence and, of course in this region, war. Beyond knowing the name of Moshe's father, the family filing cabinet stayed emphatically empty.

I became preoccupied by the Vigoda void, particularly as the more stumbling blocks I reached on Moshe's side, the more vistas opened up on his wife, Chaya Ester's. As the family tree developed I experienced moments of self-doubt about the whole enterprise. I couldn't do the Vigodas the disservice of inventing

---

6   Beider, Alexander (1996). A *Dictionary of Jewish Surnames in the Kingdom of Poland*, Avotaynu, USA.

anything about them and yet I felt guilty about allowing them to pass in anonymity. It is this absence of documentary evidence that gives people like Harry the freedom to reinvent without fear of contradiction.

The whole thing brought home how much of a role the destination of the emigrant plays in the life of an archivist. Harry's mother's family get to have a sequel simply because they were more successful in emigrating to the US than Moshe's, and if in weaving his tapestry – so full of holes otherwise – Harry had not arbitrarily chosen to retain the 'thread' of his aunt, Fannie Marmelstein, I may never have even discovered the ancestral name.

Stern means 'star' in Yiddish and it would live up to its billing in this history. Because of it I could travel back to Abram's time and start to fill in the gaps about one-half of the family at least. True, I would end up with a lopsided family tree – like one of those hawthorns bent over by coastal winds – but it would not be the stunted weed Harry bequeathed.

The US records pinpointed the patriarch of Esther's family: Moszek Berek Sztern, in Polish, or Moshe Ber Stern in Hebrew. Moshe Ber was born in about 1836 in Goworowo to Icek Dawid and Chana Ruchla, who had made their own appearances just after Napoleon's army had tramped over their land to Moscow and back.

At first blush Moshe Ber's records were a puzzle: the span of his children's birth dates seemed too wide. Aunts and uncles often appeared to be the same age or even younger than their nieces and nephews. The explanation was simple when it was found. Moshe Ber married twice: first to Malka Kraus and then Rojza or Raizel Nachowitz. He outlasted both wives which was likely something to do with all the calving that was expected of women in those days. 'Every year comes a prophet' was a common saying amongst religious Jews, and neither spouse disappointed Moshe Ber in that endeavour.

He was a few years older than Malka when they married in the mid-1850s. Four of her children – two boys and two girls – survived to adulthood but she died in the late 1860s, probably before she even reached 30. Moshe Ber must have remarried before 1870 since his and Rose's first child, Benjamin, was born in 1871. Moshe Ber was in his mid-30s, Rose barely older than the eldest child of his first marriage. Not only would she have to look after them she would give Moshe Ber at least another six children. One thing you can say about Moshe Ber, he was a committed inseminator.

I have a vision of him as a big, bearded bear of a man, no doubt auto-suggested by his second name, with a great lust for life, again probably anchored simply by the knowledge of how many children he sired. His beard was grey, not because of age but because of flour dust as he was a baker. I don't know his occupation for certain but it seems a fair bet, given how many of his descendants went into the trade.

While all the events in the preceding paragraphs happened, the dating is no more than educated guesswork based on US records. In Poland there are no birth or marriage records for Moshe Ber, Malka and Raizel nor indeed birth records for any of his eight or nine children.

There is a death certificate for Moshe Ber in Różan dated 28th November 1906. Apparently he died at three o'clock in the morning. There is also a gravestone for Raizel dated 11th December 1901. Like all the others in Goworowo it is now stored in a warehouse, the Jewish cemetery having long been ransacked. Even without these records we can be fairly certain when Moshe Ber and Raizel died because of the rush of namesakes within the family. In Ashkenazic tradition babies are not named after living people and all the Stern children honoured their parents. The patriarch's Hebrew name, Moshe, is Moses or Morris in English. In New York, Benjamin, Moshe Ber and Raizel's eldest child, called his son Morris in 1908. In 1904 his younger brother Isidor, also in New York, was the first of the family to name his daughter Rose, the English equivalent of Raizel.

The Sterns and Marmelsteins (whom two of Moshe Ber's daughters married) were bakers by trade. Over three generations a dozen or more of the men in the family would make a living that way. In my whimsical moments I see Moshe Ber ordering his sons and sons-in-law to establish an international baking empire – taking inspiration from the way that Mayer Rothschild sent his five sons out from Frankfurt to do the same thing for banking with one consonant's difference.

Regardless, it is a fact that in a twenty-year period between 1893 and 1913, eight of the nine Stern siblings and half-siblings emigrated from Poland. For anyone with any ambition it was a case of move or moulder. The only one who didn't – Yakov or Jankiel – might have done so as well if he hadn't died. His premature death would turn out to mean his children would suffer a very different fate from those of their cousins who didn't stay in their homeland.

To understand why there was such a powerful impulse to leave, one need only look at what life was like for Jews in the *shtetls*.

In the nineteenth century, modern-day Poland lay within the Pale of Settlement. The Pale was that part of Imperial Russia where Jews were concentrated because, save for an educated or ennobled elite, it was the only place where they were permitted to reside permanently. Harry's family were far from educated or ennobled.

The Pale stretched from the Baltic to the Black Sea – nearly one million square kilometres of land and the place over 40 million people called home. That number included almost all of Russian Jewry, along with Poles, Ukrainians and any other ethnic group that might have offered unwanted competition for Russian merchants and artisans.

For the Jews there was little safety in numbers, especially after the assassination of Tsar Alexander II. They had always been vulnerable to discrimination by the majority orthodox Christian population, condoned or even encouraged under different rulers, but in the wake of the 1881 assassination the Tsarists deflected public anger towards a familiar scapegoat. Jews faced repressive legislation and 'pogroms', riots named after the Russian word to wreak havoc, which became increasingly violent over time.

Mortal oppression is commonly cited as the reason for the exodus of so many Russian Jews in the following decades but the key push factors were more economic and political than the risk of physical harm. The region where Harry's parents came from suffered an economic downturn at the turn of the century, which forced many people to move from the countryside to the cities and others to emigrate. It didn't matter what your trade was – tailoring, baking, farming – it was exceedingly difficult to eke out a profitable living.

Goworowo was typical in that, although it could trace its origins back to the sixteenth century, it had not developed into the sort of place that could offer many employment opportunities to the young of its few hundred Jewish families. The village itself was mainly wooden with a few brick houses. There was no sewerage or running water – the Sterns were long gone by the time the first village pump arrived in the 1920s. It had three main streets, a bridge, a marketplace, a synagogue and, considering only a handful of non-Jewish families lived in the place, an incongruously oversized Catholic church.

The countryside was not particularly attractive or active, just working farmland and orchards. According to one ex-resident 'Goworowo was a town of shoemakers, tailors, carpenters and "balagule", that is horse drivers … Most people in the town made a living from what they produced: assorted pants, suits, shoes…'[7]

As I strived to visualise what the Sterns' lives might have been like – what forced them to desert their homeland in such numbers – I had a stroke of luck. There happens to be an oral history kept within the US branch of the family. It is a bracing correction to all those clichéd *Fiddler on the Roof* images of Yiddish popular culture that my otherwise poor imaginings might have been reduced to.

Michle or Minnie Abarbanell was the eldest daughter of Benjamin Stern and Shayna Perl Stiller, which made her Moshe Ber and Raizel's first grandchild and Harry's first cousin. She

---

7 *https://www.centropa.org/biography/icchok-grynberg?fbclid=IwAR00H01fBD2ADp-mVUxrbdVJITeEHMp6m2JbCCoPmflNN6srC9k99w-OPdI.*

was born in Goworowo in the summer of 1898 and was nine years old when she left.[8]

Benjamin was a tailor but there wasn't enough work for him so in 1900 he followed the well-trodden path to New York, leaving mother and daughter to move in with Shayna Perl's parents, Schmuel David and Chaya Sarah.

Schmuel David fished for a living but even by Goworowo's standards it was a precarious occupation as the river, the Hirsh (Orz in Polish), often dried up in the summer. Fish could only be sold alive, since none of the villagers had any means of preserving them once they were dead, so if the water level dropped so did the opportunity for making any money. Then Schmuel David was forced to become a jobbing tailor which, judging by his arthritic hands in the one surviving photograph of him, would have been a struggle.

Shayna Perl was the eldest of Schmuel David and Chaya Sarah's seven children but the last to emigrate. One by one her six younger brothers all left for the US. In the dry season the family was probably only saved from destitution by the remittances from the States. Minnie recalls thinking that she ate better than the eight or nine children in their neighbour's home. As well as the inevitable fish Minnie could remember eating potato pudding, noodles, beans, *schav* – sorrel soup – and meat or poultry once a week. Next door there was barely anything other than bread, tea and sugar.

Home for Minnie was one large room – stove in the corner, table in the centre and beds against the walls – loving but sad, she recalls, no doubt because of all the filial departures and the deaths in infancy of three of her own siblings. Benjamin returned to Poland for his mother's final illness and funeral *levaya* but still could not make a living so went back to the US. Both then and in 1904 he had tickets for Shayna Perl and Minnie to follow him but Shayna Perl refused out of loyalty to her parents. One can imagine the anguish this transatlantic tug-of-war caused.

---

8 Holzman, Ann, *Historical Recollections of the Stern Family.*

When she finally relented in 1907 it was a wrench. Minnie remembers sitting on a down quilt with her mother and baby brother, Judel, on the wagon taking them out of the village and seeing 'grandparents and the townspeople weeping as though they were mourning the dead'. They had to take an enormous wicker trunk laden with *kosher* perishables – the only thing Shayna Perl would let them eat on the ship crossing the Atlantic were potatoes. Minnie says she cried herself to sleep for a year.

Perhaps two million people left the Pale between 1881 and its dissolution in 1917. Reaching America was the dream for most of the migrants, with Britain often a temporary halt on the way. But for around 150,000 Jews – those for whom two days from Bremen or Hamburg on an overcrowded ship was more than sufficient – the stop in England became permanent.

That number included Harry's parents.

Monday 28th January

Caronia had been at anchor off Nassau since six thirty in the morning. The sound of the winches, and the ship's tenders smacking against its sides as they were lowered, had woken Harry and for once he felt hungry enough for breakfast.

He was one of the few hardy souls who had made it to dinner last night, which was a pity as the ballet involved in serving food during a rough sea was worth a guinea a minute. Harry cherished the memory of his waiter trying to stop the silver tureen slipping around on its salver while he ladled borscht into Harry's bowl.

This morning the restaurant was busy with people heading off on tour. After the storm, solid ground had suddenly become more enticing to some, but not Harry – Nassau held no surprises for him. He had holidayed there at least half a dozen times since 1947 and it was only ten days since he had made his last stop there on the transatlantic leg.

Vinnie was also very familiar with the charms of Nassau so was not venturing ashore either. Having been delayed by the storm, she was using the time at anchor to unpack properly. Harry had offered to help but she had declined. He understood her wish. By inclination, and out of professional necessity, he adored good tailoring. Hanging and folding clothes was a solitary joy, one to be luxuriated in, and he knew she had an extensive wardrobe to organise. For some of her sex, *Caronia*'s custom that evening dresses should change nightly was a challenge, one they were encouraged to meet by mixing formal separates. Not for Vinnie. She had brought along so many evening dresses and ball gowns that she would easily fill the separate bedroom she had hired as a walk-in closet. Not to mention her linen suits and camel stroller coat.

In Vinnie's absence he indulged himself with a brioche and pastry from the Balmoral's hot bun trolley. This was identical to the one in the Colony – a stainless-steel drum with a half-folding lid, and he cowed the waiter by inspecting the polish to ensure it was smearless.

He ate some green figs in syrup from another trolley and finished with grilled kidneys on toast, garnished with radishes. He had never subscribed to the notion that breakfast was the best meal of the day but this time he thoroughly enjoyed the leisurely eating. Afterwards, as an aid to digestion, he wandered over to the rail to watch the ship's tenders at work. They would be busy going back and forth for the next nine hours.

If Harry savoured a good meal just a little too readily or criticised a waiter's performance a little too forcefully, he could be forgiven for doing so as there had been not much food and certainly no chance of being waited upon as he was growing up.

*

The date when Moshe and Chaya Ester or, now they were on these shores, Morris and Esther – their anglicised names – arrived in London is lost to time. Before I started searching in earnest I had assumed their entry would have been some time between 1903 and 1905, simply because they would have both been the right sort of age to emigrate and a couple of Esther's siblings would have shown them the way.

Narrowing the date range was never going to be straightforward, since London has no equivalent of New York's Ellis Island processing centre; by and large records on immigrants from Europe have not survived.

I would have won the equivalent of the online immigration records lottery if Morris and Esther had happened to sail from Hamburg, since miraculously that port's shipping manifests have survived two world wars. It appears Hamburg was not their departure point. There was a tempting record for a Russian woman, Chya Wigoda, leaving the port for London on 1st July 1905. She was travelling alone but was *ledig* or single. Esther was almost certainly married by then – the entry is just one of the coincidences thrown up to tempt the amateur archivist off the straight path.

Neither does it appear that Morris and Esther headed for that other goldmine for genealogists: the Poor Jews Temporary Shelter on Leman Street in the East End. This laudable institution, originally just a refuge, developed into London's principal immigration and transmigration agency. Thirteen of its annual registers between 1896 and 1914 are searchable. My hopes were high: Morris and Esther would stand out, as Wygoda or Vigoda was an uncommon surname.

The closest I came to a match in the Shelter's records was a B. Wigotow, a baker from Grodno, who landed from Bremen in June 1898. I wishfully thought a harassed port agent had corrupted Wigotow from Wygoda and Grodno from Goworowo but the first initial was wrong and the date seemed a bit too early. At a pinch I speculated Morris could have left Różan to avoid being drafted into the Russian army on his 21st birthday, as at least one of his brothers-in-law had, but Esther, born in 1885, would have been too young to have been married. It would have been highly unusual for an unmarried young woman to have travelled later on her own and there is no evidence of the couple marrying here.

In fact they were married before they came. We can be certain because London was not the destination Morris initially set out for. Sad to say, it was not the city where he and Esther dreamed of spending the rest of their lives together.

Having married in 'about 1904' they had saved up for the price of a single passage to New York.[9] This was a common stratagem at the time to speed up emigration. The husband would go ahead, earn money more quickly than was possible back home and send for his spouse as soon as he had gathered enough to buy a second ticket. The plan was for Morris to join Esther's siblings and the other Różaners and Goworowers he knew already in Manhattan.

Canny Morris had timed his transit for the warmer half of the year as he would be spending the nine days of the crossing in steerage (third class). Records in Bremen show that he was supposed to be among the arrivals at Ellis Island on 6th September 1904 on the Norddeutscher (North German) Lloyd line steamship, *SS Konig Albert*.

The ship's manifest lists a 'Moses Wigoda', a married 'merchant' aged 26, whose last residence was Różan and who was travelling with a male cousin from Warsaw called Moses Gewisgold. In the document, under 'Race or People', which was determined, almost biblically, 'by the stock from which they sprang or the language they spoke', the shipping clerk had classified Morris as a Hebrew.

I was in for a shock when I saw the actual document. A line was struck through Morris's entire entry. It was like some ghastly presentiment of what would happen to people similarly classified by the Nazis 40 years later. This action would prove less fatal but still highly injurious to the couple's plan as it meant that Morris didn't actually board the *Konig Albert* for New York even though he had a ticket for it.

There is a medical note on his entry: 'conj(unctivitis) follicular', more commonly known as pinkeye. The Bremen agents would have been on the look-out for it; it was a sign of trachoma, a highly contagious disease of the cornea which was ineffectively

---

9 According to Morris in the 1911 census. His grasp of dates is admittedly unreliable – he got the ages of his children wrong.

treated at the time with copper sulphate and was often the cause of blindness. It rarely got past the Ellis Island medical inspectors and was one of the primary reasons for immigrants to be turned back. Norddeutscher Lloyd would then have been liable for the expense of repatriation. There were not usually as many passengers heading east as west across the Atlantic and a recession in the US in 1903 had brought the price of all fares down, but even so it would have cost the shipping line around £3 (£400 in today's money) to bring Morris back. So it seems that he was left behind in Bremen while cousin Moses completed the passage.

It must have been a wrenching moment for Morris to see all the other aspirants boarding the ship to the States. A lifetime of limitless possibility required little more than a forwarding address on arrival. Morris had intended to stay with his brother-in-law, Harris Cohen, at 165-7 Broome Street on Manhattan's Lower East Side, which is where records show his cousin Moses actually headed. Harris, a pants-maker, was possibly Esther's oldest sister, Rachael's husband. He had been in New York since 1893 and his address acted as a sort of post restante for all the later arrivals.

Before 1906 an immigrant could declare an intention to naturalise immediately on arrival in the US, (although they would still have had to have waited a further five years before they could lodge their second papers and the petition itself). Gewisgold submitted his naturalisation papers just a week after his arrival at Ellis Island. Having seen what had happened to Morris I suspect he was in no mood to hang about.

At least Morris was spared the even greater agony of being sent packing from Ellis Island itself. Like every other immigrant he would have been subjected to a quick examination of his hair, face, neck and hands by a doctor in the line as he was ushered up the stairs to the registration room in the main building. His eyelids would have been turned upwards for checking and inevitably 'Ct' – Chlamydia trachomatis – would have been chalked on his jacket. After that it was the holding pen until the representatives of Norddeutscher Lloyd Line would have been summoned to escort him back to Germany less than a month after he had set out from Goworowo. Morris would have been one of the two percent of Ellis Island arrivals refused entry to the United States.

Events from history, roads not taken, sometimes have a way of leaping out at you across the years. This is one such occasion for me. I look at the thick black line drawn through his name on the manifest and I can only reflect that if Morris had had better eyesight, Harry would not have been a Londoner and I would not have been here.

Balboa

Tuesday 29th January

Harry woke in a contented frame of mind. He might still be alone in his single bed but yesterday evening had been like old times. The lido pool had been kept open for swimming until midnight so they had a quick dip together after dinner – Vinnie watchful that her freshly set hair stayed out of the water. Later they had danced to Aidan McNally on the open-terraced deck illuminated by the huge sunburst effect light inside the Verandah Café.

On his way to breakfast, Harry detected a crackle of energy amongst his fellow guests. *Caronia* was sailing past the tip of Cuba. It was only three months since the threat of a global nuclear war had been at its highest – the week at the end of October 1962 that became known as the Cuban Missile Crisis. The fact that President Kennedy had successfully faced down the Russians only added to Harry's sense of wellbeing.

It was a little breezy but the weather was fine. He had the prospect of a full breakfast – he felt hungry – and a full day's sunbathing in front of him. This was the sort of day *Caronia* offered to remind him of just how far he had come in life.

*

Heading to London might have been second best for Morris but it was still better than returning to Różan. The shipping company probably suggested this alternative rather than having to refund him fully. Once he found digs in London, and perhaps with some of the fare he had saved, he sent for Esther. She would have been obliged to follow him despite the fact that all her brothers and sisters were emigrating to the US. Very possibly she could have joined him in Bremen before they made the crossing together. The transit ports acted as big dormitories at the time as the uncertain logistics of human trafficking meant they needed plenty of cheap beds to accommodate last-minute delays in sailing times, which could sometimes last weeks.

Did Morris entertain ideas about trying to get to the US again later, while never quite having the wherewithal to do it? Perhaps the two days across the North Sea in an overcrowded ship surrounded by seasick passengers put them both off travelling for the rest of their lives. Maybe Morris's experience in Bremen made him wary of officialdom forever. Neither he nor Esther ever naturalised in the UK. Neither would ever have the right to vote or to possess a British passport. Morris would have met the requirement for fifteen years' residence – non-Jews could apply after five – by the 1920s and could have managed the ten-pound fee but it seems that he didn't bother.

What is certain is that, once here, they never left the country again. Esther only ever managed to see one of her siblings – her younger sister, Fannie – again in her lifetime. And then only twice, when Fannie came to London in 1928 and 1956. There is the remotest of possibilities that she saw her eldest brother, Benjamin, when he passed through London between Poland and the US, leaving his pregnant wife with her parents in Goworowo. Records show Benjamin arrived in London aboard the *Cressida* from Hamburg on the 4th January 1905 before catching the *Friesland* from Liverpool to Philadelphia on 17th January. That gave him a fortnight wandering around London. Communications being what they were at the time, it is a long shot but I would love to imagine the three of them convening somewhere in Whitechapel to wish each other *mazel tov* one last time before he got the boat train north.

The first official sighting of Morris and Esther Vigoda in their new land came on 6th June 1908 in the copperplate handwriting of Mr E.A. Parsons, deputy registrar of the Mile End New Town District. He recorded the birth at home – 11 Sion Square – of Rose, the elder of Harry's two sisters, on 21st April 1908.

The conversation must have been halting because Mr Parsons, while undoubtedly experienced in dealing with non-native speakers, wrongly logged two bits of vital information: first, Rose is registered as Rosa (closer to the Polish 'Royza'); second, Esther's maiden name is given as Stahl instead of Stern. This latter slip, either because of a mispronunciation or, more likely, inattention (maybe that was why he was the deputy registrar), made the search for Rose's birth a century later much harder than it should have been.

Morris, not trusting his English yet, marked the register with a cross, but between them he and Esther conveyed their anglicised names and the family's surname. They were the Cohens.

The adoption of the surname Cohen came as a jolt. There is a story elsewhere in the family that Morris could not make himself clear to the landing officer when he arrived in London so in desperation the official asked the men in line on either side of him what they were called. One replied 'Cohen' and at a scratch of a bureaucrat's pen Morris had a new moniker. This is a familiar trope in Jewish family histories. Perhaps the name resonated with Morris because it was the Vigoda family's Levitical tribe or he'd heard the HaCohen honorific often back in Poland. Very possibly Morris thought it was lucky because it was the name of his brother-in-law in Manhattan, the one who had successfully got into the US. That said, despite giving it to their children, Morris and Esther's later behaviour shows that they were never that comfortable with the alias.

The Jewish Midrash, the rabbinical interpretation of the meaning of Scripture, includes the Leviticus Rabbah. Rabbi Hun held that Israel was redeemed from Egypt – obviously a big tick for the young nation – for four reasons: they did not change their name, they did not change their language, they did not go bearing tales and none of them was found to have been immoral.[10]

There is some more commentary on the observation 'they did not change their name'. Having gone down as Reuben and Simeon, they came up as Reuben and Simeon. They did not call Reuben 'Rufus' nor Judah 'Leon', nor Joseph 'Lestes', nor Benjamin 'Alexander'.

Cue a hollow laugh from anybody who has struggled with researching cross-border Jewish genealogy. Jewish families invariably altered their surnames on arrival as they searched for cognates in the English language. The use of a new surname in official annals by Harry's family name fitted a wider pattern.

In the search for the family's British footprints it was actually Annie's birth certificate that came to light first: Mr F.G. Brown, registrar of the Mile End New Town sub-district, showing his deputy how to do it. Annie was born at 4 Queen Street, Whitechapel on 18th March 1910.

In the 1911 census they were a family of five, still living at the same address: Morris; Esther; Harry, four-and-a-half years old (Morris randomly assigning a birth date); Rose, three; and Annie, one. Despite his bizarre claim to be the second born, Harry was definitely the eldest of the children.

Queen Street was a squat dead-end of a road, little more than an alley leading to warehouses. One can get a sense of the conditions the family were living in by the descriptions of the trades undertaken in the buildings that surrounded their flat. There would have been a near-constant clamour from a brass and iron foundry and a sawmill on the west side of the street, and worse, there would have been the stench of the fish-curing business at number 30. It would have been a cheap place to live and according to the 1911 census they all lived in one room.

The cramped space may have forced a move when Esther became pregnant with their fourth child. Harry's younger brother Benjamin was born at home on 5th November 1914. This time

---

10 Leviticus Rabbah 32:5.

it is Esther who marked her cross on the birth certificate. The family now lived on the other side of Whitechapel High Street at 84 Mulberry Street. They may not have known, or cared, that the street name harked back to those earlier immigrants – the Huguenot weavers would have nurtured mulberry trees for their silkworms – but it was familiar territory. Part of Sion Square, where they had been living when Rose was born, had been renamed and the houses renumbered to run into Mulberry Street in about 1912.

A sense of the family's living conditions there can be glimpsed in the trenchant accounts of the Victorian social reformer Charles Booth. Having created 'Poverty Maps' of London in the late 1880s, he revisited Mulberry Street in 1898. He does not sound overly impressed as he describes the street in his notebook as '3 + 2 storeyed, mess, fishes heads, paper, orange peel, bread, like all the Jewish Streets, boots + tailors'.

In the famous Poverty Maps, Booth coloured Mulberry Street light blue, which meant 'Poor. 18s(hillings) – 21s a week for a moderate family'. Its neighbouring streets were largely purple – 'Mixed, some comfortable, others poor' – but at least Mulberry Street was not dark blue: 'Very poor, casual. Chronic want.' In the 1898 notebook he commented that the street had become more purple than blue, a tiny step in the right direction. The north side of Sion Square had actually been coloured dark blue on the original map but it too was purple by the time Booth jotted his notes down. He described Sion Square as '3 st(oreyed), a few but very few flowerpots on windowsills – dark blue patch has disappeared.'

All this should be put in context in case it gives the impression that Morris and Esther had gentrified by 1914. In Booth's social cartography light blue was standard poverty. Household earnings averaged around twenty shillings a week in these streets, a level notionally positioned by Booth as the boundary between those just about getting by and those in want. Only when you graduated from purple to pink did you get to a level Booth called working-class comfort. It would appear that the family were just getting by and that, aside from four children, Morris and Esther had little to show for their first decade in London.

We have three home addresses for Morris and Esther in six years; very probably there were more. Families moved around a lot, especially if their income was irregular and they couldn't make the rent. They were not *schnorrers,* beggars, but young Harry must have been aware of their indigence. The rent – seven or eight shillings a week, payable in advance – would have been a constant struggle.

Of course most people Harry would have known would have been in the same boat. All the family's addresses are in the heart of Jewish Whitechapel, the junction of Commercial Road and Whitechapel High Street. Charles Booth's one-time assistant George Arkell published a colour-coded map of Jewish East London in 1899. This time the dark blue of Mulberry Street did not denote extreme poverty, it signified that over 95% of the residents of the street were Jewish. Harry, playing on the streets, would at least have been surrounded by friends with the same background and standard of living as him.

Commercial Street was a packed thoroughfare of trams and carriages passing between flower and vegetable carts lined up on the kerbs. Brick Lane, across the road heading north, offered just as much noise and bustle: not only from the sandwichmen or the street sellers of fruit, bagels and platzels, but also the barrowmen hawking catsmeat or rags, and the clothes and china shops, the kosher butchers and the shops selling chickens and fried fish.

All this commerce and industry contrasted with the lowlifes in the lodging houses (you could tell they were lodging houses by their lamps) where Flower and Dean Street joined Brick Lane. Harry and his siblings would have been warned away from that end of the lane – Morris and Esther likely highly judgemental of the drinking and brawling. Besides Bethnal Green, at the top end of Brick Lane, was a Christian area and there were certain streets you did not go down unless you wanted a beating.

In trying to imagine how Harry and his parents lived I have a problem. Given Harry's scorched-earth policy towards his family

I have no hand-me-down memories of his upbringing. In their absence I need to lean on the recollections and oral testimonies of other poor but respectable Jewish immigrants if I want to reconstruct what his life was like in those formative years.

In picturing the actual dwelling in Mulberry Street I doubt Morris could afford rent for more than two rooms. (As in a census we don't allow him to count the landing or scullery). The water closet would have been shared and outside somewhere.

In my mind's eye the front door opens onto a good-sized room but one that has to double as a bedroom at night. A coal fire and range sit opposite the door. There is a gas light on the ceiling (the room's nighttime occupants would have had to put up with the sputtering mantle) and the only furniture are a scrubbed table and chairs and a little dresser. As well as china, the dresser contains the family's prized possessions: perhaps some lace from Morris and Esther's marriage, candlesticks, small paintings, photographs of relatives in Poland. A curtain on a string suspended across an alcove opposite the window hides the bed where Harry slept. Ben would join him as soon as he was weaned, which Harry did not mind as they would keep each other warm. It would not have made for the ideal bedroom – the room was often smoky if the flue was dirty – which meant the window was always open, and the gas light was on permanently as without it the room was very dark.

One door from the parlour leads into the bedroom, long and narrow with a double bed, a chest of drawers, a small cupboard and a put-u-up for Rose and Annie sleeping head-to-toe. There is a second fireplace but it is only ever used if one of the children is sick.

Another door opens into the scullery – a single cold tap over a stone sink, a boiling copper with a small coal fire underneath, a coal bin (although, to save money, anything combustible is used to fire the copper) and the cleaning paraphernalia, brushes, mops, a bucket. There is a big enamel bowl which the family uses to wash themselves because the sink is too shallow for the job. When necessary, the family uses the public baths in Goulston Street, tuppence a time, and very occasionally Morris and Harry have a vapour bath at Shefshick's on Brick Lane before Friday worship.

Jugs of milk and butter dishes are stored under the sink in a bowl of cold water to keep them fresh. The whitewashed walls are always wet with condensation from the continuous washing. The washing itself, strung on lines across the room, never seems to dry unless the heavy iron, heated directly from the coals in the living room, is used.

All the washing – and the smoke – does not deter the bed bugs, who would crawl out of the cracks in the walls in their legions. The iron bed stands in little tins of paraffin to stop the bugs, largely ineffectively, but Esther couldn't afford Keating's Powder for the sheets. For the rest of his life Harry would hate the smell of almonds because they reminded him of his buggy nights.

That may be pushing it. While I am sure the flat was infested with bugs – a habitual problem, not a reflection on Esther's cleanliness – I have no idea whether Harry, like other tenement-dwellers memorialised by the anthologists, was repulsed by the smell of almonds. The gulf between 84 Mulberry Street and 55 Park Lane, where Harry spent the last twenty years of his life – all clubland green leather, glass-fronted bookcases and Old Masters – induces such flights of fancy.

My speculation on what their rooms were like cannot be disproved though. In Harry's time, Mulberry Street ran north-south and was connected to Commercial Street. Now it runs east-west and is cut off from the thoroughfare. Its modern façade is no guide as the road was totally rebuilt after the Blitz: it's just a few shops with flats above, offices, a hotel and a German Catholic mission. At least it still exists in some form. Queen Street is long gone: it was renamed Rowland Street, itself to be later demolished and preserved only in the name of two tower blocks on Hanbury Street, the cut-through that runs east from Spitalfields to Whitechapel.

One can cast a net a few hundred metres wide over all of Harry's known childhood addresses. It takes under an hour to walk between them, which I did, but if I expected some insight into what his living conditions were truly like I was destined to be disappointed. Decades of town planning and the close attention

of the Luftwaffe have almost completely erased the architecture and fabric of his early years.

Thursday 31st January

Harry had enjoyed a relaxing and pain free couple of days.

On the 29th they had hosted another couple of Americans at Vinnie's behest, and Harry could tell their social diary was keeping the Section Waiters on their toes. The Bartlett hors d'oeuvre trolley – like the Colony's, a great cumbersome thing with four rows of dishes on a vertical carousel – was as well polished as the hot bun trolley at breakfast. It was a jolly party: Harry's name-dropping finding a willing audience and both women looking resplendent in gold gowns. Afterwards the four went to the Gala Red and Gold Ball in the Main Lounge and Harry managed to dance a couple of very passable Foxtrots with Vinnie and their female guest.

He was still on something of a high when he woke up. He had missed breakfast so rang his steward for a cup of broth. He lounged in bed reading the *Ocean Times*, the salmon-pink digest of world events. He was not in the least bit disturbed by the lead that French President Charles de Gaulle had vetoed the United Kingdom's entry into the European Economic Community. Harry naturally genuflected to French gastronomy and adored the Riviera, especially in winter, but otherwise was indifferent to Anglo-French politics.

The breeze got up on the 30th but as more people had found their sea legs, the choppy waves didn't affect the ship's social life – the deck sports, card competitions, tea dances – all carried on regardless. He and Vinnie took in the 9.30pm showing of *Dr No* in the Theatre after dinner. They had actually been to one of the premieres at Cubby Broccoli's personal invitation – Cubby was the James Bond movie producer. But Vinnie wanted a reprise. Once again she was entranced by the action, Harry by the peripherals. He knew from the books that Bond drove a Bentley – battleship grey in contrast to the white that Harry preferred – but definitely a Bentley. In this movie he cavorted around in a Sunbeam Alpine. Harry was more taken with the Anthony Sinclair pared-down suits sported by 007. Harry did not have the physique for Sean Connery's 'Conduit Cut' but that did not prevent him from fantasising that it would be his next order from his own tailor, Cyril Castle.

Clothes, cars, jet-set travel – all fetishised in the movie but all patently within his grasp too. Like the premiere, he enjoyed watching the showing surrounded by other people for whom bespoke tailoring and exotic holidays were the norm.

At five in the morning on the 31st, *Caronia* halted briefly at Cristóbal, the port of the city of Colón on the eastern side of the Panama Canal, to pick up the pilot who would navigate her through to Balboa. The traverse of the canal was one of the early highlights of the cruise so a few hardy sightseers were up to witness the event. Under the control of the pilot, the 50-mile journey began by passing through a breakwater into the long channel that led to the Gatun Locks. As she approached the first set of huge steel gates, the ship's engines were stopped.

Harry was an old hand who had been through the canal several times before, including in both directions in 1954. Nevertheless, the theatre of the passage through the locks had brought him on deck. The cruise lecturer, Ivan Boxell, was broadcasting over the Tannoys. The ingenuity of crossing the spine of two continents at their lowest point to save days of travel had to be balanced by the cost of so many lives lost to malaria in its construction. Half-listening, Harry looked down on the famous 'donkeys', electric locomotive mules running on tracks alongside the canal that pulled the ship through the three pairs of locks, lifting her 85 feet to Gatun Lake. According to the commentary, *Caronia* was like a mouse going up the leg of a coffee table, crossing the top and down the other side.

He and Vinnie took lunch on deck at the Miraflores Locks, looking down on electric locomotives doing the same pulling job. This time they were stepping the liner down to the level of the Pacific. Houses and buildings started appearing on the shores of the channel. They passed under the Pan American Highway bridge before dropping the pilot and docking in Balboa.

The commentary had found a second wind as the ship approached its destination: Boxell closed with the fact that exactly 450 years earlier, Vasco Núñez de Balboa had crossed the Isthmus in search of gold and in doing so became the first European to set eyes on the Pacific. The reward for the Spanish conquistador shortly afterwards was a beheading on trumped-up charges of treason. As the ship rounded the waterfront statue of Balboa, bestriding the globe with his sword held high, Harry felt a kinship. It was the fearless explorer, despite his flaws, and not his stay-at-home accusers whom posterity remembered.

Balboa, the hilly northern part of Panama City, had been home to a few subsistence ranches before the US Army Corps of Engineers based themselves there during the construction of the canal. Now it was the thriving administrative centre of the Canal Zone, US territory by treaty. The evening excursion was to Old Panama to see a mainstay of local folklore, the 'Dirty Devil'. Carnival was not until February but busloads of *Caronia* tourists would be treated to the sight of oversized shamans with pink cloaks, feathered hats and devil masks whirling and warding off evil spirits.

Harry had no interest in the ceremony but Vinnie was going with a chap they had fallen in with during the Red and Gold Gala Ball. This fellow had described himself as the 'poorest man on the ship', which was probably not quite true. He had sold his farm in Texas and was fulfilling a lifelong ambition to cruise the world on the proceeds. Harry found him unusually and likeably self-deprecating for a Southerner and so, it seemed, did Vinnie. Harry had been irked by how quickly she dropped into her Texan drawl and how clearly she was enjoying the other man's company. But tonight he was glad she was not accompanying him onshore, for he had other plans. He too was leaving the ship but did not want anyone else to know his destination – the hospital.

At his doctor's suggestion, Harry had started taking Librium, a benzodiazepine recently patented by Hoffman-La Roche. Harry suspected that the upturn in his vigour and sense of wellbeing was linked to the drug regimen. For someone who valued self-reliance as highly as he did, he was loath to admit how dependent he had become on his stash of the little two-tone capsules.

His issue was that he could only get prescriptions for a month's supply at a time and was now running alarmingly low. This was the place to replenish his stock: he had a hunch that Balboa hospital would have a ready supply for all the bored and depressed wives of the servicemen stationed there.

Shortly after the port formalities had been completed, at about five o'clock, Harry took the gangway from Main Deck, the first time he had been off the boat in six days. Clutching his Panama Tourist Card – you could not go ashore in the Canal Zone without it – Harry took a taxi from the pier up Ancon Hill to the Gorgas Hospital, originally built by the French to deal with all the malaria and yellow fever cases of the canal workers.

The engineers had located Gorgas Hospital in grounds of palm and hibiscus at maximum elevation to feel the benefit of any healthy breezes. It had been improved and extended by the US authorities after they bought the French Canal Company, and by the time Harry visited it was reputedly one of the best hospitals in the Tropics. It certainly had Harry's Librium in answer to his dollars. He bought the maximum prescription – 50 capsules – which with any luck, and assuming *Caronia* worked its calming magic, would see him through the rest of the cruise.

*

By this stage Harry was in daily need of sedatives to deal with what he only ever euphemistically called his 'ailment'.

At some time around 1930, Harry had been diagnosed with Hodgkin's Disease. His white blood cells had gone into cancerous multiplication in the lymph nodes of his neck and chest. These lymphocytes, which were supposed to fight off infections, instead began to attack his own immune system. An unfathomable compound of genetic predisposition and some mild, brief illness in childhood – maybe a herpes virus – had changed the course of his life.

Like most sufferers he misattributed his initial symptoms. The weakness and fatigue he put down to the long hours of work, the same reason for his having shed a few pounds of weight (which he was secretly delighted with). Harry's natural capacity for deception meant that his illness passed unnoticed, or at least unremarked, by anybody else. But the swelling at the side of his neck and armpits, although painless, was alarming and after a couple of weeks he sought out a doctor.

The doctor ordered a biopsy, the only sure way of making the diagnosis. It was Harry's first real health setback and therefore his first visit to a proper doctor. His neck was wiped with iodine and anaesthetised with novocaine, and then a hollow needle was pushed through a tiny incision. A few cubic centimetres of bloody tissue were aspirated, left to clot on some blotting paper, dropped into a bottle of formalin and sent for microscopic analysis.

Nowadays a diagnosis of Hodgkin's lymphoma need not be devastating. Clinical research and breakthroughs in radiation therapy and chemotherapy have transformed an invariably fatal disorder into one that is routinely cured.

Harry's timing was not so fortunate. One of the anecdotes his children remember him recounting was that he had been told he would not have lived to see 30 unless he had treatment.

This was, in all likelihood, external beam radiotherapy – high energy X-rays used to shrink the cancerous cells while minimising skin damage. At the time fractionation was an empirical art, not an exact science, given the complex interdependence between dose and treatment time. Harry's regime might have been five doses a week for six weeks for a total dose of 6,000 roentgens. Unavoidably, his skin was damaged. He was treated before the efficacy of administering lower dose radiation to multiple regions of lymph nodes, not simply limiting the exposure to the nodes with the disease, was fully appreciated.

Whatever the treatment was, it worked. Even with successful radiotherapy, five-year survival rates would have been about one patient in four. Remarkably for the time, Harry had three more decades to look forward to, which is some sort of testimony to his strength of will. The probability is that in these early days of radiation Harry's 'cure' came at a price in that it seeded the cancers that were now engulfing him. At least it didn't make him sterile.

Acapulco

Monday 4th February

The cruise to Acapulco, 1400 miles north, had been just as relaxing as the cruise south from Nassau. It wasn't just because Harry's stash of Librium had been replenished. All three days had offered clear skies, calm seas and a light northerly breeze that made for perfect sunbathing weather.

On the 2nd the Main Lounge had been decorated for the Saturday Night Dance. Harry managed a couple of turns with Vinnie, who otherwise had a very full dance card. Harry could not begrudge her that. Sitting, smoking, a drink in his hand, watching Americans dancing to live music took him back to earlier times. He may have been cast in the role of spectator but he was finding that he didn't need to be the centre of attention so much nowadays.

It was seven o'clock on Monday morning when *Caronia* anchored in Acapulco Bay. In the 1920s the picturesque fishing port had been transformed into a winter playground by the construction of a fast highway connecting to Mexico City. It was a familiar resort for both Harry and Vinnie, which was fortunate as they were not getting much time to play today: just eight hours before *Caronia* departed on the 1500-mile leg north to Long Beach.

They had breakfast together, which was something of a rarity. So far on the trip they had spent far less time in each other's company than he had anticipated. By some unspoken agreement, entry to Vinnie's suite had become by invitation rather than by right. In one sense this was a relief: the prospect of moving his wardrobe if they were to start cohabiting again was somewhat daunting now that he was settled.

Harry chose the ham and eggs platter as a quick fix for his torpor although he did not appreciate the waiter warning him how hot the enamel dish was: the sound of the sizzling meat was evidence enough.

Afterwards, he and Vinnie took one of the shore tenders. It was a hot day, the canvas cabin roof of the launch had been rolled back and the all-white buildings on the waterfront glistened in the sun as they neared the jetty. They handed over half their Landing Cards, already stamped by the Mexican authorities, and picked up one of the tour cars to the El Mirador. The plan was to see the cliff divers from the hotel's terraces before a buffet luncheon in the 'Ship's Deck' dining room.

The hotel's menagerie and luxuriant gardens formed part of its draw but the real attraction was its vantage point across from the diving platform. They watched the show – the skill and bravery of the acrobats skirting the jagged rocks on their long drop was undeniable. It was a congenial morning, Harry felt strangely at home – he had been here before, of course. But at lunch it struck him that he could have been sitting in his own hotel, Rowena Court, looking out to sea over the sloping lawn. That is, if one ignored the cliffs and the intrusive Mexican orchestra.

They declined the offer of a return car and strolled back down to the quay arm-in-arm. Vinnie spoke Spanish and knew the resort well from her time living in Mexico City; she and Bob had done the same walk on the 1954 cruise. They wandered around some beachfront stores. Harry had enough Acapulco keepsakes so hadn't bothered to buy any pesos on board; Vinnie, however, bought some sombreros, ponchos and false moustaches for a dinner party she was hosting. She even purchased a couple of fake plastic cigars for the ladies.

Harry notified his bedroom steward of his return on board. He didn't expect any mail but this would be the earliest any from Britain would have reached him so he went along to the distribution point in the Forward Observation Lounge on the off chance some might have arrived. There wasn't any so he repaired to the Smoking Room for the six o'clock news broadcast. He couldn't concentrate – the excursion to El Mirador kept bringing back images of Rowena Court and therefore, Betty, his wife.

Harry and Vinnie had been snapped by a ship's photographer on the return from their jaunt, capturing the moment when they came through the embarkation doors on Main Deck. They saw the photograph later that evening on the sales board that had been put up in the Restaurant Deck lobby. The Maître D' and Head Waiters were occupied with other diners so they were escorted to their table by the Section Waiter who, in a fit of over-enthusiasm, commented on how fit they both looked in the picture. Harry hated looking at himself at the moment: he had lost weight and looked haggard. He needed a lot more sun to iron out the wrinkles. He always craved the sun in any case. He thought it might have something to do with having worked so much of his life in basements. Perhaps also because, although he had spent a lot of time outdoors, it never seemed sunny when he remembered his childhood.

*

As a child in London, like any other native of the tenements, Harry had little in the way of possessions or distractions to keep him indoors. There was not much peace in the flat anyway as you could hear people all day long through the floors, walls and ceilings and across the landing. So Harry and his mates lived on the streets.

They spent the days dodging the traffic on Commercial Street, hunting for fruit dislodged from the kerbside barrows before it rotted and playing Kick the Can. They sneaked into the movies at the Brick Lane Palace. The Saturday afternoon pictures were the highpoint of the childhood week. Not just the feature but also the serials: like *Perils of Pauline*, which was silent of course but somehow fashioned a cliffhanger to capture their imagination from week to week.

As he got older he joined in with classmates baiting the down-and-outs in the grounds of Christ Church or getting involved in yids-versus-yocks scraps with boys from the Anglican schools. He would be called into the front line in the skirmishes between Jewish Whitechapel and Gentile Wapping, chucking rubbish at each other across the cobbles. There would always be a pretext – a perceived slight or minor assault – but it happened too regularly and had too little real violence to be more than a childhood game.

This was the period when Harry decided it wasn't what you knew but who you knew that counted most in life or perhaps more accurately, how you knew them. He would tell his daughters that he acquired lifelong friends and valuable partners – men he could trust – amidst all the scrapes and trading and jaunts on the street. People like his accountant, Arnie Finer, and his personal doctor, Teddy Joystone-Bechal.

It was not all play. As the eldest he would have been pressed early into running errands for Esther to shops like Garfinkle's where she could buy in small quantities or 'on the book', sometimes late at night because it stayed open after all the other shops had shut at 10pm.

Even without visits to the grocers he would have been learning the basics of trading. Scarcity meant there was a secondary market in the use of just about any childhood possession. A ride on a scooter might cost a piece of fruit or a grab in a bag of sweets. The children would have found it natural to mimic the haggling they saw in the local markets over cigarette cards, picture-books, nuts in Passover week, anything – a penny or a ha'penny at a time in order to get the price of admission to the pictures.

My vision of the young adolescent Harry owes something to the descriptions of his close contemporary and later fractious business rival, Al Burnett. Burnett's somewhat immodest autobiography, that of a self-described 'leading impresario and entertainer', dwells at some length on those days.[11]

Burnett was born Aaron (he preferred Alfie) Isaacs in Whitechapel in 1906. Harry may well have come across him when

---

11 Burnett, Al (1963). *Knave of Clubs*, Arthur Baker, UK.

he was growing up; he certainly ran into him repeatedly and antagonistically later in life.

If Harry had written his own life story his 'voice' would probably have sounded similar to Burnett's: bombastic, competitive, shrewd, name-dropping. He would have had a fund of stories and anecdotes to mine like Burnett did. He might even have written it during his involuntary career break in 1963, the same year in which Burnett published, although there is little evidence that Harry was in an elegiac frame of mind when he set out on his cruise. Even if he were, I doubt he would have started his narrative in the East End like Burnett did – he had not spent a lifetime disowning his background to then confess it to the world in a personal history.

Burnett characterises those days when both he and Harry were in their mid-teens as 'carefree', or at least as free of cares as a neighbourhood like Whitechapel was capable of offering. The First World War had just ended, the death and misery was behind them; all everyone wanted to do was to have fun and learn to live again.

Harry, like Al, would have been one of the young men on the main drag every Saturday night – from Gardiner's Corner, where Whitechapel Road and Commercial Street met, to New Road and back. In his younger days the highlight would have been two-penn'orth of chips from Sach's in Vallance Road in the middle of the circuit. After he had left school and had a bit more money in his pocket he would have paraded in his starched Sabbath-best (which he called *Shabbos*, not *Shabbat*). He would have hoped to finish the promenade with a proposition to a girl on the same route: perhaps to meet again on Tuesday evening at the bandstand at Arnold Circus and listen to the brass band together

Burnett was a small-time boxer. He had a few six-round fights on the undercard at the People's Palace in Mile End and at Premierland in Backchurch Lane, a hall that could hold two thousand spectators. Rookies were always on standby if some of the bouts failed to go the distance, because the promoters guaranteed punters three hours of boxing. Judging by his nose,

I wonder if Harry was ever one of the enthusiastic beginners. He was certainly a fan of amateur boxing throughout his life. His nephew Malcolm Morris remembers his father, Ben, and Harry dressed in evening suits and Crombie overcoats regularly going out to the Victoria Club in the 1950s to watch – and bet on – fights.

What Harry and Al really had in common – like Harry and Bob O'Donnell – was an obsession with show business. Burnett claims he was always hungry as a child: he was one of four children whose father, a trouser presser, was in poor health and died when Al was twelve. Money would have been tight and yet he found the means to go to vaudeville at the Queens in Poplar or the Cambridge, and see variety shows from the galleries at the London Shoreditch and the Olympia. Given the similarity in their later careers, my hunch is that Harry was doing exactly the same.

The West End was a mythical area whose chief attribute was that it wasn't obviously the East End. When Harry and Al were growing up, the Finsbury Park Empire was probably as 'West End' as they could aspire to, but with cash from their first jobs – Burnett became a machinist in a tailoring workshop – they could authentically 'go up West' to see the stage shows and revues. A seat in the gallery would cost a shilling but often three or four of them would bribe the doorman with a shilling between them.

Harry, as stage-struck as Burnett, would have been bowled over by Florence Mills in *Blackbirds* or Sophie Tucker in *Playtime Revels* too. (Harry tried to sign Tucker for the Colony Club in 1950). Burnett became besotted with American acts after seeing stars like Tallulah Bankhead and the musical comedy *No, No, Nanette*. Harry likely had the same formative influences – it is striking how his own cabaret roster later would later lean so heavily on Stateside acts.

The childhood privations had another tangible benefit for Harry. His career would not have been successful were he not also obsessed with food. Like his anthologised contemporaries there surely would have been times when Harry went without it; perhaps occasions when he joined Esther, clutching a kettle and hiding his face, in the queue for the Soup Kitchen near Tenter Street.

Even if she avoided this sort of discomfit, Esther, living hand to mouth, was forever running out of essentials. Harry would run along with a dish for a penny's worth of jam, loose pickles, herrings or a screw of tea, or perhaps a jug for milk direct from the churn. Esther was a feisty customer even if she had to rely on credit. She came from a family of bakers so knew her stuff – she never went anywhere for black bread other than Rinkoff's.

Their diet would not have varied a great deal. All-day soup with greens and farfel, potatoes, barley and broad beans were the family's staples. *Vorsht* salami, in fact any sort of meat, was a treat. *Lockshen* – a sweet noodle dish for afters – even more of one. Jews from Poland had a notoriously sweet tooth, a predilection Harry kept all his life.

This sort of experience made him a reflexive gourmand. It might be trite but in all likelihood the bland diet fuelled his obsession with food or at least the desire to eat what he wanted when he wanted. I think one of the reasons the Colony would boast such an extensive choice of all-day items on the menu was Harry making up for the deprivations of his youth.

In later life his family recall the ceremony which accompanied Friday night dinners in his flat as well as his oftentimes embarrassing punctiliousness whenever he was served away from home. Harry's abiding interest and insistence on high standards were a feature of the reviews his restaurant garnered. One article in the populist daily, the *Sketch*, on New Year's Eve 1958, 'Profile of a Restaurateur' features his antidotes to Esther's all-day gruel: dishes like Poularde Souvaroff or Ris de Veau Madère – chicken or sweetbreads – that guests at the Colony could order any time the club was open. 'Harry Morris, though not conventionally trained in the intricate business of running a big restaurant, brings a natural flair to what, for him, is more of a hobby than a job', the journalist wrote. 'Always commercially interested in food, he rebuilt and opened the Colony because, like the late M. Boulestin, he was urged to do so by friends.'

Harry would have been gratified by the French in that article. Words meant a great deal to him and none more so than the menu French he associated with proper restauranting. He taught himself to use it without any sense of self-consciousness. Harry's daughters never heard him utter a single word of Yiddish, even though it was his native language as a child. His Polish accent would have been strong and might have been mocked by other Yiddish speakers. Perhaps because of this, Harry increasingly refused to speak it. This must date as one of the earliest of his renunciations but he intuitively grasped that language was the denominator of class. If he could master it, then he could move socially in a way his parents never could. In his early 20s he would completely eradicate the intonations and nasality of his accent, expand his vocabulary and learn to write properly.

Long Beach

Tuesday 5th February

Harry kept out of Vinnie's way on the first day out of Acapulco. This evening she was hosting the first of what she planned would be several soirees during the cruise – cocktails for sixteen in her suite followed by a Mexican-themed shindig in the bigger of the two private dining rooms. She was understandably tense.

He went to the matinee showing of that day's film: *Genevieve* with Kenneth More. The real star of the comedy, the veteran car, reminded Harry of those days in the late '20s when he and Betty were courting and used to take her pride and joy, her eleven-horsepower Morris Cowley, out for a spin. He seemed to be thinking a lot about Betty at the moment. Neither of them ever had to take a driving test – that would not become compulsory until 1935 – they just learned by taking turns at the wheel on those trips into the country.

There was always competition between *Caronia* passengers as to who could throw the most lavish party, admittedly a contest which was much cheaper than on shore because all alcohol and tobacco was sold at duty-free prices. A bottle of Mumm or Moet & Chandon Champagne cost barely more than $5, a hand-rolled Cuban cigar 75 cents, and, more to Harry's taste, a packet of King Size cigarettes, 35 cents.

Theoretically parties were arranged by the Purser's Office but the real actors were the Stateroom Stewards. The loyalty felt to the ship by the passengers was matched by the crew, many of whom signed up for the posting year after year, so the inter-steward competition to host the best parties spanned multiple cruises. This was especially true of those looking after the Main Deck suites who expected to be given carte-blanche by their indulgent occupants to pursue their rivalry. This cohort tested Cunard's crew policy on not fraternising with the passengers to the limit.

Vinnie aimed to put down an early marker. She had already formed a close bond with her room steward who was wildly imaginative and seemed to know everybody who was anybody on board so could be entrusted with the guest list just as he was with selecting her evening couture. He spent hours converting Vinnie's rooms into a cantina to enliven her mundane Mexican theme. His only stipulation in return was that he retain the role of awarding the prize for best-dressed guest.

Harry wasn't threatened by this intimacy because Vinnie's steward was gay, as indeed were many others. This was a period when there was a much more permissive attitude to sexuality at sea than on land. The Wolfenden Report had recommended the decriminalisation of homosexual activity between men in 1957 but it would take a further decade before public opinion had shifted enough for the Sexual Offences Act to become law.

Harry was as relaxed about this state of affairs as any other passenger. He had worked successfully with many gay performers, some more openly out than others, in his club. He didn't even object to his manservant, Torr, keeping his nail varnish and make-up in the cutlery drawer in the Park Lane flat.

Harry spent a lot of time at the party talking to Vaughan Rickard. The Cruise Director was unabashedly gay, was in a long-term relationship with another Cunard worker in Princeton, and didn't feel the need to speak Polari, the coded gay man's language flaunted by Vinnie's steward. He was also a lot more fun to be with given his inexhaustible fund of comic stories – mostly told against himself – about his wartime experience. It was a bit of a coup for Vinnie to entice him along; he would otherwise have been in the Lounge overseeing the dressing of the room for the Ball later.

Vinnie was in her element at the centre of it all. She looked resplendent in a floor-length sleeveless V-necked white dress with an orange sunburst motif, gathered at the waist to emphasise her figure: the addition of a false moustache and sombrero somehow making the ensemble even more alluring. Being partnered by the most attractive woman in the room had been Harry's single-minded aim for the last 40 years.

At 8pm the assembly trooped to the private dining room at the aft end of the Balmoral, making great play of parading through the public restaurant. The table had been laid out with menus printed for the occasion. Vinnie had selected some of her favourite dishes and requested a Mexican twist. The 'Caviar au Blinis' were accompanied by tequila instead of vodka – the alcohol splashed into Cunard wavy pattern glasses – the 'Châteaubriand sur Planque' graced by a taco salad and a Californian wine, the moulded ice cream dessert, a 'Bombe Caprice, Jubilée' surmounted by little Mexican flags. Harry avoided the latter, he had indigestion so ate some stem ginger from one of the gilded-edge shell dishes in the middle of the table. Judging by the convivial noise in the room nobody else was suffering and Vinnie's anecdotes about her years in Mexico seemed to be going down as well as the food.

The party joined the 'Mexican Fiesta' Ball in the Main Lounge afterwards. It was turning into a long night. The ship's bars generally stayed open until 1am, but as the Passenger Information put it: 'it is within the discretion of the Master to restrict or extend this time should such a course be considered desirable at any time during the voyage'. Generally that meant that if there were still enough thirsty customers around to warrant staying open, the bar stayed open. Vinnie's group demonstrated an unquenchable thirst that evening. Pleading tiredness Harry left them all still going strong in the Raleigh Room at two in the morning.

It had been a smooth night for sailing. Unarguably the evening had been a triumph but Harry was disconcerted. There had been a time, not so long ago, when he would have made a point of discovering and remembering the prejudices and predilections of all of Vinnie's guests. After all, his career had been built on just such attention to detail: that was how clients and performers had become personal friends. Tonight, however, he found he lacked both the energy and the desire to do so.

*

Harry's chameleon act may have been a key to his professional success but this aspect of his character makes it tricky to get to the truth about his childhood. Take his singular claim that his family lived in the Henley Buildings on the Boundary Estate and that he attended Rochelle School there. It must have been the specificity of these particular assertions in a childhood otherwise shorn of any narrative detail that made them stick in the minds of Mum and her younger sister. In investigating the veracity of these very precise stories, I think we get to the nub of Harry's slippery relationship with the truth.

There is a seven-year hiatus in the official record of where Harry lived between his brother Ben's 1914 birth certificate (Mulberry Street) and the 1921 census (Russell Street). Both streets are at a distance from the Boundary Estate and are much nearer schools other than Rochelle, but a gap this long enables a mythologiser like Harry. It provides him with a blank canvas on which to paint a more flattering self-portrait.

It is possible that the family moved to the Boundary Estate in the year after Ben's birth, meaning Harry could have attended Rochelle School between the ages of nine and thirteen, say. It should have been easy to check his attendance by way of the Rochelle Street School Roll. Frustratingly, the London Metropolitan Archives which holds the school's admission and discharge register for that period, deem it 'unfit for consultation'. When pressed, the archivist implied that further research would be fruitless as 'the indexes are faded to illegibility'.[12] I can't say I was surprised by the dead-end; this is Harry we're speaking about.

---

12 17 January 2014, email from LMA Enquiries.

An online search of the archives threw up only one credible school record. A Harry Cohen attended Millwall School in Glengall Road – now Glengall Grove – on the Isle of Dogs in 1915. This boy's home address was 104 Romford Street and his previous school, Myrdle Street. Both were next to Mulberry Street, Harry's last known address. This Harry left Millwall School in 1915 for another unnamed school and according to the record left full-time education in January 1918. Could this be Harry? If he could walk to the Isle of Dogs from Romford Street he could certainly walk to Rochelle Street. However, the boy's birth date – March 1904 – seems far too early as it is before Morris even tried to get into the US.

Thus I will never know for sure, but my hunch is that he made the stories up. Since Harry's lying was never pathological – there was always a reason behind it – the question that intrigued me was why Harry was fixated with these two particular places.

His wanting to be associated with the Boundary Estate is perhaps quite understandable as it became something of a talisman for aspirational Jews.

The East End of London had long been a magnet for political refugees and economic migrants, but it was only after the vast Jewish influx started in the 1880s that it assumed a reputation as the land of the outcast. This status attracted high-minded Victorian writers and social reformers like Charles Booth – he of the 'Poverty Maps' – and Sir Walter Besant. One can almost hear their words in the West End salons where thinkers, artists and hangers-on drew together to discuss the important matters of the day (and swap well-informed gossip). Speakers like Booth and Besant would have indulged the gathering with lurid descriptions of a ghetto occupied by exotic-looking people speaking a strange language: a land full of synagogues, backroom factories, little grocery stores that smelt of fish and unwashed garments and, of course, slums.

The most notorious of these was the Old Nichol Street Rookery: a crime-ridden warren of alleys and unpaved courts that was home to over 5,700 people in 700 tiny, subdivided houses. Extreme squalor, thieving gangs and prostitution might be hackneyed Dickensian images, but the reality of the Rookery would have been ghastly: its death rate was over twice that of London generally.

In fact, Old Nichol was deemed too dangerous for Dickens to visit when he was researching locations for Fagin and Bill Sykes' dens in *Oliver Twist* half a century earlier. He went to the Jacob's Island slum on the Thames instead, accompanied by a detachment of river police. He captured what he saw in his early collection of stories and articles, *Sketches by Boz*:

> *Wretched houses with broken windows patched with rags and paper: every room let out to a different family, and in many instances to two or even three … filth everywhere – a gutter before the houses and a drain behind – clothes drying and slops emptying, from the windows … men and women, in every variety of scanty and dirty apparel, lounging, scolding, drinking, smoking, squabbling, fighting, and swearing.*

Aside from the filth of the pigs and cows in the back yards, the smell from noxious activities like boiling tripe and catsmeat or melting tallow would have been an intolerable assault on the nose. There was almost no sewerage so the ponds formed by brick digging were 'lakes of putrefying night soil' according to one eyewitness.

Clearing Old Nichol almost proved beyond even the industrious Victorian do-gooders but after many false starts demolition began in 1893. The design for the replacement, the Boundary Estate – arguably the world's first council housing – was visionary. Each of the multi-storey brick tenements radiating from the central circus bore the name of a pleasant town along the River Thames. The streets between the tenement blocks were 50-feet wide and recalled the Huguenot associations of the area. There were to be over 1,000 tenements in 23 blocks, mostly two- or three-roomed and setting 'new aesthetic standards for housing the working classes'. The scheme included a central laundry, incorporating men's and women's slipper baths and two club rooms, eighteen shops, 77 workshops and 200 costermonger's sheds (for street traders to house their stock).

Twelve public houses were cleared away to ensure a 'dry' estate, an action unlikely to have recommended the accommodation to the previous incumbents of the slums. Even if they could have stomached the enforced sobriety, they may have baulked at the rent of three shillings a room. So the population turned over: the newcomers included clerks, policemen, cigar-makers and nurses but mainly Jewish artisans. The Boundary Estate could have ended up as much as 95% Jewish. Quite where the former inhabitants moved to is not clear. The only municipal housing was the estate so they probably squeezed into nearby slums, just not as obviously squalid as they had been before.

On opening the estate had 5,380 tenants – nominally. There were widespread allegations of, and investigations into, 'aliens' bribing the estate superintendent to get on the housing list. Understandably so as for many, including Morris and Esther, it offered a significant improvement in living conditions for roughly the same weekly rent.

Henley House in Swanfield Street, Harry's claimed residence, was one of the earlier blocks completed. At 70 tenements and a total of 165 rooms, it was bigger than later designs. It was also plainer. It did not have the glazed bricks on the ground floor storeys of the other blocks so the walls blackened quickly. To the modern eye it would have been pretty dull with the only relief provided by the colours in the window-boxes. But it was not damp or unsanitary and, although they may only still have had two rooms, they were bigger than the norm as the estate stipulated minimum bedroom sizes. They also had a private WC: granted, it was across the landing but they had their own lock and key.

If the Henley Buildings represented a step-up for the family, why did Harry also feel a desire down the years to be associated with Rochelle School?

The building has now been converted into a design space for artists and creatives, but one can still see the vestiges of the

Victorian red-brick inner-city school that it once was in its iron railings and separate entrances for boys and girls. It was nothing out of the ordinary for its time and there would not have been anything particularly special about his experience there.

Both sexes would have lined up in ranks in the playground for the hand bell at 8.50 every morning. The Infants Department took children up to the age of eight so Harry would have joined the set for the older boys. There was a form teacher for every 40 pupils who taught most subjects to the level of the Standards that had to be taken each year to keep moving up to the highest class in the school, aged around thirteen. After Morning Prayer there were lessons until twelve, two hours for lunch and back for lessons until 4.30 unless it was Friday, in which case the lessons ran through lunch until two and the school closed early for *Shabbos*.

Although virtually everyone was Jewish, all the lessons were in English. There was no uniform but every boy dressed the same once they were out of the Infants: boots, trousers, waistcoat, jacket and cap as a head covering – all little versions of their fathers.

Ordinary as it might have been, Harry still wanted to be associated with it. Not with the school perhaps so much as with some of its illustrious alumni. Bringing Rochelle Street School into conversations in the 1950s would have meant Harry, an inveterate, indeed professionally obligated, name-dropper, could mention some of his fellow students prominent in the business and entertainment worlds at that time. He wasn't alone in wanting to be associated with Rochelle Street: Al Burnett claimed to have gone to school there as well.[13]

I think Harry wasn't going to let the small matter of non-attendance get in the way of his stories. He wished himself there. Using the shorthand for this sort of identity disturbance from Woody Allen's allegorical movie, he zeligified himself into the early lives and schooling of these dynamic contemporaries.

Leonard Zelig is a man who wants to fit in so much that he takes on the characteristics of any strong personalities he happens

---

13 Burnett, Al (1963). *Knave of Clubs*, Arthur Baker, UK, p.12.

to be near. In the same way, I think Harry co-opted part of the life histories of two famous peers. Harry told his daughters that he knew this pair at Rochelle School and remained friends with them throughout his life. For Hearst and Chaplin in *Zelig*, the movie, read the seductive possibility of business tycoon, Charles Clore, and entertainment magnate, Lew Grade, in Harry's real life.[14]

Clore is little remembered now other than for the philanthropy that is done in his name. It was a different story in the couple of decades after the war when his hyperactive dealmaking made him as much feared as revered. Claiming him as a friend in the post-war years was to ally oneself with someone known to be shaking up the 'gentlemen's club' rules of British corporate finance. While Harry did not lack for nous and courage himself, he would have craved Clore's nickname, 'the man with the Midas touch', and admired Clore's enterprise in taking on the establishment. When Clore bought the shoe retailer Sears in 1953, it was the country's first ever hostile takeover. If occasionally his iconoclasm was too much for the authorities – another audacious bid for the Savoy Hotel Group reputedly foundered because Winston Churchill, then prime minister, lunched every day at Claridge's and set his face against it – that was fine with Harry. It brought out his scrapping side.

Grade was not a man who polarised opinion in quite the same way as Clore. He had business enemies, which was pretty much unavoidable for an agent and impresario of his standing. His larger-than-life Jewish showman act was almost a parody. Harry had no interest in emulating that or Grade's oversized Havana cigars but he would have admired Grade's sobriety and his consummate negotiation skills. There was a period at the start of the '50s when they were competing hard against each other for US talent. Nevertheless, Grade was always described as 'genial' and profiles of Harry often use the same adjective. Like Grade, Harry believed that his word and a handshake was all that was required: that the relationship trumped the contract.

---

14 Sir Charles Clore (26 December 1904 – 26 July 1979), Baron Grade of Elstree (25 December 1906 – 13 December 1998).

Israel and Yetta Clore, originally from Latvia, had a workshop on Bethnal Green High Street making clothes for their shop and barrows in Brick Lane and Petticoat Lane. Charles was a couple of years older than Harry, the sixth of seven children. It appears Israel was a bit more industrious than Morris – his workshop became a factory in Old Nichol Street where a dozen tailors made men's suits and boys' clothes. Charles attended Rochelle Street but moved up in the world – to Willesden – in 1916 which means that he and Harry would have overlapped for a year at most. Clore might have stood out – he was very blond and his nickname was 'Poppy', slang for money – but it feels to me that even if Harry was there, he inflated their relationship at school, particularly as Clore was reportedly an introverted child who did not mix well with his peers, not even with his brothers and sisters.[15]

It may have been a different story with Lew Grade, who was born Louis Winogradsky in December 1906 – the same month and year that Harry claimed he was born – in Tokmak, a *shtetl* outside Odessa.

In parallel with Harry's parental motivation, the Winogradskys' emigration followed the example set by Lew's maternal uncles. When Isaac, Olga, Lew and his younger brother Boris (Bernard Delfont) arrived in London in 1912, three of Olga's brothers were already established here, giving the new arrivals a network that Morris and Esther lacked. Consequently, while they would not have been much better off than the Vigodas – Isaac was a trouser presser and had a weakness for gambling – their assimilation was a lot quicker. Initially they rented rooms at the north end of Brick Lane, but in 1914 Olga's brother, Herschell, helped them move into the tenement where he lived, Henley House.

Lew also attended Rochelle Street School. Even though he was eight, Lew's poor grasp of English meant he suffered the indignity of starting in the Infants Department. It was only for six months though, as he proved to have a talent for language

---

15 Clutterbuck, David & Davine, Marion (1987). *Clore: The Man and his Millions*, Weidenfeld & Nicolson, UK, p.11.

and figures. Apparently he was so smart that by thirteen he had a desk in the hall, was helping the Headmaster, Mr Baldwin, to teach and had won a scholarship to Parameters College. He did not take it up: like Harry he left school at fourteen to start at Tew & Raymond, a clothing manufacturer.

The path of Grade's life and career has been well ventilated – in his own words and others.[16] Suffice it to say his start in the rag trade morphed into show business via a successful dancing career (his Charleston was legendary) and talent agency, first with Joe Collins, then with his youngest brother. (Naturally Collins, father of actress Joan, was another of Harry's close personal friends, according to Harry.)

If Harry's spell at Rochelle Street School was fantasy it would have been concocted amidst the banter and rivalry in the late '40s and '50s, when Harry was competing with Lew and Leslie Grade Ltd for talent, especially in the business of shipping American singers and comedians from New York to London. Billboard certainly pitched the two together with other active British bookers like Harry Levine, Cal Gibbons and Harry Foster.

Harry may have got to know Clore before then. He would not have had much to do with Clore in the '20s and '30s other than patronising one of his cinemas or the Prince of Wales Theatre in Coventry Street where Clore pioneered non-stop revues.

The opportunity to entrench a brief childhood acquaintance may have arisen during the early part of the war when they were neighbours in Middlesex. Clore lived at Ray Court in Maidenhead, very close to where Harry had evacuated his family. Clore held weekend parties for a revolving roster of film producers, bridge players and, invariably, dancing girls. A club owner and his vivacious ex-model wife, living nearby, would have been natural additions to the guest list. Harry's black-market contacts might have secured an invitation. Food was always a problem even for someone as well off as Clore.

---

16 Grade, Lew (1987). *Still Dancing*, HarperCollins, UK. Davies, Hunter (1981). *The Grades,* Weidenfeld & Nicolson, UK.

The Morris's invitations to Ray Court might have dried up in 1943 after Clore married his muse, Francine Halphen, and moved out to an estate called Checkendon in Oxfordshire. But as Harry's own post-war clubs became destinations in their own right, I feel confident that he often played host to these men, who were both friends and rivals. (Clore tried his hand at nightclubs, buying one on Tagg's Island in the Thames – one of his rare business failures.) This would have been particularly true for a period after the gregarious Clore split from Francine in the 1950s. He escorted many beautiful young women from his London apartment, just round the corner from Harry, at 95 Park Street; Harry's Colony was on his list of spots to take them.

Whether or not Harry poached aspects of Clore and Grade's biographies, if he was going to pick any lives to co-opt, he could have done a lot worse. Grade, Clore, Al Burnett and many of Harry's West End confrères with East End backgrounds were living rebuttals of the lazy slur that Jews were in some way partially responsible for what befell them because of a mute acceptance of their fate. On the contrary, this dynamic immigrant generation transformed those fields in which they were allowed to participate on an equal footing. Something about their marginalised upbringing – that the only way to be accepted was to work harder than any competitor – or perhaps the emphasis Jewish religion and culture places on material achievements made them all exemplars of creativity and social mobility.

Thursday 7th February

Wednesday had been a fine, clear day of gentle north-westerly breezes offering a slight sea. Vinnie had basked in the afterglow of her party. She dissected the evening over dinner with an insight and intent that Harry struggled to match. They went to the Bingo in the Main Lounge afterwards and danced to Aidan McNally's band again. For every dance he had with Vinnie, she had two with other men, a ratio that ordinarily would have annoyed Harry but he decided it was easier to allow her the limelight.

Harry's mood invariably lifted any time a ship neared a US port. He adored the States and loved Americans, whether they be performers, agents or dancing partners on the *Caronia* for that matter.

Caronia tied up at Pier A in Long Beach just after lunch. Harry and Vinnie presented their passports to US public health and immigration authorities in the Main Lounge and by mid-afternoon were ready to go onshore. They were certainly not going on one of the studio tours – MGM, RKO-Pathé or Hal Roach – nor one that took in movie stars' homes in Beverly Hills: Harry had entertained enough Hollywood aristocracy in the Colony. Instead, they were spending the night in the Biltmore where Harry planned to host a couple of theatrical agents he had worked with in the past. They were being accompanied by their wives so there would be six to sit down. Harry wanted to know who was up, who down, who was the next big thing: the price of the dinner was the cost of keeping his hand in the game and showing people he still had a future in it, he rationalised.

Long Beach itself had little to recommend it other than its proximity to Los Angeles. Oil had been discovered below the town in the 1920s and it was now a forest of oil derricks and petroleum company signs. It was the stop where many of the American passengers entertained West Coast friends on board. The stay was also an opportunity for Cunard to market its product. While Harry and Vinnie were heading in one direction, no fewer than 95 travel agents were heading in the opposite one to be wined and dined. The kitchens were expecting to serve an extra 500 meals that night.

Harry had arranged for a chauffeur-driven car for the twenty-mile drive to the hotel. It was waiting for them on the wharf: a four-door station wagon, a Chevy, appropriately the Bel Air model. It was ivy green with a saddle-coloured interior and made to seat far more than just the two of them. It could have accommodated much of their cruise luggage, not just their overnighters. Even Harry, who thought the only car ever worth owning was the Rolls-Bentley, asked the driver how long it was – seventeen feet.

As they set off they could see construction workers swarming over the arc of an enormous suspension bridge crossing the water between San Pedro and Terminal Island. The deck of the main span, hanging down from cables slung between two gigantic steel towers, had been completed but there was a gap between the road ramp, itself on pillars, and the start of the bridge. At the base of the bridge, Harry could see the bold, rectangular Art Deco front of the Terminal Island Ferry Building, its white façade cast in shadow by the bridge that would destroy the reason for its existence. Harry suppressed a shiver of recognition – the inevitability of obsolescence – but it was impossible not to get a jolt of strength from all the manic activity. If only energy were contagious.

Heading away with a grassy hill to the left and the water to the right they soon joined the Harbor Freeway north. It dawned on Harry that the last time he and Vinnie had been in the back of a car together had been when Torr had driven them to the Imperial Cancer Research Fund Gala last year. Not an evening worth mentioning in current circumstances, he thought.

Harry was always taken aback by the dazzling quality of the light on the West Coast. The colours of everyday objects seemed more intense; their edges more defined than the washed-out hues of latitudinally-challenged London. Occasionally he had a strange sensation of objects in the middle-distance flaring into blinding invisibility. He kept his gold-rimmed Aviators on for that reason.

The road was quite new and packed with cars even at this time in the afternoon. They all seemed to be V8-engined sedans: Chevrolet Impalas, Pontiac Catalinas and Ford Galaxys. He thought that the boxy Impala with its wrap-around rear window was a good-looking automobile.

For half an hour they flew over the unsavoury places of South Los Angeles – places like Willowbrook and Compton which he knew were even tougher than anything he had experienced in the East End – before taking the West 4th Street exit leading to Grand Avenue and the Biltmore.

The hotel's Beaux Arts façade, rising eleven storeys, and the massive wood-beamed ceilings, tapestries and murals inside were hearteningly familiar. Harry recognised the statue of his old friend Vasco Núñez de Balboa by the stairs. Their dinner reservation in the Emerald Room wasn't until 8pm. In the meantime they were shown up to their room, Harry momentarily disconcerted by the butterflies he felt at the prospect of sharing a bed with Vinnie for the first time in over three months.

*

Right at the beginning of my research the only formal documents about Harry that I possessed were his death certificate and his will. For wannabe family sleuths there are better starting points. In trying to fill in gaps I conflated unrelated fragments of information that led me on wild goose chases.

For instance, on the basis of Harry's dandyism and one line in the Estate of Harry Morris, Deceased, I surmised that Harry must have worked in the rag trade at some stage and that Morris must have been a tailor.

The line in question was a liability of £105 (over £2,000 in today's money) to 'Cyril A. Castle', who it turned out was Harry's tailor, first in Sackville Street and later Conduit Street.

Predictably, Harry's tailor lacked neither chutzpah nor celebrity clients. In the quarterly men's magazine, *Man About Town*, his advertisements were not bashful: *Tailors to the Stars! Patronised by top artists who understand and appreciate style and artistry in clothing, including the winner of Tailor & Cutter award for best-dressed star of 1954. The personal attention of Mr Castle at all times awaits you.*

I knew that Harry was a bit of a peacock. He was always immaculately dressed in any photograph, unsurprising perhaps for a man who had to dress up for his living most evenings. I think I understand why he chose this particular tailor as well:

the structured shoulders and swelled chest of Castle's signature cut gave Harry a more masculine silhouette than his athleticism warranted. The way the tailoring effortlessly took pounds off him was enough to ensure Harry's loyalty for over a decade. That, and the opportunity for an inveterate name-dropper to rub well-tailored shoulders with fellow clients such as actors, Richard Todd and Terry Thomas.

Once on this path, the only limit was my imagination. I constructed a vision of Morris's working life as a tailor in the sweatshops of the East End. Having started as an under-presser, opening up seams with the heavy, gas-heated irons, he graduated to second tailor, entrusted with doing chalk marks for the women machinists. With no particular skills he was often unemployed and even when he was in work, his job was seasonal: autumn hardship was an annual event for the family. Morris spent every working day in damp workshops and the steam from the pressing cloths eventually did for him as it did for many others: tuberculosis, the 'White Death'. It must have been when Harry was very young – that was the only logical explanation for why he never talked about his father and why my mum was not even certain of her grandfather's name. Morris was just one of the faceless hordes you see in sweatshop photographs of the era, lost to time, not even memorialised by his son.

With the advantage of hindsight I can see this for the nonsense on stilts that it is. In my defence, the rag trade was the natural destination for large numbers of London's economic migrants at the turn of the century. I admit to having been unduly influenced by a table in Jerry White's East End Jewish social history.[17] In the 1901 and 1911 censuses, tailoring was the occupation of almost 70% and 77% respectively of workers in Stepney who identified themselves as Jewish.

As is often the case though, a reductive approach is the right one even in the biographical vacuum that Harry preferred. Harry

---

17 White, Jerry (2003). *Rothschild Buildings: Life in an East End Tenement Block 1887–1920*, Pimlico, UK, p.199.

Morris was a street pedlar because his father was one too. He literally followed in his father's footsteps by pushing a barrow to his pitch, leaving and returning when it was dark, six days a week, his voice hoarse from all the shouting.

In Rose's birth certificate in 1908, Morris's profession was a 'hawker of fruit'. Two years later in Annie's, the entry is only a general 'hawker' but by the 1911 census, Morris was able to describe himself more accurately as a 'fruiterer with barrow'. The job would explain Morris's low or, at best, variable weekly earnings and why he chose to live where he did. All the family's addresses were convenient for the sheds and stalls of Spitalfields Market, one of the two main fruit and vegetable markets supplying London.

Morris was still a 'fruit hawker' in Ben's 1914 birth certificate. 1914 was a propitious year for the family at least because, after years of struggling, Morris proved an unlikely beneficiary of World War One. Much of the competition for the best pitches on the streets and in the markets cleared out – the borough of Bethnal Green boasted the highest record for voluntary enlistment in London. Although the sourcing of produce was erratic, the margin to be made from it once it was on the barrow was that much greater.

The introduction of conscription in 1916 might have thrown a spanner in the works. Even non-naturalised Russian immigrants like Morris could not escape – they were given a Hobson's Choice of either enlisting or returning to Russia to fight on the Eastern Front.[18] Morris may have been found medically unfit. At 39 he was on the cusp of being too old anyway. Or, like many others, he might have chosen repatriation and simply not turned up on the day. Whatever course he took, he stayed in situ and continued to make windfall profits for the duration of the war. Later, his incumbency would make it difficult for returning traders. In 1919 demobbed troops, chagrined to find the prime pitches in the street markets taken over by non-combatants, petitioned for a market exclusively for ex-servicemen.

---

18 *https://www.jewsfww.uk/russia-or-britain-take-your-pick-2709.php.*

This providential improvement in the family fortunes is reflected in the rather prosperous sheen of one of the earliest surviving photographs of the six of them, probably taken right at the end of the war. This photograph, which was handed down through Harry's brother Ben's family, is fully twenty years older than any my mother possessed of Harry, a small but poignant reminder of what their estrangement from his family cost them.

I have looked at the picture often. The faces have become familiar and I have a feeling that all their personalities survived the photographer's bleaching flash. On the left Daddy's Girl, Annie, with an enormous bow in her hair, clutching Morris's arm, the man himself looking diffident and diminutive on the throne he had been given to sit on. Esther is naturally more prominent, appraising the camera shrewdly. Ben stands straight on, open and frank. Rose looks petulant and a little sickly. And then there is Harry, precociously well dressed in a three-piece suit and collar pin shirt. He has a slight sneer, something any teenage boy might produce in similar circumstances but I think it's because he has already begun the process of dissociation.

Harry had learned the hawking trade – weighing out, bagging up, taking money, giving change – standing by Morris's side in the Sunday markets on Petticoat Lane or the junction of Cheshire and Sclater streets on Brick Lane. Morris needed help on Sundays as the Jewish markets were the only ones open since they had a dispensation from the Christian observance of the Sabbath. It was a surefire way of making money even after a difficult week's trading. Bananas from the colonies had the biggest margin: throughout his life Harry would associate this fruit with good living.

Morris's belated success at selling perishables dictated Harry's initial choice of career. Harry would have wanted to earn money at the first opportunity but Morris and Esther would have surely preferred Harry to be outside instead of in some workshop breathing in tobacco smoke and dust from the treadles. He lacked the inclination and connections to try for a grammar school scholarship even if he had been clever enough. So at some stage shortly after the end of the war his parents swore an affidavit that Harry was fourteen, bringing an end to his formal schooling and his childhood, which was much the same thing.

Harry probably had his own barrow straight away after leaving school. There were few barriers to entry in the hawking trade as any man could get an interest-free loan to buy this means of living from the Jewish Board of Guardians. The requirement for a licence was largely ignored; all you really needed was the wherewithal for a shed somewhere for the barrow and a good enough relationship with the stallholders in Spitalfields to get the day's wares on tick.

In this competitive market the young merchant would have had to venture a long way to get custom as the best pitches were fiercely defended. He told his children that he had a barrow on the Old Kent Road, over an hour's trudge from the market. For once, I think this is true: Harry must have got to know this territory well as the family moved there later on.

In the meantime he faced a hard daily slog, but father and son had a plan to make their lives easier: to graduate from 'fruiterers with barrow' to 'fruiters with shop'. Harry's walk would shorten considerably within two years.

In the 1921 census the family lived at 14–16 Russell Street, behind the Royal London Hospital on Whitechapel Road. This was more than just a flat though. Judging by the 1922 Post Office Directory, sometime in the previous year M. Vygoda, fruiterer and grocer, became the proprietor of a shop at the same address. The lodgings were probably above. It may have taken him seventeen years, but now Morris the greengrocer could stand proudly in a row with a dairyman, draper, furniture dealer, tobacconist and tailor. What is also striking is that the census entry and the shop were under his real surname, the era of masquerading as a Cohen was over. This fluidity must have left its mark on Harry in his subsequent shapeshifting.

Rose was old enough to help her parents in the shop so Harry could well have taken over Morris's old street pitches nearer Spitalfields. Within three years he too had ditched the barrow because the 1925 Post Office Directory has a new entry for a fruiterer at 2 Darling Row, a site a six-minute walk away on the opposite side of Whitechapel Road: M. Vygoda & Son.

Going into business with his son must have felt like a triumph for Morris. He had reached the point where he was humbly grateful for what life had given him. But Harry had seen the drudgery that a life selling fruit and vegetables offered and wanted more.

I feel confident in asserting this because of the interregnum in his career the following year. 1926 was a transformative one for Harry. He would join the Electoral Roll, the first of his family to do so, and he would go to the US. This solo trip is evidence of wanderlust and his questing desire for autonomy and material success. It also holds the key to his obsessive interest in *Caronia*.

Friday 8th February

The atmosphere in the Biltmore was strained in the morning. Harry had not managed to sparkle at dinner in the way in which he wanted. He hadn't learned anything of note; the evening reinforced how much he preferred New York's agents to their more reticent Los Angeles brethren. Vinnie had carried the table and both of them had drunk too much for the evening to end in anything other than recrimination and silence.

At Harry's suggestion they went shopping for headdresses for the fancy dress competition that would be a set piece of the upcoming leg to Hawaii. The theme was 'Come as a Song Title'. They found a vintage model for Vinnie with feathers and a stuffed parrot on its crown and Harry said she should go as 'Lullaby of Birdland'. This put them on better terms for the rest of the day. Nevertheless, Harry couldn't help but ruminate on those days when life amounted to more than simply placating his mistress.

They hailed a Yellow Cab, a Checker A8, back to the ship together as *Caronia* was due to leave the port at just after six o'clock in the evening for the 2300-mile steam westwards to Honolulu. After dinner, Harry could not persuade Vinnie to join him so went alone to the evening showing of *No Man Is an Island* featuring Jeffrey Hunter. He was taken with the title. It was a statement he was finding it harder to refute as he got older. The film itself was a letdown. It was a routine flag-waver about an American guerilla on Guam and Harry left early.

Making his way back to his stateroom, his mood lifted. How could it not when he reflected on the world that separated it from his first sailing? He was returning to a berth with a unique décor – no two bedrooms were exactly the same on the liner. Harry's was panelled in cream betula with bespoke maple furniture and two-toned grey-blue upholstery. Even the beige carpet and deep-pile coral and white rugs were individual to his cabin. It was all a long way from life below decks.

*

The log of passengers and crew arriving in New York on the *Caronia* on 20th June 1926 included one 'Harry Morris, Hebrew, 20', a 'G.H. Std'.

It is a tantalising entry as it could be the first instance of Harry adopting the name that he would make legal in his deed poll. The family had dropped 'Cohen' by this stage and it makes sense that Harry used the patronymic – taking Morris's first name for his surname. Putting Harry on this ship at this time in his life explains much of his behaviour afterwards. This was the trip that planted the seeds for his showbiz career and perhaps even his infatuation with a particular liner.

'G.H. Std' stands for 'Glory-Hole Steward': someone who was not entrusted with cleaning passengers' quarters – not even the Third Class cabins – only the crew's. It was just the sort of job, requiring no skill or previous experience, that someone intent on working their passage across the Atlantic would take.

This ship was the forerunner of the *Caronia* of our story. At this stage the earlier ship was two-thirds of her way through a 30-year career. She had been built for Cunard by John Brown on Clydebank, not for cruising but purely to transit 1,500 passengers a time (300 First Class, 350 Second Class and 900 Steerage) on the Liverpool to New York run.

It was a cattle run for crew and passengers alike. At least in 1926 the Glory-Hole Stewards were spared the trial of scrubbing out coal stoker's bedrooms, as *Caronia* had switched to burning oil by then, but it would have been a grinding occupation nonetheless. Being in such a lowly position could explain Harry's obsession with the ship's post-war reincarnation. One doesn't have to be a psychoanalyst to appreciate the intense gratification Harry would have felt each day that he spent on Main Deck as opposed to Glory-Hole on the contemporary *Caronia*'s cruises.

Harry could not have got work on a boat unless he had actually gone to Liverpool or Southampton and hung about, possibly for weeks, until something came up. This was a year of mass unemployment and general strikes so he would have needed to be pretty single-minded to have landed the trip. I think he was. Like many others growing up with American stars of stage and screen, he had a powerful desire to see the place for himself, but he had the powerful additional motivation of meeting his family. These were all the aunts and uncles that Morris and Esther had not seen for two decades. In the summer of 1926 he would have had plenty of his mother's relatives, the Sterns from Goworowo, to visit in New York.

Immigrants' census records are notoriously unreliable since they depend on the subject's often flawed recall, but landing documents, although trickier to locate, are not subjective, so we have a good idea of the order in which Harry's relatives came to the US.

His uncle Benjamin arrived in 1901, aiming to make enough money from tailoring to buy tickets for his wife, Shayna Perl (Jennie) and Minnie. In the event, buying the tickets was not the end of his troubles. He would go back and forth to Goworowo three times trying unsuccessfully to persuade Shayna Perl to leave her parents, and six years would elapse before she finally joined him in New York. He stands for all the Sterns in their determination to make a better life for their families and adopt the mores of their new home. Such was his drive that in 1905 he left his wife when she was five months' pregnant with Judel (Julius) to return to the US: the trip where he may have met Morris and Esther in London. And when Shayna Perl eventually landed she initially didn't recognise her husband because he had replaced his full beard with a shapely little Van Dyke, more befitting a stylish and assimilating tailor.

Benjamin's younger brother, Israel (Isidor, immediately shortened to 'Izzy'), arrived early in 1906. At Ellis Island he nominated Benjamin and the 165–7 Broome Street address as his forwarding contact.

Later that same year Feige (Fannie), the youngest of the Stern siblings, landed on the 'Statendam'; her forwarding address was also care of Benjamin, then residing at 246–8 Monroe Street. It would have been highly irregular for a teenage girl to make that arduous voyage unaccompanied, even if she was going to join her elder brothers, but the crossing may have been involuntary if Moshe Ber was dead or dying. Fannie was engaged to an in-law a few years older than her from Różan – a baker, naturally – called Eliezer (Louis) Marmelstein so either he or her brothers paid for her passage. It seems that Benjamin, Izzy and Louis all needed a couple of years' work in New York to save up the money for a second fare for their wife or fiancée.

By that stage only two of Moshe Ber's nine children remained in Poland: Frieda Granat and Sura Bejla (Sarah) Marmelstein. Sarah seems to have decided in 1911 to throw her lot in with her brothers in New York. The story is that she needed money to finish a half-built tenement in Różan – something certainly persuaded her to make the trip alone, leaving her three children, Ruben, Szejna and Benjamin, with her husband, Mendel – but it's more likely to have been a marital breakdown as she travelled under the name of Stern, perhaps masquerading as a widow. Mendel died in 1914 but her children remained in Poland.

Frieda was the last of the siblings to take the plunge. She was over 50 when she undertook the taxing journey in 1913 in the wake of her husband, Harris.

Benjamin and Jennie made up for lost time after she finally arrived. His family rapidly expanded to five children and he moved them all into a three-room apartment on the fourth floor of a walk-up on Attorney Street. Izzy moved around as he worked for different bakers, most often in Queens. Fannie married Louis in 1909 and for a while he tried his hand at something other than baking; he became a door-to-door salesman.

By the time Harry came to call, his relatives had largely moved on from the Lower East Side, that enclave of Manhattan where they had all settled initially and which, like London's East End in the late nineteenth and early twentieth centuries, could have been mistaken for the Jewish quarters of any number of Eastern European cities. Fannie and Louis Marmelstein had ventured as far as Kenosha in the Midwest before returning to New York.

His first stop may well have been at Fannie and Louis' place in the Bronx. After trying his hand as a salesman Louis had settled back into baking. At their apartment Harry would have met their teenagers, Morris and Rose, and their two younger children, Benjamin and Leo. Social, family-minded 'Auntie' Fannie was the only one Harry stayed close to down the years, and she and Louis would return his visit. The pair came to Britain in 1928 to see Esther and they are the only ones in the family who are recorded as having returned to Poland – in 1931.

In the absence of any alternative, the Marmelstein bakery at 187th Street and St Nicholas Avenue – in that part of Washington Heights at the north end of Manhattan where the island rises and narrows – would become the centre of family gossip as the century wore on.

Fannie pointed Harry elsewhere in the borough to see the now-widowed Jennie. Calling on someone who was bereaved in the manner that Jennie was might well have been difficult for a callow young man.

Benjamin's household had already had one disaster. In around 1910 his son Morris had fallen down a flight of stairs and broken his back. Morris would need years of rehabilitation to learn to walk again and would always be hunchbacked. Then Benjamin was diagnosed with liver cancer. He would battle the disease for six months, often in extreme pain, but it was to no avail. He died on 11th February 1913 and in keeping with Jewish tradition was buried the following day at Mount Zion cemetery in Maspeth, Queens.

Benjamin had made a point of keeping up with his cemetery dues so he was interred in a part of Mount Zion owned by the Goworowo *landsmannschaft*. These Jewish benevolent societies, of which there were over 500 in New York at the time, were formed by immigrants from the same ancestral towns. As well as giving their members opportunities to socialise, they offered benefits like sick pay, interest-free loans and burial rights. It does seem ironic to travel over 5,000 miles to New York only to spend the rest of eternity lying next to villagers from the Old Country but fortunately Jennie did not have to find the money to pay for the privilege.

Jennie was left literally nursing the baby as well as looking after a teenager and three other children under the age of eight – all with no money. The Jewish Aid Society covered the twelve-dollar monthly rent temporarily but she and Minnie had to find work for food. Jennie sold pieces of fabric from a street barrow; Minnie worked as a dress trimmer and then got a job packing dates in boxes in a factory in Manhattan. The family of six moved to a three-room apartment in Suffolk Street but to make ends meet a bedroom had to be sub-let to two male lodgers.

This is the backdrop for one of those agonising domestic events where family research borders on voyeurism. At the end of 1915, in a scene worthy of *Sophie's Choice*, Jennie couldn't cope anymore and gave up Julius, Morris and Rhoda. Julius, ten, was sent to a Jewish orphanage in Pleasantville, New York; Morris, seven, and Rhoda, five, both went to the Hebrew Orphan Asylum at West 136th Street. Jennie and Minnie would see the younger two each Sunday and make the trek to Pleasantville every few weeks but Julius and Rhoda would stay in care until they were sixteen and Morris until he was nineteen. Only the self-supporting Minnie and the baby, Mae, stayed at home. According to later accounts Jennie had a dour demeanour but who can blame her after this sort of capitulation.

Somehow I doubt young Harry's familial devotion stretched to a visit to the Hebrew Orphanage Asylum but there is a happier epilogue to this story. One of Jennie's lodgers – Kalman (Charles) Abarbanell from Blodwo in Poland – started to date Minnie when he left the flat and they would marry in 1921. Charles, whose first jobs in Manhattan were lugging ice and seltzer to upstairs apartments in the summer and coal in the winter, was now a trucking entrepreneur. He may not have been a baker but he was the next best thing – the Silver Flour Trucking Company, that he had started with a partner called Max Sobel, supplied flour and other ingredients to bakeries in the New York area. Close to Jennie in the Bronx, Harry could well have dropped in on Minnie – the one who later left an oral history of Goworowo – Charles and their two young girls, Anne and Bea.

In Queens Harry visited Uncle Izzy and Aunt Mollie. Their daughter Rita, who was in her early 20s and who had married a couple of years earlier, had a nine-month-old daughter to show off. Izzy had stayed in the baking trade and taken US citizenship. He and Harry looked similar, both thickset with black hair, and by all accounts Izzy was fun to be around, so they got on well.

It is unlikely Harry would have ventured up to Rochester where his uncle Abram had settled. Although Abram was already dead he had established quite a dynasty upstate. By the time of Harry's arrival there were three children and six grandchildren enjoying all the lake-effect weather. Aunt Frieda had also passed on by this time and it is improbable that Aunt Sarah's home was on his itinerary. Sarah would have little in common with Harry, and besides, her house in Grand Street was in turmoil – her marriage to her second husband, Morris Cohen, was in the process of falling apart on account of his determination to marry off his daughter to her younger son, Benjamin.

Most likely it was Izzy or Louis who took Harry back to the tenements on Broome and Norfolk Streets where all the branches of the family had lived after passing through Ellis Island. They were right in the middle of the Polish Jewish enclave on the Lower East Side, between Houston and Grand Streets, but in the way of all dynamic cities the neighbourhood was changing. It was as much Italian as Jewish when Harry visited in the mid-1920s.

Underage or not, Izzy took him to New York's speakeasies and jazz clubs; places like the Cotton Club in Harlem, an experience utterly different from anything on offer in London. Louis, older and a family man, probably avoided such haunts. But the swing dance at the recently opened Savoy Ballroom on Lenox Avenue had created a stir in the city, so Louis might have taken him there. The scale and opulence of the place, the mirrored walls, marble staircases and chandeliers – so unlike the East End's foul-smelling, stuffy dance halls – could not but have fired Harry's imagination on what nightclubs might aspire to. This may well have been the venue that inspired Harry's future calling back in London.

It is easy to imagine Harry deciding to stay in New York, seduced by the glamour and the seeming ease with which the Sterns were gentrifying. The temptation to succeed where his father had failed might have been irresistible. However, America's welcome towards newcomers had cooled considerably since his aunts and uncles had arrived. After the First World War, two Acts had been passed by Congress – in 1921 and 1924 – with the explicit goal of restricting immigration. The later one set quotas on national origins that either by design or accident had the effect of targeting those countries from which Jews tended to emigrate. Overall arrival numbers more than halved but Jewish immigration fell by four-fifths. In 1921 800,000 aliens had been registered landing in the US; by 1926 that had fallen to just over 300,000.[19] In the first half of the 1920s on average 56,000 Jews immigrated to the US each year. In the second half of the decade,

19 Office of Immigration Statistics, Yearbook Migration Policy Institute tabulations. US Department of Homeland Security, *www.dhs.gov/files/statistics/publications/yearbook.shtm.*

the annual influx fell to just 11,000.[20] Issy Cooperman, the son of another of Harry's relatives living in New York, had recently managed to get in but only via Cuba and Florida.

The paperwork would have been intimidating. And, likely as not, Harry would have had to have started at the bottom again, peddling on the streets or getting up even earlier than he was used to, to work in the bakery. Maybe he didn't fancy that or maybe, as an outsider, he might have been more sensitive to the antisemitism masquerading as American patriotism that he read in some widely distributed newspapers. He could even have felt some vestigial loyalty to his parents. For whatever reason he came home and once back he wasted no time in ensuring the disenfranchisement he might have felt in New York was not going to happen to him in London. He registered to vote.

20 Lestchinsky, Jacob (1944). *Jewish Migration for the Past Hundred Years*, Yiddish Scientific Institute, USA.

Honolulu

Tuesday 12th February

Caronia was rocked by a strong westerly gale for the first two days out of Los Angeles. The sea was rough but conditions were still nothing like the worst that Harry had experienced on the ship. That had been right at the start of the 1954 cruise when the ship had pitched and rolled in a full North-Easterly. *Caronia* had to slow to a crawl – eight knots – and it was only when they were all safe afterwards that the Captain admitted that at one stage during the storm the ship had listed to a 23-degree angle.

This was child's play in comparison, but still Harry struggled. He seemed to have picked up a chest infection in Los Angeles of all places.

He spent most of the weekend in one of his favourite spots – a place where he never failed to recover his humour – the starboard-side Garden Lounge at the aft end of Promenade Deck. The port-side lounge had an extra table, which Harry thought made it more cluttered: hence his preference for the generally quieter starboard-side. Also it was more handily positioned for the Deck Buffet Luncheon spread just the other side of the door before the line of steamer chairs started.

He monopolised one of the Lloyd Loom chairs facing the line of windows. There weren't any fruit trees in the planters but there were enough flowers and greenery to convey the vague impression of an English country mansion's orangery, at least to someone who didn't know any better. There he scanned the Los Angeles trade papers he'd picked up for familiar names in relative peace as the rain dissuaded many passengers from taking their usual circuits. Some parts of the walk – like the garden lounges – were glass-covered but it was open fore and aft so a loop in this weather required some fortitude.

On the second day out there was a break in the rain at around midday. The crew used the interlude to run the boat drill further along Promenade Deck for the few people who had got on at Long Beach. While that was going on Harry could hear the sounds of the buffet being set up. In contrast to most of the other guests on board, the increased motion of the ship had sharpened his strangely unreliable appetite. If he was going to be forced to spend more time apart from Vinnie, he might as well spoil himself with some of the dishes she denied him.

Food was coming up from the cold pantry and fruit locker below. At half past twelve on the dot Harry was at the front of the queue. He accepted his tray with its paper doily and tongs wrapped in a cloth napkin from a steward and grazed over a thirty-foot spread of antipasti, seafood, baked ham and roast beef to which he added warm potatoes – regular and sweet – from a portable oven, fruit juice from a display refrigerator and a creamy dessert. Harry handed over his piled tray to another white-gloved steward to carry back to his chair. He attacked the plate with gusto, making up for days of under-eating. And at dinner he would be able to show the requisite portion control to Vinnie, he thought, because he would still be full from lunch.

Later, after dinner, the Headdress Competition went ahead despite the heavy swell. The parade through the Main Lounge and Smokeroom and out onto Promenade Deck was usually great fun, but to general hilarity the dead parrot on Vinnie's hat detached itself in the wind and she was disqualified.

On Monday there had been some excitement as *Caronia* had acquired an additional passenger during the storm: an albatross, the 'holy grail' of wildlife sightings at sea. First spotted early in the morning aft on the port side, the giant bird followed the ship for the whole day, barely flapping its wings in *Caronia's* slipstream and seemingly indifferent to all the observers lined up along the rail with their cameras. Vinnie made a crack about it getting a free ride, Harry about its symbolism: the movie in the daily programme, *Drums of Destiny*, had put him in a gloomy frame of mind.

Tuesday was much calmer. The screening of *Bon Voyage* with Fred MacMurray seemed to sum up the sea's renewed equilibrium. Harry planned to attend the lecture in the Theatre at 11.30, 'Hawaii, the Picture Bride with a Dowery', and of course the pre-Valentine Ball at 10pm in the Main Lounge. He would have to be on top form for that. Meanwhile he wrote a short letter to his middle daughter to post when they docked in Honolulu:

> *Dearest Belinda,*
>
> *I have had to send this c/o Mummy as I could not remember your exact address – so please send it to me. Now how are you? And how did you cope in all that nasty weather? And when are you expecting the baby? Please write and let me know – I am enjoying the trip – but am still not feeling too well – I can't get rid of the swelling in my legs – how is Barry – I suppose the nasty weather must have interfered with his work a great deal – keep me posted.*
>
> *All my love,*
>
> *Daddy.*
>
> *My best regards to Barry.*

On re-reading it, he thought it more reflective than his usual missives but that was how he was feeling.

*

The trip to New York in 1926 had ignited Harry's ambition. On his return he made some decisive moves to live a different life from that planned for him by his parents.

At that time there were two Electoral Rolls a year and in the one for autumn 1926 there is an entry for a Harry Vigoda at 253 Old Kent Road. It was a shop site at the Walworth end of the Old Kent Road that Harry knew well from his hawking days but it was not he who lived there. He didn't move from Whitechapel, it was the rest of the family who moved south of the river.

In the 1927 Post Office Directory the address is listed to Morris Vigoda, fruiterer. The year before Morris had sold the lease on the Russell Street location to someone called Finegold. Malcolm Morris, Morris's grandson, remembers driving past number 253 in the 1960s so that his father Ben could point out *Zayde* Morris's old shop. Harry was still recorded at the address in the 1927 and 1928 Electoral Rolls but in reality he was living on his own above the Darling Row shop. Throughout this period the Old Kent Road shop was listed in the Post Office Directories as 'Morris Vigoda, fruiterers' and the Darling Row shop as 'M. Vigoda & Son'.

When I uncovered the entry on the roll my first emotion was one of excitement – I had discovered a staging post in the assimilation of Harry Morris and the date of his move away from his parents. Then the warning bells started ringing.

How come he was eligible to vote in 1926 when he returned from America? Suffrage was not exactly universal at the time. You had to be aged 21 or older to vote if you were a man and 30 if you were a woman; the age limit for women would not be lowered to 21 for another two years. So for Harry to be on the roll in 1926 he must have been born at least a couple of years before Rose. As well as multiple aliases, Harry now appeared to have multiple birth dates.

In the National Register taken at the outbreak of the Second World War Harry declared that he had been born on 15th January 1907. That accords with his age at death, which was given as 56 on the certificate but neither can be right as that would make him too young to have joined the Electoral Roll when he did.

In the 1911 census Morris said Harry was four and a half which would put his birth some time in the second half of 1906. Morris's memory sharpened in the 1921 census. There he wrote that Harry's age was fifteen-years-and-one-month old implying a birth date in May 1906. The truth is that he and Esther were probably not too sure themselves. They came from a culture where such details didn't have the significance that their new home ascribed to them.

Given that, all I had to do to straighten the matter out was obtain his birth certificate. He must have one – he had registered to vote without any evidence of ever having had to naturalise and he was certified as a 'natural born British subject' on his deed poll. In fact, after registration was made compulsory in 1875 a vanishingly small proportion of British births got past the efficient and financially incentivised record keepers, even in districts like Whitechapel with a heavy influx of non-English-speaking immigrants. The £2 fine for non-compliance within 42 days of the birth would have concentrated Morris and Esther's minds. Besides, they registered Rose, Annie and Ben's births so it is consistent for them to have logged Harry's as well.

In the 1921 census Morris's admittedly shaky memory puts Harry's birth in the St George-in-the-East Registry District, one that was bounded to the north by Commercial Road. This strikes me as likely to be accurate because he put his three other children in the Mile End Registry District which is where they were registered.

If this is indeed where he was born, however, his birth certificate is lodged in a form which defies retrieval. It was likely to be hard to track down given the error-strewn certificates of the others; although the gradual improvement in Morris and Esther's ability to communicate is evident between Rose's and Ben's. Harry had the privilege of being their first so it was very possible their accents or the registrar's incompetence combined to ensure his arrival was recorded under some unknown family name, certainly not Cohen or Vigoda in any of their spellings and variants.

One thousand six hundred and seventy-four Cohens were born in London between 1903 and 1907, and another 40 or so Vigodas and Wygodas: not one of them was Harry. The nearest I got to a sighting of Harry's birth certificate was an entry for one Morris Cohen born on 25th July 1906 in Settles Street in Whitechapel. The first name was an issue but the mother's maiden name, Stern, matched and the date and location fit. When the certificate arrived, this Morris had been born to Nathaniel, an insurance agent, and his wife Sarah. On multiple occasions I learned the hard way that to have one's interest piqued by an abstract in a register only to have it punctured by the arrival of the artefact itself is a genealogist's occupational hazard. Harry's ability to frustrate the answers to simple queries was turning out to be another way in which he was different from his siblings.

Naturally Harry just went his own way. He celebrated his birthday on 1st December each year but even he was equivocal – he told his children that it was his 'official' birthday, like the Queen's. I have a suspicion that he chose this date because it was easy to remember and provided a good excuse for a pre-Christmas party.

One thing is clear, however: from 1926 onwards Harry put physical distance between his family and himself. He lived in Whitechapel and the rest of the family lived on the Old Kent Road. Harry needed the space to abandon the strictures of the *Shabbos* and roam on Friday and Saturday nights.

A shilling and sixpence admission at the 'People's Palace' in Mile End got him a different girl every weekend but it was no Cotton Club or Savoy Ballroom. To recreate the atmosphere of the Harlem jazz and swing clubs he took to patronising the upscale halls favoured by gentiles south of the river or in the West End. Harry had enough confidence in his dancing and good looks to feel pretty much assured of picking who he wanted even at these venues.

This was when Harry threw himself into acquiring some new things – clothes, vocabulary, gentile girlfriends – and losing others – his 'Jewish accent', (it steadily became mid-Atlantic), and any pretence at regularly attending synagogue. If he hadn't moved out one can imagine the arguments, (meal times were when Harry had rows), after he had got dressed up to go out on Friday and Saturday nights. Not just with Morris and Esther but also with the more religiously observant Rose.

The Old Kent Road lodgings and business disappeared from view in 1929. According to the electoral register Harry's address was now 111 Upper Clapton Road, about four miles north of Whitechapel. Again, like Old Kent Road, he never resided there himself but this address – another shop with lodgings above and plenty of passing trade on a busy high street – was where the rest of his family settled permanently.

Harry retained the Clapton address for Electoral Roll purposes until 1931 but he was splitting his time between Darling Row and Fulham in those years. The Darling Row shop's Post Office Directory listing changed from 'M. Vigoda & Son' to 'Harry Morris, greengrocers' in 1930. In 1931 ownership transferred to someone called Dalton. In reality Harry had been moonlighting in Fulham for much of this time. The Post Office Directory simply reflected reality: Harry had left the East End for good – just in the opposite direction to the rest of his family.

His transformation in these years may have been spurred by the realisation that it was not just the US that had become more anti-immigrant. In a rather sinister precursor of what would happen elsewhere later, the UK's Official Public Record, the *London Gazette* of 2nd August 1929, listed 'Morris's' at 111 Upper Clapton High Street under the proprietorship of 'Morris Vigoda, Fruiterer and Greengrocer', as an 'Alien's Business'.

This inclusion in the *Gazette* related to exemptions to Section 7 of the Aliens Restriction Act of 1919, legislation that had extended the powers of an emergency wartime act into peacetime. The act contained clauses restricting aliens' employment rights – barring them from certain jobs in the civil service, for example – and in Section 7 banned aliens from changing their names: 'An alien shall not use any name for themselves or for a business they own other than that by which they were ordinarily known on the 4th August 1914.'

The Secretary of State could grant an exemption to the prohibition so long as the name proposed to be assumed was a suitable one. A further stipulation was that the exemption should be published in the *Gazette* as soon as possible after its granting. Naturally there was a fee for the privilege: ten guineas, a small fortune for Morris and Esther. There was also a requirement to put an advert in the local paper at their own expense announcing the name change.

No wonder the family were keen to drop 'alien' trappings. Morris appreciated the commercial logic of calling the shop after his forename but otherwise he and Esther contentedly reverted to Vigoda. Cherished or not, Poland was the baseline of their lives and they found it hard to shed its impedimenta. It was different for the children. Vigoda, like Cohen, was a passing phase. They felt more at home being Morrises. Even though Vigoda was in occasional official use until the late 1930s, one by one the children stopped using it during the decade.

By the time of the Gazette announcement, Harry's mutation had gone well beyond a simple change of name. Although he still dated widely, one relationship in particular had become serious.

Betty Houben was the eldest of Herbert Houben and Mary Ann Workman's four children. Her father's family were Dutch, her mother a true Cockney laced with Scottish and Irish blood. As the only daughter, Betty was spoiled by her father, a lady in the making who was spared housework to save her hands, something which must have made her less than popular with her mother.

Betty was a bit of a revisionist too, although not in Harry's class. She had already amended her rather Edwardian Christian name, Ivy May, to Elizabeth – always shortened to Betty or Bet. She had learned typing and shorthand but she preferred to work in upmarket dress shops, throwing in some modelling on the side.

Betty liked a good time. She had always gone out with Jewish boys as she found they belied the stereotype and were the freest spenders of her contemporaries. Harry was a natural fit. The two of them were both attractive and well dressed – two ambitious 'twenty-somethings' who liked to dance and dine out.

The evidence that Harry's personal diaspora had started almost as soon as he had returned from the US lies in a browned and spotted, gossipy letter Betty's brother, Bertie, sent to Mum in 1980:

> *I first met Harry Morris around about 1928. We were living in Putney at the time. It may even have been 1927 because we moved to Southall in December of 1928 and I can remember Harry visiting us at the Putney house several times. Anyway, Betty asked me one Saturday afternoon to take a message to a fruit and vegetable shop in Dawes Road close to the Salisbury Hotel. Having lived within a stone's throw of this spot, it was no trouble to jump on my push bike and pedal down to Fulham. I found the shop without any trouble but did not recognise it because it had not been a greengrocer when we lived in the district. I asked the man who was running the shop if he was Harry Morris and he said he was, so I gave him the message from Betty, and after talking with him for a few minutes, cycled home.*

As encounters go, it's not exactly Stanley meeting Livingstone but the anecdote does make clear the extent to which Harry had diverged from the rest of his family as early as 1927. It may only be eight miles on the map but this westwards shift in Harry's orbit was doubly significant. Not only was he moonlighting from Darling Row, he was working on *Shabbos*. There were quite a few greengrocers close to the Salisbury Hotel at 154 Dawes Road in the Post Office Directory. Harry wasn't listed as a proprietor in the directory but a greengrocer with a Russian-sounding name, F. Vorobieff, at 147 Dawes Road, was his most likely employer.

The stage was set for his relationship with Betty to move to something permanent. There was just the rather significant issue that she was a *goy*, or non-Jew.

Wednesday 13th February

Caronia docked at Pier 9 in Honolulu harbour at 11.30am. In the nine years since his last visit Harry had forgotten about the hulking example of Hawaiian Gothic, the Aloha Tower Lighthouse, which loomed over the ship's berth. Seeing it took him back to 1954 when they had sailed in from the west and had been greeted with a band and cheering crowds. A Hula troupe had come aboard to sing and dance and one of the girls had thrown a lei around his neck. After days at sea the ship had had a sudden tropical fragrance.

There was much less ceremony this time but at least there were no embarkation formalities as their Landing Cards from Long Beach remained valid. Even if he hadn't been at sea for the last four days, Harry would still have been eager to disembark. The verdant, balmy mid-ocean halt was one of his favourites – supposedly the all-year-round climate was so perfect that the Hawaiian language possessed no word for weather.

He and Vinnie planned to retrace the trip to Waikiki Beach and Pearl Harbour that they had taken with Bob in 1954. Between the two visits Hawaii had become the 50th state, which had set off a building boom. Harry remembered from their earlier drive that there had been lots of hoardings along the roadside offering land for sale. The plots must have been ridiculously cheap given how much more developed the route was now.

Back then, at Bob's insistence, they had spent time at the Pearl Harbour Cemetery set in the punchbowl crater of an extinct volcano above the city. When they had been standing in front of the memorial to the fallen, Vinnie had talked about her brother Merrill's wartime service in the navy, which had made Bob quite emotional. Much later Vinnie had admitted to Harry that Merrill's naval rating had been CM2, a construction mechanic 2nd class, so not quite on the front line (although it would entitle him to a burial at Fort Snelling National Cemetery in Minneapolis).

This time they skipped the cemetery in favour of the sands of romantic Waikiki, but typically Vinnie spent most of the day avoiding the sun in their cabana.

That night Vinnie and Harry weren't tempted by the 'Aloha Party' excursion to the Royal Hawaiian Hotel despite the promise of a Gala Dinner and full programme of dances from the 'Lands of the South Seas'. Instead they had dinner back on board and afterwards were entertained by the soaring falsetto of Hawaiian hula singer Bill Lincoln and his backing dancers. Lincoln was far better than the traditional tourist fare; Harry conceded that he was one of the few 'entertainments' on board that he would have considered booking for the Colony.

*

Harry was not a spiritual man, *Shabbos* held no special meaning for him and the closest he came to religious iconography was a green stone head of a deity which he brought back from one of his trips to the Tropics. Hence the bafflement – and disruption – he caused by his last-minute refusal to participate in my parents' Christian marriage ceremony. Uncle Bertie gave Mum away instead.

I doubt very much that Harry's misgiving had anything to do with the strict Rabbinic teaching of the Talmud that embargoes entering non-Jewish houses of worship. Nor do I believe the hindrance was the timing of the wedding – four o'clock on a Saturday afternoon – which meant it was too early to mark the end of *Shabbos* with the *havdalah* blessings. I think Harry's no-show had less to do with some late-in-life conversion than petulance at the cost of the ceremony.

Harry was well aware of the obligations orthodox Judaism placed on its adherents and how incompatible they were with the life he chose. Anne and Ben's children remembered Morris and

Esther as *frum* or devout but not ultra-orthodox. The modern dress in the 1918 family photograph endorses this but they were religiously and culturally orthodox enough to feel at home in Upper Clapton, an area renowned for its Hasidic community.

It is impossible to think of the urbane, well-dressed Harry pictured in the newspaper profiles of the 1950s ever being bearded or wearing the black hat and coat and earlocks of a Hasid, let alone the traditional undergarments with the tzitzit, the fringe, outside his belt. I can picture him in a yarmulke but struggle with him owning a tefillin with a head strap.

My poor imagination does not mean Morris and Esther were not observant. I think it is fair to say that Judaism underpinned their way of life: they ate kosher and honoured all the festivals and holidays. They went to synagogue (which they would have referred to by the Yiddish word *shul*) almost every Saturday, but over the years their practice, and their sense of separateness, softened.

Morris was a taciturn man who apparently did not speak about his own childhood. However, his grandson David can remember being impressed by Morris reading from the prayer book and enunciating the Hebrew words without vowels. Clearly Morris had had religious tuition in Poland, probably the only education he ever received. Nevertheless I invest Morris with the archetypical Jewish fervour for study. Thus in his mind *shul* was a place for erudition as much as devotion: somewhere to go every week to argue over the Talmud with his cronies. As soon as he was old enough Harry would have gone with him. East End schools with big Jewish contingents finished at 2.30pm on a Friday – Morris would park the barrow, come home and then both he and Harry would wash and go to *shul*.

Which *shul* exactly is lost to memory, as is the case with many of the synagogues that once distinguished the East End. The nearest one to home was the New Hambro Synagogue on the north side of Adler Street, or Union Street as it was called, when the family lived round the corner in Sion Square. Street names were seemingly as fickle as family ones back then.

I am not sure Morris and Esther would have felt very comfortable amongst the New Hambro's overtly Anglo-Jewish congregation. Charles Booth's impressions of Union Street in his 1898 notebook were of 'the constant whirr of the sewing machine or tap of the hammer as you pass through' and 'the feeling as of being in a foreign town'. That wouldn't have been off-putting to Morris and Esther, but the general good repair Booth noted – it was a cut above Mulberry Street – may have intimidated them. The synagogue itself was one of London's oldest, having moved from the City of London under Chief Rabbi Dr Hermann Adler. They worshipped in a substantial four-square Italianate building facing Union Street, with two entrances for men, one for women and seating for 370. The ladies gallery was at the western end of the temple and, in an unusual arrangement, there was overflow seating upstairs for men at the east end where the ark was.

If they did not attend the New Hambro, where did the family pray? The synagogues in Great Garden Street or Fieldgate Street might have been close to home but I like to think that the family attended a *shul* in Princelet Street. It was only a small congregation – just over a hundred worshipers – but it is one of the few buildings from that era that survive today, if only as an exhibition space. The East End once boasted almost 200 synagogues but most, including the New Hambro, closed as their congregants headed for the suburbs. Today, aside from Bevis Marks, which has held regular services for more than 300 years without a break, there are just a couple of small neighbourhood *shuls* left.

Locating the family in the Princelet Street *shul* is not just wishful thinking on my part: the synagogue's heritage was Polish – Morris and Esther would certainly have felt more at home there than the New Hambro – and it was handily sited for all the places in which the family is known to have lived.

When Morris and his family attended this *shul*, the building had already been around for almost two centuries. It had been a Huguenot master silk weaver's home but a small synagogue had been erected in the garden in 1869 by a group of earlier arrivals from Poland called the Loyal United Friends Friendly Society (which must be about as many different terms for comity as it is possible to fit into an organisation's name). By 1891 the roof had become so dilapidated that the Federation of Synagogues declared the building unsafe. Redecoration and refurbishment followed and it was reopened in 1893 – with a new façade – funded by that prolific benefactor, Sir Samuel Montagu.

While Morris sat downstairs in the main seating area, the women and children of the family sat on the balcony which ran around three sides of the interior. The ark was at the far end, a bright azure blue with gold stars. A glass skylight illuminated the *bimah* – the altar – and the elaborate brass candelabra that hung from the ceiling.

The names of those who had contributed to the reopening of the synagogue were commemorated along the balcony panels: a roll-call of Anglo-Jewish 'aristocracy' such as the Rothschilds, Mocattas and Montagus. Perhaps that fired Harry's ambition at a young age. On the other hand much of the service would have been unintelligible to the young boy and he may have been shaken by the emotionalism in the room. The congregation shouted and wailed, they moaned and shook and they sang. That may have been what put him off organised religion but I think his aversion is more likely to have been caused by his experiences at *cheder*, Hebrew school.

There would have been periods in Harry's childhood when he spent three nights a week between tea and bed, and possibly Sunday afternoon as well, in *cheder*. In return for a few pennies a week, a rabbi would teach Hebrew and the Talmud to reluctant, fatigued boys who quickly learned to chant in rote or risk a clout. Collective memory puts these lessons in cellars and disused workshops and has them smelling of boiled cabbage, the rabbis remembered as zealots and sadists. Harry probably forgot everything he had learned within a month of his *bar mitzvah* although the endless repetition did at least train him in the practice of retaining large amounts of information, a skill as valuable as any showman pizzazz in his line of business.

In any case, before his time as a club owner, Harry had firmly rejected the tenets of his religion with his clandestine marriage to Betty in a registry office in June 1931.

The catalyst for formalising their union might have been the shock of his Hodgkin's Disease diagnosis or his work, which at the time was increasingly taking him away from home. In any event it would be fully six years before Harry informed his parents that he had married 'out', a combination of innate stealth and foreknowledge of the likely reaction. The event would be an embarrassment to the observant Morris and Esther. Only the birth of his daughter Susan made the deception no longer tenable. Until they were let in on the secret, as far as his family was concerned Betty was just another of the *goyim* he dated, something not to be mentioned along with his drinking alcohol, gambling and not keeping *Shabbos*.

It is a moot question but what would have happened if Susan had been a boy? Harry made no secret of wanting sons; how would he have told his parents if he was not going to follow the traditional Jewish rituals for newborn boys? One can readily imagine Morris and Esther being much more disappointed if there was no *bris* or circumcision to welcome the boy into the faith. In a sense it was fortunate that Susan was a girl. Perhaps if she hadn't been, Harry would have continued to keep his marriage a secret from his parents.

Harry and Betty's honeymoon was split between the beauty spot of Symonds Yat in Herefordshire and a stay at the Arlington Hotel in Bournemouth with the rest of her family.

While the Houbens didn't have to wait six years to find out about the marriage, there was a contrasting reaction from Betty's parents. Her mother, Mary, a latent antisemite typical of her time, was not happy, while her father, Herbert, a fish and chip seller turned West London property developer, was delighted with Betty's choice. He could identify with the entrepreneurial energy of his son-in-law.

For a decade Harry and Betty would be inseparable. It was a marriage of dovetailing desires and aspirations. They would create a family and a business together and Betty would be invaluable support for Harry as he recovered from his health scare. He showered her with gifts in this period including the perfume that would become her signature scent. Even I remember the square bottle of 'Joy de Patou' that was ever-present on her dressing table: she smelt of its jasmine and rose in the evening. She always maintained that it was the most expensive perfume in the world, an unscientific but impressive claim to make in front of an ingenuous grandson.

I do not ever recall seeing the circular glass bottle filled with a champagne-coloured liquid that was 'Je Reviens' by Worth. Apparently the orange-blossom and jasmine bouquet was Betty's favourite day perfume but it may have evoked painful memories if she associated it with Harry. It translates as 'I will return' which, after a while, he no longer did.

Yokohama

Saturday 16th February

Most of *Caronia*'s major expeditions involved Eastbound traversals of the Pacific. When the International Date Line was crossed, passengers 'gained' a day, in effect an extra day that had to be relived. Not so in 1963: everyone on board skipped the whole of Saturday 16th February because the ship crossed the International Dateline travelling west. Friday became Sunday over the course of a single night.

The day lost because of crossing the Date Line was a spur for creative jollity in the ship's print shop. 'We had a full day's programme scheduled for you,' the spoof daily programme starts, 'but unfortunately today does not exist. However, we would like to tell you what you missed.'

The timetable that followed was full of in-jokes and innuendo that fix Harry's cruise in its time and place. There was Breakfast at Tiffany's (champagne naturally) followed by a deck hike hosted by Bea Lillie and deck sports, the highlight of which was a hula-hoop demonstration by Mae West. If that didn't suit, Juliet Prowse and Fred Astaire were available for free dancing lessons.

For those on a diet, the Deck Buffet Luncheon was cancelled. After lunch, diamonds for the ladies and Cadillacs for the gentlemen were prizes for those with the lowest card-party scores, gift-wrapped by none other than the number one host, Lorna Yost. Beer was available at Afternoon Tea, especially for those who hate tea. Even Elvis Presley got in on the act, apparently providing Music for Cocktails.

The feature of the day was a Grand Pyjama Ball in the Main Lounge with an absolute galaxy of film stars none of whom, in their finery, would have been out of place aboard the Green Goddess. If the clock advance time was to be believed, the cruise would almost be over the very next morning.

*

For all its clunky pastiche, Harry and Vinnie's 'lost day' became something of a metaphor for me. Harry left so little correspondence behind that my attempt at visualising him at play on his last trip and divining what he thought and felt was starting to feel more fanciful than real. In desperation I reasoned I could add some verisimilitude to my writing by recreating his journey on board a modern cruise ship.

That was before the world, and certainly travel writing, was brought to a near-standstill by a microbe: I did not just lose a day, I lost a voyage.

To follow in Harry's footsteps I had selected a ship whose route most closely matched that of *Caronia*'s: the *MS Viking Sun*, departing from Los Angeles on New Year's Day 2021. I would be on board for longer than Harry was – not disembarking until Singapore on 24th March. I found out that I would be part of a flourishing travel sub-segment called 'heritage tourism', catering to those who want to retrace a forebear's experience, say. Family memoirs often sport such trips to allow the writer to reconnect with their ancestors on the page. My three-month sabbatical would just be taking it to the next level.

My journey had a head start on Harry's; I would be at my first destination, Hawaii, about five weeks earlier in the year than him. Then the timetables started to synchronise as the *Viking Sun* took a long loop down through Polynesia and Australasia while *Caronia* kept to the same latitude, heading to Japan. After Australia the *Viking Sun* sailed north to the Indonesian islands;

at the same time the *Caronia* was steaming south via Hong Kong and the Philippines. The closest the two would come to being in the same place on the same day of the year was in Malaysia. I would be arriving in Koto Kinabalu in Sabah on the 5th March exactly 58 years, give or take a day, after Harry. Except when Harry visited the city it was called Jesselton and Sabah was still known as British North Borneo. This felt to me like the pivotal point to connect with Harry across the years.

Alas, my planning was for nought. The cruise liner industry was one of the worst affected by Covid-19. This was not just because of bad publicity at the start of the contagion. The lockdown reversed a consensus about the irresistible rise in demand for cruising and led to many operators racking up unprecedented losses.

It was the *Diamond Princess*, a vessel operated by one of the biggest players in the business, Carnival, that was the harbinger of doom. In February 2020 it gained unwanted notoriety as the single biggest cluster of Covid cases outside China. Japan quarantined it off the coast of Yokohama. In a modern twist on the legend of the *Flying Dutchman*, ships were forced to wander between ports as country after country refused to let potentially infected vessels land. In a public relations disaster liners were described in the world's media as 'floating Petri dishes', those little glass bowls that scientists use to culture bacteria. It stuck because, even at a time when relatively little was known about how the virus was transmitted, it was unarguable that thousands of people sharing small amounts of common space was not likely to be best practice.

As a consequence the majority of the 32 million passengers who were due to sail in 2020 stayed at home, the ships themselves hibernating in dock or mooring offshore. Viking cancelled *Sun*'s 2021 Grand World Tour and my scheme to bridge the years to *Caronia*'s 1963 tour was gone.

I comforted myself with the thought that trying to authentically recreate his final journey was hopelessly quixotic anyway. After all, the industry and the nature of its passengers have changed out of all recognition in the intervening 60 years.

Take the nature of the cabins. No two staterooms were exactly the same on *Caronia*, not even things like drawer handles, let alone the wood of the cabinets or the pattern of the curtains. (Each one was fitted out by hand by H. Morris & Co., a Clyde-side furniture manufacturer founded at the start of the century by a Russian *émigré* named Harris Morris. I like to think that Harry knew this and was tickled by the coincidence.)

On the other hand, modern cruise operators believe that holidaymakers will accept uniform-sized cabins with prefabricated plastics and laminates so long as they also offer a private balcony. *Caronia*'s staterooms had ample space – how else could the occupants throw all those private parties – but it was all internal. Almost twenty percent of my 338-square-foot cabin on *Viking Sun* would have been outside. Rightly or wrongly – and record industry profitability would suggest the former – meeting the minimum requirements of the cruising public such as verandas, mini-bars, coffee brewers, flat-screen televisions and USB ports is viewed as being far more important than any sort of bespoke offering.

My fellow passengers would have been very different from Harry's too. They would have been younger, polyglot and more cosmopolitan than *Caronia*'s complement. In seeking the reliable pockets of affluence that existed in her era, *Caronia* had a singular focus on US consumers.

Relatively speaking, nowadays a world cruise is not anywhere near as expensive as it was in Harry's time. Vinnie would have paid around $28,000 for a suite on the 1963 cruise, the equivalent of $230,000 in today's money. Even the $9,500 that Harry – or, more accurately, Vinnie – paid for his cabin is worth around $80,000 today. And they didn't even get balconies.

It wasn't the cost that made *Caronia* the exclusive preserve of the idle rich however. It was because, unlike modern tours, *Caronia*'s passengers could only buy accommodation – in US dollars and in full, three months before the departure date – for the *entire* cruise. In effect all *Caronia*'s guests had to be in a position to commit to around 100 days of leisure, which made for a much more loyal, homogenous and famously social passenger list than any liner can boast today.

The itinerary and written archive of *Caronia*'s Grand World Tours smacks of the tail-end of colonialism. British power may have been in decline but its realpolitik could still determine destinies in far-flung regions. The Malaysian Federation only came about in the year of Harry's tour because the British shot-gunned the Malay populations of its colonies in North Borneo and Sarawak to the Chinese of Singapore. The real objective was to ensure Malaya and Singapore remained allies in the fight against communism but the resulting hotchpotch of nationalities was doomed to fall out. Manufacturing a racial balance in such a hubristic way seems inconceivable today.

There is a hint of the conditioned superiority and casual racism of the passengers in the splashy titles of the pre-arrival port lectures given by Ivan Boxell who was an experienced journalist and newspaper publisher from Pennsylvania. He described Japan as 'Risen Phoenix-like from the Ashes' and Singapore as a 'Ferris Wheel with a Chinese Circle'. Would a speaker on a cruise today give presentations with titles as patronising as 'Headhunters, Pirates, Birds' Nest Soup' (about Sabah) or 'Japan: No Goodbye as Wistful as Sayonara'?

I didn't need to make a cruising pilgrimage to know that Harry would have shared the sentiments on board. His trips were as much about reinforcing his self-image and his perceived membership of the 'elite' than about uninterrupted leisure.

A contemporaneous report of *Caronia*'s visit to Japan in 1954 under the headline 'The Hon. Dollars' encapsulates the prevailing attitude of the moneyed leisure class on board. The tone is ironic but the gulf between the visitors and the visited is stark.

Officials of the Japan Travel Bureau are quoted as saying that the arrivals had come 95% to buy souvenirs and only 5% for sightseeing, 'a tedious business anyway' The 'Japanese had looked forward eagerly to the well-advertised arrival of the *Caronia*, for its staterooms were filled with the most expensive collection of dollar-heavy souvenir hunters ever to hit the Ginza'.

The Great Circle department store in Tokyo had its entire stock of high-priced screens, dolls and kimonos bought out. A taxi driver in Kyoto was given a 3,000 yen ($8) tip for a 100 yen (28¢) fare. By the time the *Caronia* headed for Honolulu and home, she had left behind some $300,000 in good convertible currency, a truly staggering sum. Another official is quoted: 'They were so nice, so charming and so very, very rich.'[21]

Passengers on *Caronia*'s cruises in the '50s and early '60s would have got used to seeing headlines in the local papers at the ship's ports of call saying something along the lines of 'Millionaires' Yacht Arrived In Port Today', an unlikely sobriquet for any modern liner as none can match the relative concentration of spending firepower that *Caronia* represented in her day.

In the end, it is all too easy to fall into the trap of judging the mores of the past by the standards of today. Harry was a man of his time and I must try to understand his behaviour in its context. Good intentions aside, I realise I am almost halfway through Harry's final voyage and I have managed to create little more than a simulacrum of the man based on his actions on board interspersed with gobbets of the family backstory. My limited facility means that I have barely scratched the surface of his thoughts and feelings at this point in his life. Nor am I much closer to understanding why he was so determined to keep his families apart.

I resolve to spend more time in his company in the second part of the narrative and concentrate on his heyday. It would be a gross misrepresentation of the man not to dwell on the time when his vigour and prosperity were both so different from the broken specimen witnessed on board *Caronia*.

Thursday 21st February

The pattern of all *Caronia*'s world cruises included at least one unbroken period of seven or more days at sea. The 3,500-mile

---

21 19 April 1954, *Time*.

arc across the Pacific from Honolulu to Yokohama was the segment for 1963.

These interludes were popularly known as 'Hate Weeks'. Passengers' nerves usually frayed, especially if their sleep was affected by the clocks going forward on consecutive nights or if the weather kept them from venturing onto the open decks for any length of time.

Caronia's travellers were fortunate with the weather that February. There may have been some depressions on board but climatically speaking it was a period of high pressure. The light, fresh breeze came from the west; the sea remained moderate. It was overcast in the middle of the week but it didn't rain once.

On board, the ship's company split into two camps during the crossing. One group fought the longueurs with hyperactive gaiety: its members were reliable participants in all the card games, sports tournaments and fancy-dress parties that the staff laid on. The other surrendered to extended meditation, perhaps precipitated by the feelings of personal insignificance brought on by the immensity of the ocean.

This may have been the year that Harry transitioned from the active crowd to the reflective one.

Valentine's Day got the week off on the wrong foot for him. It was Ladies' Night so he faced competition from other aspiring 'knights' for a place on Vinnie's Dance Card. Harry wondered whether Vinnie still viewed him as her soulmate; he had the uneasy feeling that the patron she was praying to was not Valentine but Raphael, the saint for those seeking love.

Every night saw invitations to private parties with themes and dress codes that reflected where they had been and where they were going. Harry made an effort with some – he wore some tropical shorts for a Hawaiian cocktail party but all that did was call attention to how swollen his ankles were. Common sense prevailed for the Cherry Blossom Party as that would have required him to wear a kimono. Vinnie went alone. They did attend an evening concert of light operatic arias together, but Vinnie went solo to the Aloha Ball, the pre-George Washington Ball and even the Pairs Dancing Competition.

In each case Harry excused himself on the grounds of fatigue and his painful back and legs. After each dance he made a point of asking how the evening had gone but steered well clear of asking who accompanied her. Harry's ennui was such that he found he wasn't even interested in who Vinnie was choosing to dance with. Instead he concentrated on planning their Japanese shore excursions, a more likely setting for his rehabilitation in Vinnie's affections. His priority now was to gather his energy for those exertions.

*

It feels appropriate at the end of 'Hate Week' to move Harry's story on to that 'low dishonest decade', the 1930s.

After their marriage he and Betty set up home in Santos Road, Wandsworth. In an early sign of their aspirations the couple, both working full time, took on a housekeeper. She was 'Auntie Flo', Betty's mother's sister, Florence Gunning.

Betty set about trying to make a success of a lingerie shop in Fulham bankrolled by her father and a haberdasher friend of his, Charles Parsons. The shop was called 'Bensons', a portmanteau of the two backers' surnames.

Meanwhile Harry was managing two greengrocery shops but, short of ownership, this would not make the sort of money he wanted. So he changed tack. He gave up the Darling Row lease – the commute made it untenable – kept on the Dawes Road position and started other ventures.

He joined John Blundell Ltd. Blundell's was well known at the time as a department store which sold furniture, household goods and clothes to the working classes on a weekly tick. For every pound – twenty shillings – an article cost, customers put a shilling down and paid a further shilling a week for twenty weeks. It was a business strategy that survived fluctuations in interest rates and decimalisation and remained largely unchanged until the company went bust in the 1980s.

Harry's initial position was as a 'credit draper', a job title that sounds as archaic as costermonger or cordwainer. It was a fancy term for a tallyman, a traveller whose job was to sell and deliver goods and then collect the weekly rental. The company incentivised credit drapers not only to sell but to enlarge the account if the customer looked like a good bet. Harry's mix of charm and pugnacity must have proved a winning combination because he quickly became an enforcer, collecting rent from bad customers, and then a supervisor overseeing an army of tallymen in London and Birmingham.

It's possible he then moved on to become a regional manager for Victoria Wine; he was a man in a hurry. Victoria Wine, which had pioneered off-premises drinking in the eponymous queen's reign by offering customers bottles or quarter-pints in their own jugs, had expanded to nearly 100 shops by then and been taken over by the brewers, Taylor & Walker. It had diversified into other liquors and tobacco so Harry, with his background in managing people and consumer goods, would have been a natural fit.

Herbert Houben must have seen enough of Harry's work ethic and success in building up capital in the early years of the marriage, because in 1935 father and son-in-law partnered in Harry's first truly proprietary business: 'Harry Morris Ltd (Fruits)'. Morris's, a fruit and vegetable shop, opened at 118 Putney High Street that year. In the family fashion, Harry, Betty – and from 1937, their daughter Susan and her live-in nursemaid – occupied the flat above the premises. It was a well-chosen site on a busy road, right next to a pedestrian crossing graced by a black-and-white Belisha beacon, only introduced the previous year.

Harry had learned something about the value of clustering in his business – owning shops close together so that perishable stock could be swapped around to meet differing demand. Within a year he had opened a second store, a minute's walk away on the other side of the road, at 85 Putney High Street. He soon added a third shop on the Quadrant in Richmond.

Once he had come clean about his marriage, Harry took on his sisters as part-time employees. Both were saving to get married.

Rose and Harry did not get along. In 1938, after she married Nathaniel Banks, predictably another greengrocer, she quit to join her husband in his own shop in Hendon. It was not a happy union: Rose's inability to conceive eventually led to separation in 1950 and divorce. While sweet-natured, she would cut a melancholic figure in the 1950s, a decade as unremarkable for her as it was eventful for Harry but in the year of Harry's final cruise she met and married Hymie Levy in Edmonton. They met in a 'convalescent home' – Hymie's wife, Hetty, had died the year before – and he would prove an even-tempered partner over the years.

Anne persisted at work, however. She toiled the whole week for Morris *père et fils*: on Saturday, when the Clapton shop was closed for *Shabbos,* she had to get up at 5.30am and take two buses in order to work a full day for Harry in Putney. She and Alec Gopstein, a furrier and jeweller, finally married at the start of the war; theirs would be a more fruitful union – Anne would have two sons, Michael and David.

Harry's venture may have been a success but this was not the time for any business to flaunt its Jewish ownership. As a Jewish shopkeeper he may even have been targeted as it wasn't uncommon for offensive remarks to be chalked on the pavements and walls of Jewish-occupied houses and businesses.

Did an antisemitic message or a placard on his door accelerate Harry's heathenism? Was his rejection of his Jewishness just a commercial calculation or born of something deeper like personal fear, worries about the security of his family or even dismay at establishment Jewry's conservative response to the affronts? If so he went well beyond the degree of assimilation necessary to diminish commercial vulnerability, for this was the period when Harry the chameleon abandoned any remaining signs of his Jewish identity and heritage.

He lived in dangerous times. In parts of Europe it was not the least bit unusual for people to hide their Jewishness to avoid persecution. Not having experienced racial hatred in any form, I have no right to judge Harry. That said, it should not prevent me from trying to understand whether mortal fear is the explanation for his ethnic concealment.

The Jewish community that he was part of had been built up in layers by waves of immigration. There were the Sephardic Jews who had settled in England in the seventeenth and eighteenth centuries, and *Yekkes*, Jews of German descent, who had followed them. By the mid-late nineteenth century, many of these pathfinders were assimilated and anglicised and had become relatively prosperous bankers, stockbrokers, merchants, traders and tailors. As the century wore on there was a steady flow of less affluent Jews from Holland, North Germany and Eastern Europe but it was the annual migration of tens of thousands of Jews – many poor and unskilled because of the proscribed list of Jewish occupations in the Pale of Settlement – that led to a backlash at the turn of the century.

Sadly this was true even among their more established Jewish fraternity. Assimilated Jews were concerned that the new Jewish immigrants would give them a bad name and erode the reputations and status they had worked hard to achieve. The new arrivals were sufficiently numerous and different in appearance and way of life to act as an irritant to the majority population. Outside the mainstream uneasiness, the British Brothers League marched and petitioned. Foreigners were the 'scum of Europe', and described as 'dirty, destitute, diseased, verminous and criminal', all antisemitic tropes. Assaults on Jews were not limited to London: there was also anti-Jewish unrest in South Wales in 1902 and 1903.

In a sense it was fortunate Harry's parents arrived when they did. They got in just before the bar for migrant numbers dropped following the Aliens Act 1905, legislation which introduced controls and registration for the first time. While the act was ostensibly designed to prevent paupers or criminals from entering the country, the actual objective was to control Jewish immigration from Eastern Europe.

Far more restrictive provisions were introduced during the war – the ones that forced Morris to disclose his business's change of name in 1929 – as suspicion of aliens was coupled with resentment over the failure of Jewish refugees in the East End to 'do their bit' for England. In 1917 there was a fight between more than 2,000 Jews and Gentiles on Blythe and Teesdale streets in Bethnal Green.

Antisemitism simmered away but it would have been more and more obvious to Harry in the 1930s. As a small business owner he would have been well aware of the individual acts of vandalism and Jew-baiting of the British Union of Fascists ('BUF') founded by that political apostate, Oswald Mosley.

In attracting disaffected youth in the aftermath of the Depression, it seems that the BUF's distinctive trappings – emblem, uniform, salute, hierarchy – was enough to overcome the contradictions inherent in much of its antisemitic ideology. The BUF perpetuated the myth that Jews were behind the Bolshevik Revolution in Russia and that there was an International Jewish Communist Conspiracy to destabilise whichever country they lived in. Although its active membership peaked in the low tens of thousands in 1935, its reach through the weekly *Blackshirt* paper and the risibly-titled *Fascist Quarterly* was far greater.

Less than one percent of the British population was Jewish but their concentration in three major cities – London, Manchester and Leeds – meant they became the focus of the BUF's rallies. The march to the BUF's headquarters in Bethnal Green was a weekly provocation and the brutality of the BUF stewards, notorious. In one of the rallies in 1936 William Joyce, notorious later as the Nazi propagandist Lord Haw-Haw, declared the Jew to be an Oriental subhuman creature. Matters came to a head in October that year in a mass brawl, the 'Battle of Cable Street', after which a Public Order Act restricting processions and banning political uniforms accelerated the decline in the BUF's standing. Pre-war antisemitism wasn't quite done – the influx of Austrian and German Jews fleeing Nazism was vilified in the popular press in 1938–9 – but the threat of personal harm was lifted.

I don't think antisemitism or any fear of harm caused Harry to repudiate his roots in the 1930s. That would award him a prescience about the rise of Nazism that he probably didn't possess. My impression is that his fudged identity was less about betraying his roots than simply disowning the poverty and grubbiness of his childhood. He might really have been an outsider but he could strive to become an equal citizen by disavowing his heritage. Everything points to him doing this without any obvious dissonance: no tortured psyche here. In essence he made antisemitism into someone else's fight. If Zionism was the vehicle for creating and developing a proud Jewish identity, there is no evidence he was ever a Zionist.

Would Harry's distancing have mattered if the Nazis had occupied Britain in 1940? He had denied his origin to the point of managing to lose all consciousness of it but the orthodox rabbinate formula holds that if either your mother was Jewish or you have converted to Judaism in accordance with the religious law, you are Jewish. The decades Harry spent denying his birth, marrying 'out' and rejecting the Jewish God counted for nothing. His mother had a marriage contract, a *ketubah*, and that was that.

If he had wanted to protect his children from the fascists he would have been in for a disappointment. The practice of tracing Judaism only through the maternal line means I could never have been Jewish by birth, since only my grandfather was, but matrilineal descent was a subtlety lost to the Nazis: I don't think they trafficked in quartered Stars of David. I would have been a *Mischling*, if only 'second degree' in the absurdly pedantic nomenclature of the Third Reich. That would have meant that I would have been faced with the prospect of sterilisation or, if I were deemed to have looked too Jewish, deportation.

Consequently I may be a bit more engaged than the average gentile. While people of my generation should not feel responsible for the Holocaust, I believe strongly that Jews and non-Jews alike should challenge the deniers and do our utmost to ensure such an atrocity never happens again. I want to be the obverse of Harry. Just as he sought to obfuscate his Jewish connections, I want to laud them. The more I found out about Jewish relations across the world, even if only distant, the more I wanted to shout about it to balance Harry's reticence.

As a bonus, under Israel's Law of Return, expressly modelled on the persecution criteria in the Nazis' Nuremberg Laws, I can claim citizenship since I have at least one Jewish grandparent. Admittedly the State of Israel might think it was a bit of a cheek given the alacrity with which Harry denied his ethnicity.

Friday 22nd February

'Hate Week' officially came to an end at seven o'clock in the morning when *Caronia* swung into Yokohama harbour.

There may have been a frisson on the bridge on passing the breakwater. Five years earlier *Caronia* had been driven ashore and holed here – the ship's signature, oversized funnel always had a tendency to act as a spinnaker in cross winds – but there were no mishaps this time.

Japanese officials came on board shortly afterwards to issue shore passes. They sat in the Smoking Room and went through all the passports with grave formality. Harry used the delay this caused to buy some yen from a money exchanger who had set up in the Forward Observation Lounge.

It was all a bit workmanlike and underwhelming compared with their arrival in 1954. That visit, the first by a cruise ship since the war, was headline news and the ship and passengers were feted. Thousands of locals had gathered on the flat roofs of the quayside buildings to witness the tying up and a US army brass band serenaded them in. The sending off had been even more of an event: the Mayor of Yokohama gave a speech, the Captain replied and geisha girls danced. When the tugs had pulled them off the dock there were fireworks and not one but two bands playing. Harry remembered it as the best farewell of his entire time on *Caronia*.

After a decade of dollar-laden cruise ship arrivals in the wake of that first grand entrance, tourists were not quite the celebrities they had been back then. Still, when he and Vinnie finally disembarked, Harry was surprised by the number of onlookers – their welcoming smiles might have been a bit more synthetic but there were a lot of them. As a first step in recreating the chemistry of that first visit he was off to a promising start and they were staying at the best spot in town: the Imperial Hotel.

Unfortunately their impressive room, overlooking the moat and twisted pines of the Emperor's Garden, could not prevent the tension between them sparking an argument over the thermostat. As ever, Vinnie insisted on air-conditioning; Harry found the room wretchedly cold. He subsided with bad grace, which persisted until later, when she took his arm as they walked through the nighttime streets, excited by the thrill of the unknown while fully confident they were not in any physical danger. He cheered himself up with the thought that he had Vinnie pretty much to himself for four days in the next five.

They were following a route to the restaurant that the hotel concierge had recommended. It was a cloudless night – looking up they could see colourful cones and whirligigs of light on top of the skyscrapers. On the ground the older locals were muffled up against the cold in quilted kimonos while the young were in western-style overcoats. The young Japanese seemed slavish in their desire to dress like Yanks, which made Vinnie laugh, but Harry also detected a strut in their step: a renewed sense of self-confidence that might have come from Tokyo having been chosen to host the Olympics the following year.

Their path took them past *pachinko* halls with their pinging bells and sandwichmen advertising bars and nudie shows. Ginza was a blaze of light and beer halls spilling customers, many of them American sailors, onto the street. Harry spotted the restaurant by its oversized lanterns – red ones with big black characters.

They took off their shoes and walked across a wooden floor that had been polished to a shine by years of stockinged feet. They were led to a private room and sat at a counter on the edge of the tatami opposite the chef. A serving girl in a bright kimono and sash knelt behind them and gave them hot towels to wash their hands and face. They started with clear soup, then soybean paste and other sauces were placed before them. The chef selected raw prawns from a bowl, rolled them in egg yolk batter and fried them. He picked them up one at a time with chopsticks and placed them on a metal grill set into the counter for them to pick up and dip into their sauces. He did the same for white fish, cuttlefish and vegetables.

By this stage Harry's back was aching dreadfully. No matter how much he tried shifting position, the pain was undeniable. The only anaesthetic on offer was the warm sake so he knocked back lots of it. They raced through the rice course and stumbled back to the hotel. Suffering back spasms on top of the swelling in his legs was a lot to bear. Still, being able to stretch out in bed came as a welcome relief despite the cold room.

*

Harry, Betty and Susan were issued with brown National Registration Identity Cards – number, name and address – in September 1939, Susan's saying 'Under Sixteen Years' on the front. The family got their first ration books in December the same year: the adult ones were buff coloured, Susan's green.

Running a chain of greengrocers was not easy during the war but it wasn't the worst occupation. At least he wasn't a baker like his US uncles and cousins so didn't have to serve up those loaves made with National Flour that everyone agreed somehow tasted grey. Fruit and vegetables were never rationed but were always in short supply: precisely the sort of marketplace in which someone as venal as Harry could flourish. He supplemented stocks from the traditional wholesalers by building up a network of corruptible contacts both at the docks, for imported produce, and at growers within drivable distance from London. Not only was he sending his own vans out into the country to buy vegetables directly from farms, he felt no compunction about using the services of others who did the same.

Picture the scene in 1940: after a sleepless night worrying about being bombed, you happen to be walking down Putney

High Street before dawn. Odds-on you would have witnessed vans delivering supplies to numbers 85 and 118, cash on the spot. In the first two years of the war it would have been Harry, incongruously well dressed for a greengrocer, that you would have marked overseeing the exchange. With the lure of easy profits he would have dealt in more than just fruit and vegetables. There would have been nothing to stop him buying rationed items like eggs or butter when his vans were at the farms to sell on the black market to restaurants and catering businesses.

Covert, uncertain supply chains were one thing, but Harry also had to deal with the Ministry of Food, the bane of any shopkeeper's life in the war. It demanded he display their posters in place of his adverts in his shop windows. 'Your courage, your cheerfulness, your resolution will bring us victory' was one. 'Help win the war on the kitchen front' was another. Fortunately he did not need to advertise; he could rely on discreet word of mouth about his ability to supply sought-after produce. There was an endless queue of housewives, without the garden space or temperament to 'dig for victory' – and with their own newspaper for wrapping because the shop did not have any – whispering 'AUC', 'anything under the counter'. These usually upright citizens wanted more than a 'Woolton Pie' of carrots and parsnips and were not above bending the rules if it meant they could get hold of life's little luxuries like an out-of-season tomato or fruit shipped from overseas.

Harry never saw profiteering as a crime. If it was a crime, who was the victim? He might have been charging inflated prices but he was doing society a favour. Many people in the neighbourhoods where his shops were located could afford to pay a little extra. There was always more demand – and the money to back it up – than goods available to match it. Black marketeers were like eighteenth-century Cornish smugglers, giving people a little bit of what they wanted away from the eyes of the Excise. Coping with this sort of duality was child's play for someone with Harry's ability to compartmentalise.

He had to be careful though. Undercover officials from the Ministry of Food posed as customers to see if small shopkeepers could be persuaded to break the law. High-profile figures were frequently shamed in public for doing so. In 1941, Nöel Coward was fined £200 for not handing in the dollars he earned in the US on a goodwill tour. Even George Arliss, almost 80 years old, was fined and publicly humiliated for not declaring his overseas bank accounts like Coward had been.

Two years later, Ivor Novello went to prison for four weeks for not being able to explain where he got the petrol to keep his Rolls-Royce on the road, a punishment that would have caught Harry's attention because by then he was making serious money and dreaming of buying his own Rolls.

It was as if his life until now – the distancing from his family, the self-reinvention, the *chutzpah* – was preparation for this moment, two years into the war. In the biggest non-sequitur of his whole career Harry parlayed two years of grocery profiteering into the running of a big-time nightclub. There can't have been too many others who followed this particular career path.

He and Betty enjoyed nights out in clubs even after Susan was born, but being a patron of nightclubs is no qualification for running one. He would have had a smooth sales patter but, again, so would many others. My bet is that a club proprietor who used Harry's black-market goods backed him. Perhaps they recognised the overweening ambition and amorality of their supplier. Both sides would have been taking an enormous gamble but it turned out to be a very good call. Harry had found his vocation.

Saturday 23rd February

Harry and Vinnie took a sedan to Asakusa Station and then a fast electric train to Nikko, 90 miles north. Stewardesses selling snacks and drinks walked up and down the aisles but Harry was still in too much discomfort to pay them any attention, instead he concentrated on the green rice paddies flashing by.

They had lunch in the Kanaya Hotel, crossed the bridge at the end of the high street and walked upwards underneath a canopy of pines and cedars to the tombs of the House of Tokugawa. The main draw was the Toshogu Shrine, the Shinto equivalent of the Taj Mahal. It was a riot of gateways and lanterns, huge stone guardians, scarlet-faced monsters and, guarding one entrance, twin samurai seated on either side with their bows at the ready in their laps.

They made a point of searching out the wooden carvings of three monkeys in the roof panels of one of the outhouses. Here were the originals of the immortal monkeys who see, hear and speak no evil. Harry identified with the macaques – refusing to acknowledge impropriety by 'turning a blind eye' had been invaluable in his career. He was also buoyed by a story about the resilience of the sculptor, Jingoro. The legend was that jealous fellow carpenters had cut off his right arm but he had carried on anyway left-handed.

Afterwards they took a taxi to Kegon Falls. The road up there past Lake Chuuzenji reminded Harry of the Alpine passes at Arosa, a sense that was reinforced by the lift inside the cliff that took them to the base of the falls. A viewing platform overlooked the plunge pool. He didn't know which was louder: the sound of the 300-foot-high, but narrow, waterfall or the thousand cameras' shutters clicking at the same time.

On the train back to Tokyo they agreed it had been a memorable day's sightseeing. Harry's back had held up and they had not argued once.

*

The only reason I know that Harry's nightclub was called the Knightsbridge Studio Club was because of a throwaway comment from Mum that he had made a great play of owning it when the film, *Carve her Name with Pride* was released in 1958.

This biopic of the secret agent Violet Szabo, played by Virginia McKenna, was one of the highest-grossing films in Britain that year. My mother would certainly have seen it at the time as she was an avid moviegoer. This was the year that she was obsessed with the actor, Tony Perkins, and the John Wayne Western, *The Searchers*, which she ended up seeing a dozen times. I can imagine her excitement when she found out that her hitherto unheroic, medically-exempt father had had something to do with the war effort, even if tangentially.

Violet Szabo was initially recruited in the Knightsbridge Studio Club in the summer of 1943, six months after her legionnaire husband Etienne had been killed in El Alamein. Her fluent French and athleticism were spotted there by an agent, Harry Peulevé, who referred her to F Section, that part of the Special Operations Executive responsible for running intelligence networks in France.

The film plays around with the chronology but nods towards the enlistment. At the end of Violet's training the fictitious captain Tony Fraser, played by Paul Scofield, utters the immortal line: 'Do you know the Studio Club?' After Violet admits she does not, he replies: 'Have a drink. Do a theatre maybe?', activities that would undoubtedly have commended themselves to Harry, the proprietor. About six minutes later in the film there is an interior shot of the pair arm-in-arm in the 'Studio Club'. Deuce tables surround the dance floor and there are pictures with frame-mounted lights on the walls behind.

Sadly, this is 1957 Pinewood, not a celluloid souvenir of the real thing. Interior shots of the Studio Club would have had to have been taken on a soundstage because the club itself was located in a basement. It had an impressive mailing address – 116a Knightsbridge – but in reality was off a cut-through to Hyde Park called Park Close.

Once upon a time this little alley would have looked like one of those London lowlife scenes depicted by Hogarth: full of street sellers and fruit hawkers outside the 'Lifeguardsman' pub. They were cleared away by the second Duke of Wellington in favour of that engine of Victorian social mobility, a riding school, which in turn was demolished in the 1890s to build a block of mansion flats, rather unimaginatively called Wellington Court.

This mansion block was a trophy address at the turn of the century – full of well-heeled bachelors entertaining in their suites and communicating with their servants on the top-floor via speaking tubes. The design incorporated a club below where the young gentlemen could indulge their depravities in the 'naughty nineties'.

Of course in 1940 when Harry first set eyes on it, like much of central London, the building had seen better days. The decorative iron gates had gone, the red brickwork had faded and sections of the ornamental stonework had fallen off in the bombing so the façade looked like a series of broken shelves according to one eyewitness.

The basement was just as run-down. At the time it was the 'Wellington Club'. In February 1940 the gossip column of the weekly music and variety newspaper, *Band Wagon* ran a story that owing to the club's chronic unprofitability it was being relaunched as a 'Bottle Party'. Bob Rose was to compère a new floor show in front of a five-piece band.

Converting a club into a 'Bottle Party' was a well-known wheeze at the time. The ruse went like this: patrons would order cases or bottles of liquor from a nightclub's partner wine store during licensing hours but would not take delivery immediately. In the nightclub they would sign a chit authorising delivery of the bottle or case from their 'stock'. The wine store compared the signatures and sent the drinks back. That way the nightclub was not selling alcohol – it only stocked ginger ale, soda water and other mixers – and the wine store was simply fulfilling an earlier, legitimate order.

Some switched-on club owners owned the wine store as well. Harry's later partner at the Astor, Eustace Hoey, was one such. He ran the New Paradise Club in Regent Street and supplied it from his own wine store in Warwick Street. Harry might have part-owned one – in his will he still retained shares in a business called Gloucester Wine Stores Limited.

Whether or not they went that extra step, the commercial incentive for a club owner was compelling. A bottle of whisky, which might have retailed at 30 shillings, would cost £3 to deliver to the table, an extra ten shillings to the wine store for staying open into the night and a £1 'commission' for the nightclub.[22]

22 Burnett, Al (1967). *https://player.bfi.org.uk/free/film/watch-al-burnett-1967-online*.

This loophole in the liquor licensing law was well known – it had been around since the early 1930s – but it was not until the first year of the war that a wave of 'Bottle Party' openings in the West End alarmed the authorities sufficiently to take action. The exact number of Bottle Party Clubs open every night was unknown but it probably ran into the hundreds. Many were simply 'Clip Joints', populated by hostesses rather too practised in the art of separating callow soldiers from their service pay.

The Metropolitan Police revived its 'Bottle Party Squad' in January 1940 to reassert control. It was equipped with the power to summarily close any undesirable nightclub under Defence Regulation 42c, a wartime emergency regulation that would actually stay in place until the early 1950s.

Regulation 42c fast became notorious in the industry as the definition of 'undesirable' was solely in the eyes of the police. Being found to operate a drunk and disorderly establishment was one thing, but many clubs were closed down seemingly at the whim of the Met.

The impact more intrusive policing had on Bottle Party numbers can be seen in a Written Answer on 1st April 1940 in the House of Commons. The Home Secretary, Sir John Anderson, was responding to a question from Alfred Denville. Denville, who had been an actor and impresario before becoming an MP, wanted to know how many Bottle Parties remained in the Metropolitan area. Sir John's fusty response deserves to be reprinted in full:

> *The Commissioner has made orders under Defence Regulation 42c directing the closing of six Bottle Parties, known respectively as Boogey Woogey, El Morocco, Hi-de-Hi, Macs, Paradise and Stork. The number of known Bottle Parties now in existence in the Metropolitan Police District is seventeen, but I do not think it desirable to give them a gratuitous advertisement by reading out a list of their equally peculiar names.*

That same month it was decided that if troops on leave were going to go to clubs, the spots should be supervised. Licensing hours were extended to 2am and the police undertook to draw up a list of 'good' Bottle Parties.[23] The four-hour extension was a potential goldmine but in effect every venue had to walk a nightly tightrope to remain in the Met's good graces.

The *Band Wagon* column ran a bit of a puff piece on the Wellington Club in March, which was also the first time the club's change of name to the 'London Studio Club' appeared in print. The *thick-gutted businessmen of Knightsbridge were finding life tedious in this blackout* and wanted *a little bit of amusement.* So: *Arthur Bowler, popular clubman, has opened up a new day club called the London Studio Club. I have a feeling that all these businessmen will eventually toddle along to Mr Bowler and beg him to make them members. He tells me that he intends to put all the surplus cash into bigger and better floor shows. Judging from what I saw there last week he's going to make his members very happy and comfortable.*[24]

This is all a bit coy, or perhaps regular readers of gossip-column fodder understood the innuendo. There was a variety floor show and cabaret but the main attractions of the club are clear from the gossip snippets above the cabaret cards section in the newspaper. One read: *Young lady who is coming much to the fore is Marcia Dillon, sixteen-year-old dancer who last week was at the London Studio Club. She has now signed a contract to go out on tour with a road show.* Another announced that: *Miss Pamela Harris makes her comeback to the entertainment world when she makes her cabaret debut Monday next at the London Studio Club, 116 Knightsbridge, SW 1 as a striptease artiste.*

Why Harry chose this particular venue to launch his radical change of career is not clear. He may have had an introduction through one of the performers there: Lennie Felix played piano in the club and happened to be another first-generation Polish

---

23 Thomas, Donald (2003). *An Underworld at War*, John Murray, London, p.251.
24 March 9 1940, *Band Wagon*.

Jewish immigrant. It might have been that Harry knew the club through his black-market customer list. Or it might have been pure happenstance of knowing the existing management socially.

Predictably for anything involving Harry's business activities, there is a whiff of deception and underhand dealing around the transaction. Exactly who he bought the club from is a bit of an enigma. The Arthur Bowler referred to in *Band Wagon* might have only been the club's secretary, and the owner possibly someone called Stanley Leighton. Neither appears to have stayed on good terms with the Met, which might explain why Harry changed the name again to the 'Knightsbridge Studio Club' when he took over. But forgetting Bowler and Leighton for a moment, there seems to be a better candidate for Harry's vendor: someone who would not be outed until nearly a decade later in Arthur Helliwell's showbiz column in the *People*. This person provides a link between the different phases of Harry's nightclub career:

> *One of London's plushest nightspots changes hands this week when club owner Bertie Green takes over the Astor Club from his old friend Harry Morris. There's an odd story behind the switch. Back in 1941, when he was called up, Green gave his Studio Club in Knightsbridge to Morris as a present. Morris, who until then had been running a couple of fruit shops, did well in the club business. He made a fortune and today owns a swanky Mayfair restaurant, a luxury seaside hotel and a glittering Rolls-Bentley. And now as a friendly gesture he has sold the Astor to Green at a bargain price. But knowing how business is around the golden square mile I'm wondering whether Morris has done his old pal a good turn or not!*[25]

One does not need to be aware of the hard-nosed reputation that Bertie Green would earn later as an agent and club owner to

---

view this story with some scepticism. Michael Black, the singer Matt Monro's agent, has been quoted as saying 'Bertie wasn't one of nature's gentlemen' and 'You'd get a bad name just through being associated with him.'[26] Neither Green nor Harry were ever the sort of people to sell assets at below their market value let alone 'give' them away.

A gift would helpfully do away with the need to explain how Harry raised the money to buy the club. It does stretch credulity for him to have built up the capital required in two years of wartime trading, even with the opportunities available to make black-market profits. Money aside, there is still the conundrum of why anyone would entrust a club to someone with nothing to recommend them other than a career in greengrocery.

Harry was a good salesman – a predisposition to lie undoubtedly helped – maybe the combination of shmooze and pushiness in his pitch impressed Green. Green would go on to build a reputation as an excellent judge of performers, perhaps this was a very early example of his ability to spot talent.

On Harry's side, what induced him to take such a risk? It would have been impossible to run a nightclub and the shops at the same time – he had to sleep – he had a pregnant wife, a four year-old and no obvious qualifications for the role other than audacity. This, however, was his once-in-a-lifetime opportunity to become rich in a way the fruit and vegetable business could never offer and in the process become 'somebody'. I think this explains the conundrum at the heart of his choice of career. His actions throughout his life betray an immense egoism; he always placed his interest before those of anyone else. Yet success in his line of business required an authentic attempt to put the needs of customers first. The point is that it was utterly in his self-interest to do just that. Sadly he couldn't see a corresponding benefit in acting the same way towards his family.

26 Monro, Michele (2011). *The Singer's Singer: The Life and Music of Matt Monro*, Titan Books, UK, p.129.

Sunday 24th February

Neither Vinnie nor Harry had any interest in joining other passengers on the ship's shore itineraries – to Kamakura to see the giant bronze Buddha or Hakone to view Mount Fuji. Vinnie was more interested in shopping for souvenirs. After checking out of the hotel they browsed the electronics stores and Vinnie persuaded Harry to buy some photographic equipment, plausibly claimed to be the most advanced available in the world by the salesman, but in reality just something with which Harry could impress his daughters back home.

Any intimacy that they had generated last night seemed to evaporate during the shopping trip. The nearer they got to *Caronia*, the more distant Vinnie became, almost as if she resented sharing the ship with him or that she regretted having agreed to another overnight stay in Kyoto tomorrow. Preparing for that was the pretext she gave for demanding an evening to herself. Not for the first time he wondered whether she had found another beau among the eligible bachelors on board.

At a little bit after 6pm, Harry felt *Caronia* turning under the motive power of the tugs. She was making the short hop overnight to Kobe, 350 miles away. Normally Harry would go for a drink before dinner in the First Class cocktail bar. He rarely frequented the Raleigh Room right at the aft end of the ship as it was quite a long walk away from the main activities taking place in the Lounge on the deck above. Tonight, however, it was a place to escape to. After a very unsatisfactory dinner he watched the evening movie alone. It was *Kill or Cure* starring Terry Thomas.

*

The extension of the licensing hours was a boon for operators. It created a backdrop in which Harry could not only learn how to run a members' nightclub on the job, but also flourish. He became adept at putting on a floor show, making guests feel at home (and pay more) and above all, serving drinks in a way that meant that the Knightsbridge Studio Club stayed on the Metropolitan Police's list of approved Bottle Parties.

It didn't hurt that London was a wonderful place in which to do business in the lull between the end of the Blitz and the start of the V rocket attacks, especially after the influx of all the moneyed and adventurous US air crew in 1943. This was doubly true for someone like Harry who was comfortable making deals, marking up prices and turning a blind eye if necessary, particularly when dealing with the perennial labour shortage. I doubt the Studio Club was anything other than fully staffed at all times because Harry had few qualms about taking on those young men who had simply opted out of the war before they had been called up. His permissive attitude probably even stretched to deserters so long as they were able-bodied enough to serve as waiters and bouncers. He would not have enquired too closely about identification papers or whether applicants had a fixed address. Counterfeit identity cards, complete with green class IV medical exemptions, were relatively easy to come by in any case.

Maintaining a regular supply of staff was one thing; doing the same for booze – naturally a key aspect of running a successful club in wartime – was another. I am not sure Harry would have been happy wholly delegating this aspect of the business to the wine store, even if he part-owned it. The margins to be made from less legitimate suppliers such as looters, smugglers and service outlets like the NAAFIs (or their US equivalent, the PXs) would have been too tempting. He would, however, have drawn the line at peddling hooch, industrial spirit broken down on illicit stills and sold in bootleg bottles, despite the astronomic profits on offer. One bad batch would have meant instant closure.

The Studio Club benefited from the widely-held misapprehension that basement clubs were the 'best air-raid shelters in town': underground havens for those who wanted to eat, drink and be entertained through the blackout without having to worry about their safety. The belief that ceilings of steel and concrete were ample protection survived even the bombing of the 'Café de Paris' around the time Harry took over his club. Revellers barely paused despite 30 members of the Café's clientele and staff being killed, such was the demand for any relief from wartime tension and boredom. The original location of Harry's rival Al Burnett's 'Nut House' club in Greek Street was also bombed out. Fortunately it was empty at the time and Al reopened within weeks at a new site on Piccadilly.

Like all club owners, Harry would have worried more about rule 42c than bombs. His nightly duel was not with the Luftwaffe, it was with the Metropolitan Police: a struggle that required him, as named owner, to be on site virtually all the time the club was open. He had to ensure members always showed their cards to gain admittance, that no members' guests were allowed to buy drinks and that known drunks, even in uniform, were actively discouraged from entry. On one hand, girls coming off the streets with a reputation for prostitution, even if in the company of a member, had to be barred, but on the other, Harry had to ensure a nightly draw of nubile female company and dancing partners.

Like Al Burnett, he steered away from paid hostesses. The girls were members of the Studio Club, granted entry and paying their way like any customer, although at discounted prices. In the club they had to behave impeccably but in return had the freedom to dance with whomever they wanted. Harry took the view that whatever happened between clients and their dancing partners off the premises was none of his business. He screened hopefuls personally for known call-girls, choosing the ones who both looked the part and could also look after themselves. No doubt he did a bit of talent scouting for himself as well.

He always had to have security on hand to deal swiftly with the inevitable violence, whether it be rival gang members using his premises to stake their turf or internecine strife amongst Allied servicemen. Having a reputation for disorder was equally as threatening to the club's continuing operations as drunkenness.

Harry's job was to be at the centre of all things in the club: cajoling staff, charming customers, occasionally bribing officers from C Division of the Met to tip him off about lightning raids and overlook transgressions. He did not aspire to be a flamboyant Master of Ceremonies in the Al Burnett mould, but he still had to look the part. Luckily he would have had no difficulty flouting the cloth-saving provisions of the Making of Civilian Clothing (Restrictions) Order through his East End tailoring contacts.

Harry was never shut down under 42c, which was much more of an achievement than it sounds. Witness Al Burnett's chequered wartime experience in contrast: the Nut House's replacement premises near Piccadilly Circus was raided under the regulation, found to have 'undesirables' and shut down. There was no redress; Burnett was banned from reopening for twelve months. Like Harry, Burnett was unfit for army service, so he had another go. He launched another club in Regent Street called the 'Merry-Go-Round' with his wife Celia as the named owner. That too was closed down under 42c. He bounced back with the Nut House after a year but was shuttered down yet again. A particularly violent brawl at another of Burnett's spots, the 'Shangri La', ended his involvement there as well.

Somehow Harry navigated all these shoals. It did not hurt that his aim was to offer an upmarket US-style night spot, no doubt heavily influenced by the venues he recalled from his trip to New York. His ambitions went well beyond simply mimicking the black walls and pink curtains of Soho chic. While the interior of the Knightsbridge Studio Club itself was simple: a platform of tables overlooking a dance floor and a back room, Harry did not stint on the band – drums, bass, clarinet, pianist, a vocalist – playing Glenn Miller, Benny Goodman and Tommy Dorsey tunes. When the band was off, a cocktail pianist would take requests.

Harry listened to the V-Discs the Americans brought over. The ambience and the choice of music – not just dance music but jazz as well – was designed to evoke Stateside memories of girls and dates from before the war. He went out of his way to find vocalists with a style and 'girl next door' personality that would appeal to the imports. In 1943 his lead vocalist was Kay Harding, singing six nights a week. Under a headline 'Kay for

Krooning' in *Good Morning*, the Submarine branch's daily paper, her nightclub work didn't stop her recording with Felix Mendelsohn's band, laying on troop concerts for ENSA and cooking sausage and chips at an American Eagle Canteen.

The club was a hit, vying with the Crackers Club or Shepherds in catering to US servicemen homesick for jazzy sounds. Word-of-mouth recommendations meant that Harry could rely on a steady stream of flightcrew coming up to London from their bomber bases on 48-hour passes and demanding instant memberships. The Yanks may have been immaculate guests – all servicemen were given a little booklet when they shipped over advising them not to make fun of British accents, criticise the King or Queen or complain about the food – but relations with the residents of the mansion block must have been strained. The club kept late hours and inevitably there were altercations outside when Americans tried to bring in escorts, oblivious to the risk their entry would pose to the establishment.

Most nights the room was a sea of airmen in their 'pinks-and-greens', Class-A uniforms with 8th Air Force patches on their sleeves, dancing with the pretty girls that Harry knew would both be attracted by, and attract, his target audience. The availability of covetable dancing partners would have garnered the attention of both the pomaded, padded-shoulder types and RAF air crew so there was no shortage of domestic custom either.

Undoubtedly there were a lot of people involved in creating a popular nightly destination, the sort of shady characters who get lost in time, but Harry set the tone for the Studio Club. This was his calling; this was his vision of what a club should be like. Thus I am sure he would have been gratified by the reminiscences years later of one American pilot who got one of those instant memberships, even though he managed to use it only once.

In April 1944, Bill Schock was a B17 pilot on a 72-hour pass from Grafton-Underwood Airfield with his bombardier, Jim Garrett. They had heard of the Studio Club and went there on the last night of their leave. Schock was shot down over Denmark on 9th April and became a prisoner of war. Garrett, who had not gone on the raid, got some of Bill's personal items from his footlocker. After the war, both went home – Garrett to Denver and Schock to Nebraska where he became publisher of the *Falls City Journal* and wrote a weekly column into his 90s. In April 2013, Garrett's widow sent him some memorabilia including Bill's pristine Knightsbridge Studio Club card – member #596 – which triggered memories of that night in his column. 'It was very nice, kinda upscale but not swanky,' he wrote.[27] 'Jim and I got a table and sat down to watch other people having fun… military guys—Royal Air Force and Yanks—were dancing. Jim and I wondered to each other where those good-looking girls with them came from.' It might have taken 69 years but Harry would have loved that testimonial.

---

27 2 April 2013, *Falls City Journal.*

Harry's mother and father, Morris & Esther.
Photo reprinted courtesy of Beverly Danan

The latest family portrait, probably taken in 1918 or 1919. Left to right, they
are Esther, Harry, Ben, Rose, Morris and Annie. While still officially the Cohens,
Esther and Morris had increasingly reverted to using the surname Vygoda.
Photo reprinted courtesy of Beverly Danan

The earliest family portrait, taken in 1915. They would still have been the Cohens at this stage. Left to right, they are Rose, Harry, Annie, Morris and Esther with Ben sitting on Esther's lap.
Photo reprinted courtesy of Beverly Danan

Harry's original greengrocery shop on Putney High Street, probably in 1936.
Photo reprinted courtesy of Beverly Danan

The Morris family's ancestral village in Poland, Goworowo, burning after its
capture by the "Kempf" Panzer Division on 9 September 1939.
Image from the Imperial War Museum archive

On holiday in Deal, Kent Easter 1939. Betty is on the right at the back, Harry, with a centre parting in his hair, on the left.

Betty and Harry enjoying the winter sun in the Bahamas, 1947

R.M.S. CARONIA.
Photographed on board.

Harry in auctioneer mode on the Caronia, probably on the 1951 cruise

*Vinnie, third left, and Harry, on the left, at a gala dinner in London,
either in 1961 or 1962*

Harry, second left, Bob O'Donnell, sixth left, and Vinnie, extreme left, at a Japanese tea ceremony on the 1954 cruise, the trip when Harry first met Vinnie

Harry, second from the left, looking uncomfortable outside Westcott church at Mum and Dad's wedding, 1962

Kobe

Monday 25th February

Kobe lay at the eastern end of an inland sea, its port protected by enormous seawalls. Harry was on deck after lunch to see *Caronia*'s approach. In 1954 they had sailed in from the opposite direction – from Manila – but the impression of mile upon mile of shipyards, warehouses, mills and factories stretched out along the waterfront was just the same. Virtually all of the industrial buildings were new; during the war three-quarters of Kobe had been bombed.

As if in sympathy a pall of smoke and haze hung above the city. It was trapped by the hills behind: poor air quality was the price the inhabitants paid for a sheltered location and full employment.

Harry coughed productively into his handkerchief – his chest infection from Los Angeles still lingered. Spitting out pinkish-yellow phlegm was becoming a regular, if furtive, occurrence in public – much to Vinnie's disapproval. His back hurt as well but as was his habit he downplayed how unwell he felt.

The last time they were here they had started much earlier in the day so they would have to leave promptly if they wanted to revisit as many of the old sites in Kyoto as possible. That meant skipping the arrival ceremony of Miss Kobe 1963 and her Maids of Honour, which was no great loss to Harry's mind. He had seen enough Japanese girls in garish kimonos to last a lifetime.

Vinnie wanted to go back to the Heian Shinto Shrine, with its beautiful gardens, and Nijo Castle. She also wanted to return to the geisha house they had visited before, despite Harry's reservations. He had managed to extract one concession from her though: there would be no repeat of the interminable Cherry Dance spectacle they and Bob had been subjected to after lunch in '54.

Imperial Kyoto's palaces and temples might have been spared Kobe's wartime aerial bombardment, but the city had still suffered the ravages of fire over the ages – to Harry's eyes everything looked reconstructed. The enormous wooden edifice near the station, the Higashi Honganji Temple, was actually less than 70 years old, having burned down four times. What a monument to human resilience, Harry thought. Far more becoming than similar symbols in London, such as the modernist monstrosity, Bowater House, which had been put up on a bombsite near the Studio Club.

It was said that the stout wooden pillars supporting Higashi Honganji Temple's flowing tile roofs had been dragged there using three-inch thick ropes made from the plaited hair of devout Buddhist women. It was a centre for evangelical Japanese Buddhism: no need to struggle to cleanse the self, just constant invocation of, and belief in, Amida Buddha. A sure route to salvation.

In the shadowy, cool great main hall, worshipers fell on their knees at the rail even though the Buddha's image was concealed behind large screens. The pious on the tatami seemed more than satisfied by the aniconistic display, judging by the regularity with which notes and coins were being dropped into a giant wooden treasure chest.

Back outside, Harry sat down gratefully in the courtyard amongst all the bus tourists. Vinnie had wandered off somewhere in the complex so he bought a drink from one of the booths selling coloured postcards and Fuji films and ignored the many guides proffering their services. Amongst all the advertisements, one for 'Night Club Buddha' caught his eye. He didn't think a night spot extolling God would fly in London.

Time was short so they decided to give Heian a miss and go directly to Nijo Castle. The roads were teeming – trams, buses, three- and four-wheel trucks, motorcycles and bicycles all competing for the same space and seemingly oblivious to the countless pedestrians. The castle itself, behind its moat and gleaming white walls, was a serene contrast. It had been built for the first shogun – Tokugawa Iyeyasu, whose tomb they had seen in Nikko – and its curved roofs were supposed to ward off evil spirits who could only move in straight lines. They sat down at a vantage point overlooking the castle's Zen garden. There was a large pool and a humped bridge. Meticulously placed boulders simulated islands and mountains, dotted here and there with stone lanterns and tiny bent pines. A rounded bank of grass reminded Harry of Parliament Hill, which he knew was the purpose of such microscopic harmony and precision – to evoke a remembered landscape. It brought on a novel emotion for Harry – homesickness.

In the evening they went to the Geisha Quarter in Kyoto where the lantern-lit verandas of the tea houses looked out over the Kamo River. The house they revisited had both geishas and *maikos* – apprentice geishas under contract to the *okasan*, a surrogate mother to the girls. Vinnie made some arch comments about having to be on her mettle now she was surrounded by women – some younger than Anabel – all trained in the art of pleasing men. She needn't have worried. Two *maikos* danced interminably to the sound of a plucked samisen behind a screen. Tiny doll-like white hands peeked out of their kimono sleeves and what must have been precise gestures just looked to Harry like two white doves fluttering in their death throes. The utterly expressionless, rouge-streaked faces of the dancers added to the macabre effect that they crowned with a graceful swoon in their oversized kimonos.

They were followed by the *Tayu*, the elite geisha. Her get-up made the beswagged *maikos* look underdressed. She moved with slow dignity to the mat, slipped off her wooden sandals and immediately lost four inches. Two little girls emerged to be taught how to make tea: the red gashes of their lips a ghastly presentiment of puberty. The *Tayu* faced them kneeling on the floor, put some leaves in a bowl, added tepid water and agitated the mixture with a bamboo whisk. The bowl kept getting turned to ensure it was presented to the guest in the right fashion. Harry accepted a cup. It was tepid and gritty.

Like in 1954, they stayed at the Hotel Kyoto, only this time in the same bedroom. Vinnie was very solicitous. She said she'd enjoyed the sights and the show so the day had not been a total waste of effort.

*

Harry may have had a good war – in a financial not martial sense – but no one could escape such a cataclysm unscathed. One event must have brought home the reality of the conflict to him: the night Betty's brother Dennis was killed in action.

Den had always been the baby of the Houben family, born in one war and destined to die in the next. He was a decade younger than Betty but already matched her in the parenting stakes, having married Joan Ford in 1938 when barely out of his teens and becoming a father to Judy a few months later. He joined the RAF, trained as a bomb aimer and by the summer of 1944 was a Flight Sergeant.

A few minutes before midnight on 21st June he and the six other crew of Lancaster DV360, of No 207 Squadron, took off from RAF Spilsby in Lincolnshire to bomb the synthetic oil plant at Wesseling in the Ruhr, or 'Happy Valley' as the aircrews called it because it was so heavily defended. A hundred and thirty-three Lancasters took part in the attack, 38 failed to return including five from Spilsby. In Bomber Command annals it is a notorious raid: with a 28% 'chop rate' – to use the chillingly euphemistic term for aircraft losses – it was proportionately the worst of the war.

On an unusually bright night, enemy fighters penetrated the stream from the rear and then steadily worked their way forwards, shooting down bombers as they went. Dennis; Pilot, Edwin Goodman; Wireless Operator, David McDonnell; Navigator, Joseph Shaw; Flight Engineer, John Pierce; and Air Gunners, Eric Evans and George Lackie crashed between the villages of Grosshau and Kleinhau, 40 miles south-west of Cologne.

Dennis had just turned 27, the same age as Shaw; Goodman, a South African, was 22; and McDonnell, an Australian, nineteen. Seven men with an average age in their twenties driven from the corners of the world to join the battle, now lying with over 3,300 other Commonwealth servicemen in Rheinberg War Cemetery. One crew, one sortie: a symbol of the incalculable loss war brings.

To add insult to injury, the oil plant was only slightly damaged. A German report quoted in the British official history records a 40% production loss at Wesseling but, if so, it was only for a short duration because Wesseling had to be attacked again within a month. The second raid was more successful in terms of production destroyed and at the cost of just one aircraft.

I doubt very much that his brother-in-law's death made Harry feel guilty about not fighting. He was a legitimate non-combatant because of his Hodgkin's Disease. He might even have rationalised that between the club – offering vital rest and recuperation to soldiers and airmen – and the greengrocers he was aiding the war effort. In truth, having discovered his *métier* there was no way he was going to change his course.

What the Studio Club showed was that Harry could build a business in the most trying of circumstances, meeting the demands of exacting customers and not falling foul of the authorities in the process. His backers made money because, judging by the change in his lifestyle, he made a small fortune for himself in the space of three years.

Business would become tougher after the war when the Americans started heading for home. Bottle Parties would be done away with in the 1949 Licensing Act and the last one closed in December 1950. But by then Harry had moved on to much bigger enterprises.

Tuesday 26th February

They left Kyoto in the morning to return to Kobe to see if goods were still as cheap as they were in 1954. Harry recalled the souvenir stalls set out all the way along the quayside then.

He thought Vinnie was more nostalgic about Bob today than she had been since they had got together. She brought up the way the three of them had visited Motomachi Street: the shopping centre decorated with artificial cherry blossoms that were so perfectly made that they looked genuine. They had hired an English-speaking driver and had him drive them up Rokko Mountain. The road was a masterpiece of highway engineering. Vinnie had squealed at the speed the driver took the endless hairpins only to be denied the view from the revolving platform at the peak by a haze that covered the city, then as now.

Bob had been obsessed with a sales pamphlet they picked up before going ashore. It was by 'Mr K. Mikimoto, famous gentleman of Japan, and inventor of the cultured pearl' and promised a perfect necklace of these 'lustrous gems of the ocean' for 'a song' in terms of US dollars. He wanted to buy one for Vinnie but they ran out of time. In Bob's memory, Vinnie bought herself some cultured pearl earrings this time.

They handed in their shore passes and record of purchase forms on the gangway and, Harry, with some relief, headed to his separate cabin. The sightseeing stops had taxed his body to breaking but he now had the rest of the week to recover for Hong Kong.

*

Unlikely as it would have been to find Harry fighting for a noble cause, he might have felt that Den's death in combat had meaning at least. Could he have said the same for his Polish relatives?

It seems neither he, nor his family, ever tried to find out what had happened to Esther's family under Nazi occupation. Charitably, one might argue that he believed he had no cousins left in the Old Country. Of Moshe Ber's nine children, eight had emigrated and the one who stayed – Jankiel – was from his first marriage so might have been only distantly known to Esther and, therefore, Harry. Perhaps, less forgivably, he had moved so far from his parochial Jewish roots by that stage that he convinced himself he would never have had relations caught up in the Holocaust.

Many of Harry's relatives outran the demons in their own country and the monsters never caught up with them in Britain or the US. But the history of Harry's cousins – the children of Jankiel, the one who stayed behind – brutally demonstrates what would have happened if they had not quit their birthplace.

Jankiel died not far from Goworowo in 1908, a couple of years after Moshe Ber himself. His widow, Cyrla, and the youngest of his six children, Josel, died from a contagious disease like typhoid or diphtheria within a fortnight of each other in 1911. One daughter, Sura Ryfka, emigrated to Israel. That left four sitting ducks when the Nazis rolled in. The atrocity suffered by one of them – Harry's cousin, Szmul, serves to demonstrate the fate which befell that part of Harry's family who remained in Poland.

Szmul – like many Stern males, a baker – and his wife Sura – the daughter of a rabbi, Yaakov Shepsil Truchnowski – had moved to the picturesque old town of Pultusk on the Narew River. During the occupation, the town, renamed Ostenburg, saw all its Jews, about half its population, deported to concentration camps.

Szmul, his wife and six of their eight adult children – Malka, Ester, Mojsze, Liba, Rachel and Elka – were murdered.

I know their fecundity was overwhelmed by the nihilism of the Nazis because of the testimony lodged by the two survivors of the family – Szmul's daughters, Shoshana and Chaya – in the central database of Shoah victims in Yad Vashem. The family is also in the necrology of Pultusk's *Yizker Buch* or Yizkor Book, the volume of memories collected by former residents of the town or village that has to act as the substitute gravestone for the martyrs who did not have a proper burial.

Even in Szmul's family, the motivation to leave Poland was strong, albeit in a different form. Shoshana and Chaya came of age when Zionism was becoming a powerful force in the *shtetls*. They both immigrated or, in Zionist terms, made *Aliyah* – ascended – to what was then Palestine before the war. Chaya married Moshe Zemel and had three children in that tumultuous period for Israel between the end of the war and the Suez crisis. Shoshana married Menachem Blum and had two of her own. To bring children into that uncertain world after what had happened to their aunts and uncles speaks to a pioneering human spirit and a refusal to be bowed. Symbolically, Chaya and Shoshana settled in Rishon LeZion. The name translated means 'first to Zion', which in the context of the family is undoubtedly what they were.

The two sisters' witness differs. Shoshana's is more extensive as it includes members of her husband Menachem Blum's family; Chaya's is the more detailed and includes photographs of her parents and siblings – images of youth and beauty before the outrage.

Understandably there is confusion about what exactly happened to Szmul's family in the immediate aftermath of the forced expulsion from Poland at the end of 1939. They were expelled from different places – Putulsk, Bialystok and Ciechanow. Chaya thought part of the family ended their days in Baranowicz, in what is now Belarus, and part in Sarny, in what is now Ukraine. Chaya could have alighted on these particular towns because both became notorious for their ghettos and massacres after the war. Just as possible is that they died of starvation en route, were shot by the roving *Einsatzgruppen* death squads after the German invasion of Russia or were shipped back to Treblinka to certain death. Chaya is only certain about the end for one of her siblings – Malka and her family were degraded and murdered at Auschwitz in 1942.

More Jews were killed in 1942 than in any other year in the Holocaust. Treblinka exterminated almost 900,000 Jews in five months. The insult added to injury of their being later dug up and tossed onto open-air cremation pyres as the Nazis sought to hide the evidence of their genocide only adds to the crushing sadness.

It would be improbable to think that they were the only members of Esther's extended family to have suffered this fate. I know that two granddaughters of Esther's much older half-sister Frieda had narrow escapes. Taube (Tillie) Goldberg got out with her husband and two children on the *SS Batory* from Gdynia in May 1939. Her younger sister, Malka (Mollie), actually went back to Poland in 1938 to marry Mosher Karwat, who must have been a childhood sweetheart. She too got out in 1939 but seems to have travelled back to the US alone – no more is heard of Mosher after the war started. Another of Frieda's grandchildren, Fannie, never left Poland – the only one of her family not to emigrate. She married Zelik Hercberg in 1931 and they both perished in the Holocaust.

It may be a banal insight, but a high likelihood of tragedy always stalks any twentieth-century Polish Jewish genealogy. I had good reason to feel a sense of trepidation when I started digging up Harry's roots, but it is my inestimable good fortune that I do not have to write a Jewish family elegy. Having re-searched Jankiel's family and recorded their fates, I do not feel some inauthentic love of all things Jewish, just the shared sense of loss common to all humans at this outrage, whether they have Mitteleuropa roots or not. His ancestral home lay behind the Iron Curtain after the war so information would have been very difficult to come by, but I like to think that if he had had access to the facts, Harry would have felt the same.

Hong Kong

Saturday 2nd March

Caronia left Kobe in the very early hours of Wednesday morning for the 1500-mile passage southwest to Hong Kong.

The sea had been rough when Harry woke, but he had been more anxious about the state of his pyjamas. His itching and night sweats had been getting steadily worse and that morning they were soaked. His bed clothes were being changed daily, a state of affairs his room steward had shared below decks: in crew slang he had told his fellow stewards that his 'blood' was 'minty'. In other words, Harry, normally so fastidious, had turned malodorous.

Despite the ship's rolling, Harry had been happy at the prospect of an extended period at sea. All the frenetic sightseeing in Japan had drained his reserves to empty. That first afternoon out, he and Vinnie had braved the swell and taken tea. It was not a favoured meal for either of them although Harry's sweet tooth usually overcame his lack of appetite. He had made a pantomime of inspecting the silver pans and clean cloths on the tea trolley with his restaurant manager's practised eye but, in truth, his heart hadn't been in it: he felt too fatigued.

On Thursday he had woken with a frightening presentiment that willpower and denial would no longer be enough to repel his cancer. He had a strong sense of what other people had noticed but, other than Vinnie, were too polite to mention: that his body was slowing down and not functioning as it should. His mind turned to the prospect of going into St Mary's again. Or perhaps a hospital in New York when they docked. He thought he might need another blood transfusion like he'd had November, although it hadn't seemed to work very well then. He would find the money for it from somewhere.

Consultations with the ship's doctors were always available before lunch and dinner but the location of the waiting room, forward of the Purser's Office on Main Deck, was too conspicuous for Harry's taste. He preferred the alternative service offered before regular consultation hours in a converted port-side stateroom on A Deck. He resolved to make a discreet appointment directly. In all his voyages on *Caronia*, he had never had to resort to telephoning the hospital for medical attention and he was not going to start now.

Of the two medical officers on board, Harry preferred Dr Winer, the ship's surgeon, to Dr Cuthbert. Both were reassuring presences, highly experienced and in truth overqualified for the majority of cases that might present on board, but he had more of an affinity with Isaac Winer. He knew him from previous voyages and his 'bedside' manner brought Harry's personal physician, Joyston-Bechal, to mind.

Whichever doctor he had chosen, the outcome of the examination would have been the same, the diagnosis of advanced Hodgkin's Disease unarguable. What neither Winer nor Cuthbert would have mentioned at this stage, in a bid to spare the patient's emotions, was that Harry's lymphoma had denuded his bone marrow to such an extent that his body was struggling to make new white blood cells. To a doctor, the chest infection Harry had picked up in Los Angeles, which he had never really shaken off, was a strong indication of neutropenia.

Winer prescribed an antibiotic, more for a placebo effect than anything else. He could only hope for stabilisation as there was little he could offer by way of remedy save advising Harry to increase his consumption of fresh fruit and vegetables and to exercise caution over future shore visits in order to reduce the risk of infection. Harry was to make another appointment immediately if he saw signs of further deterioration, in which case the best course of action might be to cut the cruise short and head home for specialist treatment.

That night 'Beluga Malossol Caviar' had been on the menu for Thursday's dinner. Harry had ordered it in defiance of the doctor's prescription of more fruit and vegetables. He fancied it as much for the presentation – the silver serving tray, ice bowl, crushed ice, shredded egg and chopped onion accompaniments in porcelain shell dishes – as he did for the fish eggs themselves. When the delicacies arrived, however, he noticed with some alarm that he could barely taste the saltiness of the dish.

Afterwards he went along to the movie – *Jigsaw* with Jack Warner. He had no desire to patronise the 'Gay '90s Ball' even though he knew Vinnie was attending with some other escort. The film brought to mind some of his more obvious gangster customers in the Colony, and the policemen who expected similarly complimentary entertainment.

Because he had lived with lymphoma asymptomatically for so long, Winer's diagnosis that Harry's chest infection and la-boured breathing were related to his disease was a concern. He had to admit that he had been lowered by the doctor's prognosis that his condition was not going to improve quickly and that he should think seriously about staying on board. By the end of the film, however, Harry had come round to the view that this was simply another obstacle cast in his way that needed to be overcome. Besides, he had never been to Hong Kong Island so was not about to miss the opportunity.

On Friday the cruise lecturer, Ivan Boxell, had done a late-morning talk on the British Crown Colony. It was entitled 'A Dot Between the Tiger's Claws' and had proved very popular. Harry and Vinnie could not get into the Theatre so had to listen to a broadcast in the Main Lounge. Vinnie, bored, dozed off but after all the obligatory facts and figures, Harry was transfixed by the echo of the war in the theme of the lecture – a tiny island standing up to a continental menace.

He learned that the colony was made up of Hong Kong Is-land, Kowloon Peninsula, and the New Territories (on a 99-year

lease granted by China in 1898). The border with 'Red China' –
which Boxell, mindful of his largely American audience, insisted
on calling the Communist monolith to the north – was about
twenty miles from Kowloon.

The colony was indeed a dot: 400 square miles that was
home to almost three million people. Since reoccupation the
population had grown fourfold, despite the immigration quotas.
Government housing projects had been completed, and more
were under construction, but the population was multiplying so
fast it was difficult to keep abreast of the problem. The irony was
that land being reclaimed from the sea – the extended runway
and brand new terminal at Kai Tak airport, for example – was
simply accelerating the pace of new arrivals

Here were people leaving everything behind to seek a better
life – like his parents, Harry thought. If anything, they were even
worse off: Morris and Esther never had to squat in the streets or
in shanties on the hillsides or on the tops of buildings.

Harry's attention only tailed off at the end when Boxell, as
was his wont, reverted to shopping advice. The tailoring business in Hong Kong was world famous for its speed and quality,
he said. You can get a suit of clothes made to order in 24 hours.
The leather goods manufacturing was even more remarkable:
a Hong Kong cobbler could take your measurement, make a
last and deliver shoes in two days for a fantastically low price
compared with similar custom-built items in the US. Although
if you did have some shoes made during the ship's stay, you
were advised not to wear them until they were fully dry. Harry
thought ruefully about how many months he had been waiting
for his second fitting at Cyril Castle's.

At least Cyril would be pleasantly surprised by his slimmed-
down physique. Later on, one of the hospital attendants came
to Harry's room to give him some physiotherapy – basically
just vigorous massaging – to reduce the swelling in his legs and
ankles. No doubt that helped with slimming too.

Caronia steamed into Hong Kong just as dawn was breaking.
Harry had spent a restless night so was up to witness the arrival.

Even at this early hour, as the liner navigated the freighters at anchor and turned towards its dock on the Kowloon side, there was a great deal of water traffic to observe: ferries and launches, flat-bottomed sampans and junks with their taut brown sails heeling in the wind. He knew from yesterday's lecture that Hong Kong meant 'fragrant harbour'; he wondered what the Cantonese for 'busy harbour' was. Harry could see the grey silhouette of a destroyer next to the smooth white lines and yellow funnel of a Lloyd Triestino passenger ship. To the south, on the island, it seemed that the Praya was one long line of junks all the way along to Kennedy Town. Looking up, above the warehouses and offices and bank skyscrapers, Harry could see the white houses and apartments on the 'Peak', perched serenely over the mass of the city below.

The swelling in his legs was not resolving itself. Something was blocking the lymph fluids and blood supply in his lower body, making it painful to walk. He and Vinnie had planned to join the driving excursion, but in the end the prospect was too daunting so Vinnie was to go on her own.

They were in Hong Kong for two full days so he would use the day to rest, write some letters and take a truncated tour with Vinnie tomorrow. There would be lots to see but they would avoid those areas where the Hong Kong Chinese lived in back-to-back tenements. Boxell had warned his listeners that in March, which fell towards the end of the dry season, there was always a water shortage. The sight of women and children queuing at taps in the slums to get water would have brought back too many unpleasant memories of his own childhood.

By mid-morning the ship was largely deserted. Harry had the *Caronia*'s library, an intimate space at the aft end of the Smoking Room, to himself. The desks, chairs, deep-pile carpet and burr wood veneers were designed to make the room feel like the private study that, no doubt, many of the passengers possessed on land. Artfully spread magazines were close at hand and books displayed behind wire grilles. The bookcase, with its curved corners and contrasting frieze, and the chairs with their bold decorative pattern were late-1940s Art Deco chic at its peak.

The library was designed to be more looked at than used. The chair had an overly narrow squab, trading comfort for style, but frankly any inconvenience was minor in the current scheme of things and Harry felt at home; the décor reminded him of his own flat. It was one of his favourite places on board, its charm only enhanced by the fact that all the furniture had been built by his namesake, H. Morris & Co. So it was here that he wrote his airmail letters, 'blue flimsies', with their imprinted stamp and stern injunction that any enclosures would be surcharged. One was to his middle daughter:

March 2nd, Hong Kong.

Dearest Belinda, I was so pleased to hear from you after all this time and to know you are feeling so well. Your mother seemed to take a hell of a long time telling me about the address of yours I wanted, and as a matter of fact I have not heard from Anabel at all. Does she keep the cards I have been sending Anabel – please find out for me as I would love to hear from her and you. I entertained Susan in New York and she looked lovely now her teeth have been fixed. We are having a very nice trip except that I am far from well. I may have to go into hospital as soon as I return as I have to get my complaint cleared up. I am glad you were able to get over the hard winter without any illnesses – you seem to be looking forward to the baby very much. I hope it's a boy and please send me a cable as soon as it happens – so I can drink to both your health. The puppy sounds fun and must be tremendous company for you, especially with Barry being away all day. I am glad he is doing well and hope he is in good health. By the way did you get the card I sent you to the house? Look after yourself and give Barry my best wishes. I am due back mid-April unless they send me back sooner – keep me posted and I will, you.

All my love,

Daddy.

Mrs O'Donnell sends her love to you.

Later on he took tea in the echoing Main Lounge where he was entertained by recorded rather than live music and the white-gloved stewards outnumbered the passengers.

While the ship was quiet Harry went to see Dr Cuthbert for a second opinion. Cuthbert was more assertive than his colleague. It was quite common for people with bone marrow issues to die from an infection, he said; if one got into Harry's bloodstream he could risk sepsis. He was at greater risk than normal of bleeding and bruising were he to have an accident; in fact the bleeding could be internal and invisible, heightening the risk of a stroke. Harry wasn't cowed. He would still be going onshore with Vinnie tomorrow. He had never felt unlucky.

The same was true for his whole family, he thought.

*

The consequences for the Sterns if they had not left Goworowo is clear from one of the Polish volumes of the Encyclopaedia of Jewish Communities. The *shtetl* lay about an hour's railway journey from Warsaw on the line to Lomza. That, and its proximity to the highway, was its raison d'être but also its undoing. The German tanks arrived within a week of the outbreak of war.

At the same time that Morris and Esther were celebrating the marriage of their younger daughter, Anne, to Alec Gopstein, everybody they knew in their old villages was fleeing for their lives:

> *When the Germans entered Goworowo they made sport with the Jews and began to rob them of their possessions. On September 21st the Germans took all the Jews out of their homes and pushed them into the*

> *town's shul. Every Jew who tried to remain in his home*
> *and not go to the synagogue was shot on the spot. Then*
> *the Germans burned the homes of the Jews and set*
> *the synagogue on fire. The Jews who were inside were*
> *saved after a German officer who chanced to appear*
> *and who, after hearing the cries from inside, ordered*
> *them to be released from the burning building.*[28]

Goworowo has a Yizkor Book, only partially translated into English but still making for grim reading. It has an account of the same inferno but through the prism of Yoelke, the baker. Yoelke was 65 and 'still a strong man'. In a life dogged by tragedy – all thirteen of his children had died – this was obviously one outrage too many. He broke out of the *shul*, went to his bakery and returned with a sack of *challas* for the children. Miraculously he wasn't shot. The respite was only temporary. During *Chol ha-Moed Sukkot*, the intermediate days of the Feast of Tabernacles, which in 1939 occurred between September 30th and October 3rd, all the Goworowo Jews were expelled to the Soviet half of annexed Poland.

When those territories were themselves overrun by the Nazis in 1941, many of the exiles were exterminated by the *Einsatzgruppen*; the remainder, including the last rabbi of Goworowo, Rabbi Burstein, were shipped westwards to end their days in Treblinka Death Camp, chillingly close to home.

It strikes me as unlikely that Morris or Esther didn't talk about Goworowo to their children, even if only to compare it to the relative comfort of Whitechapel. If they did, however, the oral history has not been passed down the generations. Other than Minnie's account the same is true of the US family. However, 30 years ago one of the US descendants decided to fill in the gap in his heritage. In 1990, Benjamin's great nephew, Shale Stiller, the grandson of Jennie's younger brother Baruch, returned to Goworowo. He called it by its Yiddish name: Govorova.[29]

---

28 Wein, Abraham and others (1989). *Pinkas Hakehillot,* Yad Vashem, Israel, pp.152–154.
29 Stiller, Shale D., *Journey to Govorova.*

Things were a bit rough around the edges in the village as the Communists had only just fallen from power, but what irked Shale the most was the suspicion with which he was viewed by the inhabitants: an attitude he assumed was driven by the belief that he had returned solely to reclaim his family's stolen inheritance. Perhaps it is natural for a lawyer from Baltimore to think in terms of property rights. But I like to think it was not guilt on the part of the villagers, more bafflement that anyone would be interested in their tumbledown dwellings.

Shale admitted as much in not hiding his disappointment at how his family birthplace looked. His first impression might have been coloured by taking the first signposted route from Różan: 'The road to Govorova is dirt all the way,' he wrote, even though there was a metalled road to Goworowo about a mile further along. 'The town is very poor with only one paved street … with dirty old houses, no fresh paint, dispirited, unhappy, backward-looking people who came from nowhere and are going nowhere.'

He was shown the site of the old *shul* and visited the Jewish cemetery. Across a bridge, a dirt lane led to a 'field formerly known as Vilke Govorova and now known as Vilke Brzinska … No stones remain from the old cemetery. The Nazis took them all away,' he recorded. Nevertheless he recited the *El Malei Rachamim* – the prayer for the souls of the departed – for Schmuel David and Chaya Sarah and all of the Stillers who may have been buried there.

What Shale could not have known in those pre-internet days was that a man called Wojciech Henrykowsk had already catalogued and photographed twenty or so of the surviving *matzevot* that had been stacked up in the courtyard of the local library.[30]

I am not sure his mood would have improved if he had. The tombstones had previously been 'recycled' elsewhere in the village. During the occupation they had been used to pave the road and driveway to the garage of the Catholic presbytery and after the war they were used by some residents for construction.

---

30 Jewish Historical Institute in Warsaw, *http://cmentarze-zydowskie.pl/goworowo.htm.*

Apparently, even into the twenty-first century Hebrew inscriptions could be seen in the foundations of one of the buildings in Goworowo's Market Square.

At least by 1988 the *matzevot* had been removed from the presbytery. They and a couple of hundred others – nearly 90 were discovered by the petrol station in 1999 – went to the warehouse of the Community Administrative Office and were still there fifteen years after Shale's visit.[31]

Shale was barely more impressed with Różan – it might have had some factories and tall apartment buildings but had little else to recommend it. Again he sought out the Jewish cemetery, now 'just an empty field with a few trees' and recited the *El Malei Rachamim*. At the end of the day he sums up his emotions by quoting the title of the Thomas Wolfe novel: *You Can't Go Home Again.*

After reading his account I think Shale's trip couldn't have been anything other than anticlimactic. He had dreamed of visiting the mysterious Goworowo for 35 years so I think his expectations were too high and he happened to arrive at a particularly dysfunctional period in the country's history.

I believe that you can go 'home' again. I didn't want Shale's grim descriptions to be the final word on the subject so even though international travel was still constrained by the Covid pandemic, I organised my own quest in the summer of 2021.

I did not visit alone. One unambiguous blessing of the research for this book has been the discovery of so many relatives across the world. I went to Goworowo in the company of my second cousin, Richard Keen, who lives outside Warsaw, and his bilingual daughter, Nicola. For one day at least there would be a Jewish contingent in the ancestral village again.

We could have picked a better day to go. After a hot July the weather had broken. As we drove up from the city the rain fell heavily from a steel-grey sky. Urban sprawl gave way to stands of birch and fir and then cultivated fields and orchards. Unlike

---

31 *https://iajgscemetery.org/eastern-europe/poland/goworowo.*

Shale's visit I didn't see any horse-pulled carts on the roads, which was just as well as they were all awash in spray.

Just like Shale we entered Goworowo across the bridge over the Orz into the Market Square, although it would be fair to say that our entry did not quite generate the stir that he did. No one gathered around us, strangers no longer the curiosity that they were in 1990. People were intent on doing their shopping in the stores dotted around the square. All the streets are paved now and although there are still a few wooden houses, they act as picturesque adornments, setting off their brick and concrete neighbours. Goworowo looked like it was: a quiet, unremarkable centre for a dispersed farming community: not a place that anyone would go out of their way to visit unless they had a connection as strong as ours. The *shul* was now a mini-market. The synagogue, like any signs of Jewish occupation, is long gone.

There was a slightly jarring note just off the square, a towering Catholic church built in the 1880s in exaltation of the Holy Cross and on a completely different scale from all the other buildings in the village. Perhaps it is just a coincidence, but this was the decade when the pogroms began and Jews started to leave. It is a reminder that antisemitism in the region predated the Nazi occupation. At any rate, the impact of the church on the incumbent population is clear from Minnie Abarbanell's oral testimony. As a child she was taught to lower her gaze when she passed it, lest something horrible would happen to her as a non-Catholic.

We enquired about the Jewish Cemetery in the Municipal Office. They had no knowledge of its location but fortunately we could fall back on Shale's account for rough directions. We recrossed the bridge into Wólka Brzezińska and struck out across the fields to the left. We followed a long, straight track for about a kilometre. Walking it, one could easily imagine the *levayas* to the cemetery on this route, the community following the coffin out of the village to the grave site, processing and pausing three times in the ritual manner.

When we got to the place there were no visible signs of it ever having been a cemetery. It was simply an unkempt field indistinguishable from all the others save that in place of what would originally have been a masonry wall, it was now screened from the world by a belt of trees and dense undergrowth.

We split up to see if we could find any headstones or other markers. The space felt neglected and dead. It felt as if this was a field which citizens agreed could not be touched but at the same time, preferred to forget the reason why. It certainly no longer bore witness to an extinct community.

Needless to say, I didn't find any memorial stones. After all the rain the ground was inundated. Somehow wading through the weeds and mud connected me with all the unmarked graves underfoot. While I was looking, I felt a frisson from the sound of a long goods train rattling over a rail bridge beyond the trees: I was clearly in a highly suggestible state.

I had the same feeling at the site of the Jewish Cemetery in Różan, a similarly inert field again hidden by trees. We went there to honour the unknown Vigodas on Morris's side, doubly unknown now as the locations of their final resting places are lost forever.

Apparently, in the municipal warehouse, some of the Goworowo gravestones are still decipherable. One is that of a Rojza, daughter of Benjamin, who died on 11th December 1901. The date fits, the travel record of Rose's own son, Benjamin, ties in – it is quite possible this is the marker for my great-great grandmother.

It doesn't feel right that gravestones should end up stacked like paving slabs in a builders' merchant. It also feels wrong that cemeteries, even stripped of their masonry, are not signposted. That said, in the complicated relationship that Poland has with its twentieth-century history, it is not surprising that the artefacts are orphaned. They are a continuous and awkward reminder of a period the country would doubtless prefer to forget. If it is remembered, it is most often in a way that equates the suffering of Poles and Jews under the Nazis. To combat this collective amnesia, the state-condoned promotion of one version of the events, I would argue that it is imperative that if you can, you do go home again. In this, I think Shale was wrong. I would also agree with Harry that he was a lucky man to have had parents who left their homeland for a better life elsewhere.

Sunday 3rd March

The film on board today was *Scrooge*. Alistair Sim's portrayal of the title character was not dissimilar to Dr Cuthbert, whom Harry had seen for a consultation yesterday. They ran close in terms of misanthropy. But despite medical advice he was determined to venture ashore with Vinnie; he had not spent his entire life taking risks only to duck one now.

Vinnie confided that he hadn't missed much by skipping yesterday's driving tour. The Pagoda in Tiger Balm Garden had been ruined by the plainly visible squatters' shacks on the steep hillside to the east. Vinnie could see children carrying water up the slope in slopping buckets. The only highpoint had been the fishing village of Aberdeen to the south, not so much for its waterfront where the activity seemed to be simply drying things – both fish and fishing nets – but for the fleet itself. The tide was out so the thousands of junks and sampans sitting on the muddy sea bottom were in such proximity that you got a strong impression you could walk far out into the sea simply by stepping from the deck of one junk to its neighbour. Apparently this permanently floating population numbered over 100,000.

Harry felt much more able to walk after the physiotherapy, so directly after breakfast they headed off to the Star Ferry Terminus along the quay. There were no immigration formalities: the Master-at-Arms merely advising them to keep the ship's white landing card on them at all times and to be wary of the unscrupulous behaviour of unofficial guides. On the short ferry ride across the bay they looked back at their ship and got a shock: she was covered in a web of bamboo from the water line to her top. They had been warned that she was going to have a coat of paint – she had left her home port in January without having one during her annual overhaul because the painters had been on strike – but they hadn't realised it was going to be so extensive. At each stop some prominent discolouring had been covered over but in Hong Kong the job was going to be completed. She would emerge in her new coat in less than a day, something that would have taken at least a week back in Liverpool.

Harry's musing about the work ethic of Asian painters versus their British equivalents was interrupted by the sound of the telegraphs clanging as the Ferry Master came alongside the wooden ramps on the island side at speed. The passengers were deftly disgorged. 'Beware of Pickpockets,' the Tannoy intoned.

In front of the terminal a new building was going up covered with the same scaffolding as *Caronia* – bamboo poles lashed together with fibre. There was no crane, all the building materials were being hoisted by human hod carriers with poles over the shoulder and baskets tied to each end. Again, Harry was struck by the industry of Asian workers compared with those back home.

They wandered aimlessly around the Chinese business district of North Point, Harry unsettled by the brightly lit shop windows full of watches, jewellery and cameras. His sense of smell had not been good recently but it was strong enough to know the burning joss sticks were not masking the aroma of putrefying rubbish in the alleys between the shops.

At Vinnie's insistence they took a green tram to K-Town to see the Waterfront Market. The tram was full to overflowing with commuters so Harry had to stand, which he bore stoically. He had a sense that Vinnie's frank perusal of how he was carrying himself was somehow a test. He couldn't help but feel he was in competition with some unnamed rival.

In front of the warehouses the junks rose and fell on the tide. Labourers, bent over by their burden – a basket or a crate – at each end of their t'iao poles, navigated the narrow loading boards onto the junks, each crossing rewarded with a tally stick. Heavier cargo was swung over on wooden derricks to be met by the sharp baling hooks of the men on deck. It was as oriental a scene as you could imagine apart from the billboards pointing out that it was 'Coke Time' or urging them to 'Fresh Up with 7Up'.

If he was in competition for Vinnie's favour, Harry wasn't going to cede his position without a fight. He had asked Lorna Yost for something out of the ordinary for lunch – somewhere other than the Castle Peak Hotel with its courtyard full of shiny American motors where the rest of *Caronia* would end up. Yost had recommended a hotel on the Tai Po Road called the Carlton, whose position on the Heights offered an unmatched viewpoint.

Harry and Vinnie took the ferry back to the mainland and the fast tarmac road up. From the roadside they saw an angular white building with large windows and tea tables on the lawn. At the rear, the restaurant terrace looked out over Kowloon and across the bay to Victoria. The spot lived up to the Number One Hostess's billing.

The location was not exactly a well-kept secret though. The dining room was busy. Even so it was impossible not to eavesdrop on the animated discussion being conducted in English by a pair of property developers and an investor on the next table.

There were opportunities aplenty in simply addressing the colony's housing problem, Harry overheard. If you could raise the capital there was no more certain return than Hong Kong property. Apartments were the best bet as your average middle-class Chinese spent half his salary on rent. The payback was three to five years and after that it was pure profit. The bet was simply that things stayed roughly as they were for that length of time and, since it was wealthy Chinese who were backing all the building at the moment, you could be sure nothing much was going to change. The site they were talking about was somewhere in Kowloon overlooking the harbour and the swamplands being reclaimed from the sea.

The conversation turned to the perennial theme favoured by Hong Kongers and presaged by the lecture on board: political uncertainty. The consensus was that while there were Communist cells all over the place, they weren't recruiting like they used to. The refugee crisis visited on the colony when the Kuomintang were thrown out of the mainland had made the ideology a lot less appealing. The Chinese on the island would concentrate on making money and leave the rest to the Government. The Formosa lot – the nationalists on Taiwan – were trying to stir up trouble but they would never get back in.

Harry had to admit the property pitch was seductive. Perhaps this was a sign he should switch horses, career-wise. He made a mental note to discuss it with the money men when he got home. In the taxi back to the ship Vinnie had suggested he might think about cutting short the cruise to get some expert doctors in London to look at his chest. His response was to float the idea of relocating to Hong Kong and trying his hand at property development. Even as he was saying it though, he felt daunted. Best to enjoy today and not worry about the future. He would think about the arrangements to come back and investigate the opportunity properly when his ailment had been treated. Whether it was the prospect of this or the day's exertions, in the taxi he felt a wave of fatigue as powerful as any he had ever experienced after the late nights of the Colony. He craved nothing more than his stateroom bed.

*

All the effort Harry expended in making the Studio Club a success (and keeping it on the right side of the law) came at a cost: despite having two war babies, he and Betty drifted apart.

In 1939 they were living together above the shop at 118 Putney High Street. It would not have been the most stable of environments – they had an uneasy relationship with both sets of parents-in-law – Susan having finally been presented to Morris and Esther – and with each other, given Harry's wandering eye.

The Phoney War newsreels of evacuee children, some the same age as Susan, queuing up in 'crocodiles' at the stations may have spurred them into action. The sense of paranoia would have only been increased by getting leaflets in the post like 'If the Invader Comes' telling them to hide their maps and food (fat chance for a greengrocer) and not to give the Germans anything. Harry took the Ministry of Information posters literally – 'Be Like Dad – Keep Mum' – and shipped Betty and Susan out of London for good. After leaving Putney High Street, Harry never lived with his family again.

Wartime fuel restrictions limited how far the family could move and still stay in touch. Eventually they plumped for a place called 'Limes'. It was an eighteenth-century farmhouse with a stuccoed front and a double-pile roof in the Middlesex village of Laleham.

This was admittedly a fairly dubious choice if family safety was uppermost in Harry's mind, as the village was near Northolt Aerodrome, an obvious bombing target, and right alongside a landmark as easy to follow from above as the River Thames.

He was probably swayed by what the house's solid Georgian façade signified in terms of how far he had come from the tenements. In a sense it was the apotheosis of what he'd been striving for since Susan's birth. Even when they were living above the shop in Putney, there are photos of Susan in a brougham-sized Silver Cross pram (as used by royalty) or in the arms of a nanny on days out at Chessington Zoo. The nanny may have originally been Betty's auntie Flo, but she was still made to wear a wimple and starched white pinafore apron.

In her mid-30s, Betty didn't object to becoming a full-time housewife as her career in fashion had stalled. Before the war she had managed an upmarket lingerie and gown shop but the demand for 30-guinea frocks had disappeared. Wearing clothes that were obviously showy was not the 'done thing'; the emphasis was more on 'make do and mend' now. This meant repurposing coats as dresses and men's suits as jackets and skirts rather than buying new. There was a particular issue with the mainstay of her old shops: stockings and underwear. The use of silk was banned from 1940 and there were never enough rayon ones to go round: it was the baggy wrinkles of Lisle Utility stockings or nothing. No wonder so many women took to staining their, (shapely in Betty's case), legs with tea or gravy.

In hindsight she made the right decision to retire from her chosen occupation. From June 1941, rationing meant that most adults could buy the equivalent of only one new outfit a year – counting clothing coupons would have taken all the fun out of selling dresses. Even more so when the Board of Trade introduced 'Utility', governing things like the number and length of pleats for skirts, in 1942.

By that stage she was firmly ensconced in the 'Limes' and, counting the servants, running a household of four – soon to be five – as she was pregnant with her second child, my mum.

Harry had moved too. He rented a flat in Park Lane that was convenient for the Studio Club and more in keeping with his new-found status as a nightclub owner. Fifty-Five Park Lane was a trophy building that had been built half a dozen years before by Western Heritable, the property arm of the Mactaggart family. Harry started on a low floor at the back of the block – the cachet of the address counting for more than its amenity – and he never left, instead upgrading flats within the complex until he acquired number 81, a prime third floor set overlooking Hyde Park. That was where, in his pomp, he would entertain the rich and famous, and occasionally his wife and daughters.

Eventually the combined impact of the U-Boat attacks and the loss of Malaya meant the allowance of petrol for 'pleasure' motoring was revoked in the summer of 1942. Tyres were in critically short supply too. Harry could prove a business need because of the greengrocers so would have been allowed a supplementary ration. There were penalties for misuse but that would not have stopped him motoring out to Laleham, particularly if he and Betty were paying a weekend call on Charles Clore.

Betty, to everyone's surprise, had proved herself more than capable with the house's vegetable garden, asparagus beds and fruit bushes. Between the garden produce and Harry's greengrocery contacts the children were spared any of the hunger he had felt at their age. The girls had a bedroom each as did the nanny and the cook-general, Molly, who also had exclusive use of a downstairs sitting room. A third daughter, Anabel, arrived in 1943 and meanwhile Harry was free to pursue his energetic womanising. He made up with Betty on his weekend visits by bringing her face powder and lipstick from the black market in defiance of the Toilet Preparations Order. He fell short when it came to sourcing her favourite fragrance, 'Joy', but he could lay his hands on some counterfeit Yardley perfume instead.

This set-up seemed to satisfy all parties for the duration of the war, but after hostilities finished, Harry found Betty's jealousy and increasingly desperate attempts to intrude on his affairs irksome. Betty was not a neglectful parent but was not above her own subterfuge when it came to chasing after Harry. Her daughters remember on one occasion they tracked her down to a spa and when she finally came to the phone she denied being their mother and pretended to be French, complete with a comedy accent. She was probably spying on Harry, incognito.

Harry was not afraid of being seen to work like some of the nouveau riches he bumped into in café society, but he was entitled to play hard as well. He womanised, bought himself a Bentley Mark VI and took Betty to the Bahamas in 1947, eye-wateringly expensive for the time and quite the contrast with their last holiday in Kent just before the war. With his socialising, spending and generally defying Austerity, the last thing he wanted was a watchful and possessive wife.

He needed to create a diversion. Such was my eagerness to fill the gap and find out what that diversion was that I ended up pursuing the biggest red herring in all my research. It is hard enough to avoid succumbing to Harry's inventions without creating a fool's errand for oneself.

Typing 'Harry Morris' and 'club owner' into a web browser brings up lots of references to 'Club Eleven' a nightclub that, although it only operated for eighteen months, is remembered as the first venue in the country that was dedicated to modern jazz.

The club was named for its eleven founders: ten British Bebop musicians, (including a couple that went on to be household names, Ronnie Scott and Johnny Dankworth) and their business manager, Harry Morris. Surely my grandfather's business nous, pedigree in managing clubs and contacts in the jazz world – many jazz players had dodged conscription and Harry did not enquire too closely into service eligibility when hiring for the Knightsbridge Studio Club – meant it was him.

In 1948 this Harry Morris opened the Metropolitan Bopera Club with a sextet led by jazz pianist Dennis Rose. It proved short-lived. At the same time, Scott and Dankworth started practising in a basement club in Ham Yard in Soho. This was close to Archer Street, a sort of open-air job centre for musicians and it created quite a stir in the fraternity. Ten jazzmen came together; Harry spotted a commercial opportunity and the new club opened in December 1948 with two house bands, one led by Scott, the other Dankworth.

Word of mouth amongst jazz fans aware of the modern music being produced by the likes of Charlie Parker and Miles Davis saw people from all over the country flocking to the club. There were broadcasts and recordings and within a few months Harry had to relocate to much larger premises at 50 Carnaby Street. The club opened in the afternoon as a meeting point for musicians and was now operating six evenings a week, booking other acts to perform, including bands from America.

The wild success led to problems – the two rival bands began to quarrel about their share of the take – and worse was to come. Management had always turned a blind eye to the pot and cocaine circulating in the club on most nights, but on 15th April 1950 it was raided by the drugs squad. About a dozen musicians and customers, including Ronnie Scott, spent a night in the cells and were handed fines of between £5 and £15 in the morning. Denis Rose was arrested by the Military Police as an army deserter. The arrest and conviction of some of the Club Eleven members was front page news. That did nothing to lessen attendance but the club folded shortly afterwards.

In my excessive enthusiasm to backfill Harry's chronology, I rationalised that, naturally, he would never have mentioned an enterprise like Club Eleven to his family since it had closed in such ignominy. Moreover, I stumbled across some reminiscences in 1967 from the saxophonist, Don Rendell, who was a stand-in for Ronnie Scott when the latter was touring, in which Harry Morris was described as a good businessman who took care of the financial side and, more corroboratively, was already dead by the year of the interview. That fit. A contemporaneous anecdote had Harry turning up at a flat in the early hours with the legendary jazz guitarist Django Reinhardt. Musicians used to gather after gigs in each other's flats – a jam started, until an altercation with a neighbour cut the session short. What I liked about the story was that Harry arrived with Reinhardt despite neither being able to speak the other's language. It was said that Harry Morris never played an instrument but loved the company of those who did. This was the social, club-owning music lover that I was familiar with.

Then again, one of Ronnie Scott's biographers, John Fordham, portrayed Morris as a 'garrulous, wisecracking street-hustler'.[32] If Harry had a fun-loving work persona, he hid it very effectively from his children and I think he would have been a bit upset to have been described as a street-hustler by this stage in his career. More problematically, this Harry Morris was described as a photographer who had a studio in Soho and apparently looked like Chico Marx behind the big portrait cameras. Harry could only have been mistaken for Chico Marx in a very dim light. One story about Harry was particularly jarring: it was said that on a drive to the country with muso friends he only got as far as Marble Arch where the green expanse of Hyde Park caused him to say, 'I've had enough of this, let's get back to town.' That might have been amusing to basement jazz types but doesn't sound like something someone who was actually living on Park Lane at the time would have said.

So tempting as it is to fill in life's gaps neatly, I have to admit that the Harry Morris with Club Eleven on his curriculum vitae was a different man with the same name.

---

32 Fordham, John (1995). *Jazz Man: The Amazing Story of Ronnie Scott and his Club*, Kyle Books, UK, p.20.

The wild goose chase proved one thing at least: Harry was not the sort of person whose defences would be breached by a keyword search on Google. Throughout his life Harry took a magician's delight in deception. I had to be on my mettle not to become one of his dupes, taken in by the same sleight of hand that fooled so many others.

Harry's scheme to keep Betty away would prove to be both more prosaic and devious than launching a Bebop jazz club. So I suppose more in keeping with the man himself.

Manila

Tuesday 5th March

Harry spent the whole of Monday in bed, something that would have been inconceivable at any other time in his life but now held a distinct allure. He felt dizzy and light-headed and his abdomen was distended and uncomfortable.

What should have been a respite proved to be anything but. He was bone-tired but slept fitfully. His attacks of breathlessness were getting more frequent and his chest infection made every inhalation painful. He dozed on and off all day and only talked to two people – his steward and Vinnie. He had to request an extra blanket as, despite all the sweating, his hands and feet felt icy.

Vinnie recoiled from the smell in Harry's cabin. It was overheated and yet Harry's face looked pale and blotchy. Even he had to admit her visit was perfunctory. It was little more than her poking her head round the door, asking how he was feeling and telling him that she was going to the Cherry Blossom Concert featuring those *Caronia* workhorses, the resident vocalists, Miss Aliani and Mr Diard. He was able to joke about her not needing to push him to lose weight anymore but the truth was he did not want her to see him this way. If she had shown any signs of wanting to stay, he would have sent her away.

Caronia docked in Manila just before midday on Tuesday. The temperature was in the high 30s and yet Harry still felt cold and disoriented. When Vinnie stopped by, en route to the gangway, he needed no persuasion to stay on board. He preferred to conjure up happier memories of 1954.

They had steamed into Manila from Bali. He remembered a Fancy Headdress party the night before and the fuss about having to take malaria tablets before going on shore. Bob had got up early to witness the passing of the Bataan Peninsula and the Island of Corregidor as a personal salute to the bravery and suffering of the US servicemen who had fought there during the war.

Back then the ship had anchored three miles offshore and they had taken the launches to a berth – next to the Presidential Dock – in front of the Manila Hotel.

The three had their own car and a guide from the Golden Taxicab Company. Bob was a Catholic and the tour was initially a bit heavy on Christian churches for Harry's taste, but he was happy to simply be in the same vehicle as Vinnie. They all agreed that the ancient Spanish Walled City and Fort Santiago with its lurid torture chamber, both ruined in the war, were a disappointment. The visit to the War Cemetery on a beautiful plateau in Fort McKinley was more successful. Bob was sufficiently emotional at the sight of the countless white marble crosses that he had to be consoled by Vinnie.

The guide then took them to Quezon City, twenty miles away on a fast highway, a detour seemingly designed to show off some industrial development and the new site of the University of the Philippines. If the guide had wanted to emphasise the resilience of the Filipinos, Harry thought, he could have simply pointed to the other taxis on the road: mostly converted ex-army jeeps, customised with glitzy paint, chrome and woven roofs.

After lunch and being treated to a programme of native dances, they boarded the launches back to the *Caronia* for a bath after a hot day. What made the day stand out in Harry's mind was none of this – it was the glorious sunset and then the full moon rising in the east over Manila Bay, spent alone in Vinnie's company.

It was the remembrance of that night that finally persuaded Harry to leave his stateroom. Besides, the steward needed him out to do his cleaning. Harry's consideration came at a cost: he found each step was laborious in the extreme. He attributed his shortness of breath to his lingering chest infection. Actually the lymphoma was making him anaemic, preventing his organs from getting the oxygen they needed to function properly and leaving him dangerously weak.

*

There was never any question of Harry and Betty getting a divorce: they were united by the antipathy shown to their union by the rest of their families – a dissolution would have given the nay-sayers too much pleasure for Harry's liking – and their mutual physical attraction somehow survived Harry's abuses. But he needed a diversion for her: something to keep her busy and allow him to pursue both his career and other women unmolested. Just when her interventions were starting to curtail his freedom of movement, he stumbled on the solution.

In making the Studio Club a hit, Harry had conclusively demonstrated that he didn't need experience to make a success of a new business. Perhaps that is why he had the audacity to make his next venture another radical departure: he bought a seaside hotel.

He holidayed in the Bahamas in May 1948 – without Betty but not alone – and on his disembarkation from the Queen Mary in Southampton he described himself on the form for the first time as a 'Hotel Proprietor'. The hotel in question was Rowena Court, overlooking St Mildred's Bay in the Kent resort of Westgate-on-Sea. The rumour in the family was that it was a gambling debt that he didn't know what to do with, but I think he was cuter than that.

Running a hotel would satisfy Betty's entrepreneurial drive and, more importantly, mean her hands would be full managing an establishment a three-hour drive from London.

They motored down to Westgate-on-Sea in Betty's Sunbeam Talbot – a long excursion which required a stop for lunch at the Grasshopper in Westerham – and, as Harry had hoped, Betty was seduced by the opportunity.

She inherited a tired but graceful building, beautiful lawns and a locally famous rose garden. A prominent Victorian surgeon called Sir Erasmus Wilson – famous for financing the shipping of Cleopatra's Needle from Egypt to the Embankment – built a suite of rooms on the side of the original bungalow to house his personal museum (no doubt filled with terrifying Victorian surgical tools). The agglomeration was later sold to Sir William Ingram, multi-millionaire founder of the *Illustrated London News*, and on his death in 1924, stood empty for seven years until a Lady Pearson converted it into a guest house.

Its position and design, 25 bedrooms capable of sleeping 40 people and a dining room for 70, were better suited to a hotel, which is what it became in 1937 under the control of Mrs Susan Austin. She managed to keep it open during the war despite Westgate's front-line coastal position. The much-loved classical singer Kathleen Ferrier stayed there in February 1943 and called it a 'lovely hotel'. It was also where William Temple, Archbishop of Canterbury, died in October 1944. Even Harry might have heard of him as he made a widely reported speech in defence of Jewry the previous year in the House of Lords: 'We stand at the bar of history, of humanity and of God,' he rightly judged.

Because the hotel offered terms all year round it was full of long-term residents who had been bombed out of their houses in the war and were disinclined to create a home again. Worse, the hotel may have been a well-known feature on the Westgate Front but it had been starved of investment. It made no financial sense to stay open over the winter unless the offering could be moved upmarket and charge accordingly. In attempting this Harry did not provide Betty with any additional funds to close and redevelop; she had to refurbish around the incumbents.

Her first advert illustrates her dilemma: alongside 'On Sea Front', 'Every Comfort' and 'Excellent Cuisine – Central Heating – Cocktail Bar – Dancing – Golf – Television' there is the grudging concession that the hotel offered 'Summer and Winter terms on application' and 'Residents Reduced Rates' along with the direction to 'Telephone 591'.

It is tempting to conjure up the pathos and melancholy of these permanent guests, reminiscent of a scene from a Terence Rattigan play of the time. Very likely Rowena Court had its share of bogus army officers and repressed spinsters wintering by the seaside and leading lives of quiet desperation on separate tables. Maybe Rattigan was inspired by a stay at Rowena Court, although in truth he could have been to any one of the similarly genteel establishments of that era and his drama, *Separate Tables*, is set in Bournemouth. Nevertheless, I like to think of Betty as a prototype for the hotel manager, Miss Cooper, encouraging her guests to face the future with courage, and generously bringing people together despite the personal cost.

In spite of her best efforts, Betty would never get to grips with the seasonality of her business. She created a Stillroom where breakfasts, tea and snacks could be prepared away from the main kitchen for passing trade, but that always fell off sharply in winter when the lugubrious residents reasserted control. She added rooms in a bungalow annexe and upgraded all the bedrooms, but the clientele refused to follow her upmarket.

Every year the hotel traded at a loss, which Harry covered because of the value of keeping Betty diverted. It was also a handy weekend getaway from the stresses of the Colony. Lounging in one of the hotel's outdoor wicker chairs, like those in *Caronia*'s Promenade Deck Garden Room, was a particular pleasure. Rowena Court could be a useful asset for hospitality on occasion as well. Years later, his nephew David remembered a family holiday there one summer. But David's cousin, Beverly, had never heard of Rowena Court so clearly Harry didn't ever invite her father, Ben. As his daughters can attest, Harry's generosity was never spontaneous: it was conditional and mostly concerned with how it made him feel about himself. To that end it suited him to offer Rowena Court to limited family members. Just as it suited him to keep Betty afloat. In the 1950s he was making more than enough money in his other ventures to do so.

Jesselton

Thursday 7th March

Yesterday, after 48 hours of rest, Harry had felt a little better. He wasn't going to miss another port – especially one he had never been to before – so he made his way to the Theatre before lunch to hear the cruise lecturer give a talk on North Borneo: 'Headhunters, Pirates, Birds' Nest Soup'.

As ever, the lecture had proved heavy on facts – latitudes, longitudes, square mileage, legal tender – and the best places to hunt for souvenirs. Harry did glean that the roughly triangular British North Borneo, contiguous with Sarawak, made up the north-western part of the island. The biggest tribal group were the Dusuns – although they didn't use this name themselves – described as physically small, pleasantly featured and friendly. The Muruts in the interior were a bit more primitive – they were the headhunters that gave the lecture its eye-catching title but they had stopped hunting heads a generation or two ago and, no need to fear, were even smaller than the Dusuns: almost a pygmy race. The Bajaus were sea-loving natives on the east coast, too distant to see, given time constraints. The Chinese were the largest non-indigenous group but there were also Sikhs, Cingalese and Indians in the population of half a million, all governed by a small white community.

One interesting fact was that the Malays called Jesselton Api Api, Town of Fire, in recognition of the torching of the original Victorian settlement by Mat Salleh. Salleh was a folk hero to the natives but dismissed by the colonial British as little more than a troublemaker who got his just comeuppance in a battle in the interior a few years after the conflagration.

All this went down very well amongst Boxell's overwhelmingly white, well-to-do Anglo-American audience. What Boxell neglected to mention, or possibly hadn't even apprehended, was that the majority Malay population was a handy bargaining chip in British efforts to engineer a merger of the various Malaysian states as a bulwark to Chinese communism. The colonial administration was in wind-down: any new arrivals had to be sanctioned by the Government and, even so, they needed a guarantor willing to put a deposit down on their behalf. The Colony Restaurant diaries still granted Empire Day the status of a 'notable date' each May but if Harry and *Caronia*'s time was passing, so was that of the British Colonial Empire.

Harry's sleep pattern was now completely disrupted. On the morning of their arrival he was out on deck early. Jesselton's waterfront was a long thin line: new shops and offices in the centre giving way on either side to the lower profiles of the old kampongs – part concrete, part corrugated iron – amongst the palms and mangroves. Some new high-rise apartment blocks stood on the cliffs above the city. Behind them, across the plain and jungle and running roughly parallel to the sea, the Crocker Range dominated the skyline. The ridge rose to a peak at the sacred Mount Kinabalu, over thirteen thousand feet above sea level.

Harry knew from yesterday's lecture that the hinterland of the island was jungle-ridden, mountainous and largely unpopulated. One of the excursions offered was through rubber gardens and rice fields to a native village called Penampang which served as the road-head for the paths into the interior but it had sounded like a lot of palaver. Instead he and Vinnie planned to take a walking tour of the city including some time on the beach at Tanjong Aru Point to the south and lunch at the Turf Club.

The ship moored in a channel of deep water opposite a busy fruit market. Harry could see the tour buses and red taxis already lined up on the pier. It would be a short shuttle for the ship's launches. A couple of the boats – with their tarpaulin roofs rolled back – were already being lowered into the water.

At the last moment, overcome by a wave of nausea, he decided he wasn't up to the walk and would just take a fifteen-minute ride by taxi to join Vinnie for lunch later. When the time came there was no immigration procedure, just the landing card his bedroom steward had put in his room.

The taxi from the harbour to the suburb flashed past office blocks and shops and then, slightly further out, Government houses evenly built in wood and asbestos. These in turn gave way to coconut palms, banana plantains, papayas and Casuarina trees and the shiny limousines on the road changed into old boneshakers and bicycles. Harry stopped the taxi by the lawns and grandstands of the Turf Club, in front of whose gates was a box from which policemen directed traffic on race days.

The Tanjong Aru Hotel stood opposite on the corner of a U-shaped parade of shops. There was a market in the middle doing brisk business with the housewives and amahs. Harry was early so he drifted among the stalls of bamboo and atap, stopping to look at some green coconuts on one. He smelt joss sticks and heard the sound of transistor radios competing with the Ke! Ke! shriek of little geckos under the thatched roofs of the stalls. He walked unsteadily away, passing an open green, a Chinese middle school and some coral tracks leading away to mangrove swamps through the palm trees. He stopped for breath at a little chapel in front of which a notice board proclaimed in Chinese and English that prayer meetings were held regularly. Harry read the text from Isaiah. It seemed appropriate on this baking day: 'They shall fear the name of the Lord from the west, and His glory from the rising of the sun.'

The menu for the late lunch in the restaurant – curried chicken, ice cream, bottles of cold boiled water – was inoffensive enough but even though he hadn't touched breakfast, Harry found he had no interest in it. He was aware of mosquitos around his knees, the incense coils on little tin stands dotted around the room offering no deterrent. He was strangely sensitised, seemingly hearing each of the flying white beetles careering into the shutters and glass. The cicadas in the grass outside must be gigantic, he thought, given their knife-grinding intensity. He felt sick again.

In this hypervigilant state, Harry was fortunate it was not an evening meal on offer. After the party had left the restaurant and the sun started to set, the geckos with their incessant rat-tat-tat chatter joined the cicadas. Moths with half-foot wingspans invaded the room and then foundered pitifully in the light from the lamps. Harry would have been overwhelmed.

By that stage he was back on board. Getting on the launch had proved almost beyond him. He wasn't going to accept any help from Vinnie, but the shore excursion staff, ignoring the prohibition on touching passengers when they were off the ship, helped him without any ceremony. He arranged an appointment with Dr Winer and went straight to bed, oblivious to the evening safari of the monkeys coming out of the jungle and down to the shore to see the big ship sail away in the twilight.

Because of the lymphoma, Harry's liver was no longer producing bile to digest fatty food. From now on nausea and loss of appetite were all he could look forward to.

*

When Harry was growing up, the 'West End' – that imaginary area bounded by Park Lane, Oxford Street, Charing Cross Road and Pall Mall – held mythical status. In his teens, after leaving school, he used to walk there on a Saturday night, usually to the Coliseum in a group of three or four. None of them had much money, a shilling or two from the week's labours, to buy cigarettes, have a puff or two on the walk and imagine themselves a bunch of swells out on the town. To work in the West End was something to aspire to, to own and run your own successful business within the enclave, the stuff of dreams.

Having said that, the limitations of a private member's club like the Knightsbridge Studio Club in terms of competing with the larger, entrenched cabaret venues became obvious after the Americans went home. Harry hung on to it – living the aphorism of his friend and business idol, Charles Clore, 'sell and regret' – but at the end of the 1940s the imminent closure of Bottle Parties and the emergence of a couple of suitable sites finally forced his hand.

He partnered with another experienced nightclub manager, Eustace Hoey. In a sense Hoey was one of the reasons for the Studio Club's success, as in supplying wine from his store in Warwick Street to his club – the New Paradise – in Regent Street, he was one of the earliest adopters of the Bottle Party licensing loophole. In fact, it was the decision in November 1944 by the Chief Magistrate at Bow Street, Sir Bertrand Watson, that the New Paradise's Bottle Party was perfectly legal so long as the customer reserved their drink at the wine merchant before going to the club that lifted the scourge of imminent prosecution from all such establishments.[33]

The Licensing Act of 1949 swept their reason to exist away though. That summer, Home Secretary James Chuter Ede accepted that nightclubs could serve drinks until 2am so long as they were accompanied by music and dancing.

With this concession it was an auspicious time to launch a nightclub. Harry's entrance can be dated quite accurately from the section in the US music trade paper *Billboard* devoted to nightclubs and vaudeville. The paper said on August 6th 1949 that Harry Morris had recently acquired both the Lansdowne Restaurant and the Nightingale Club in London.

The Lansdowne was a restaurant and nightclub on the south side of Berkeley Square which had been in operation since the mid-1930s. Brian Lawrence and his Orchestra were long-time residents. Its near neighbour the Nightingale Club was located, somewhat confusingly given the name of Harry's other acquisition, in Lansdowne Row just behind Berkeley Square.

The article stated that the Nightingale Club's resident bands were to be Paul Adam and His Mayfair Music and Edmundo Ros

---

33 Thomas, Donald (2003). *An Underworld at War*, John Murray, UK, p.252.

and his Rhumba Orchestra, both of whom would be moving from their current spots to the Nightingale, which would be renamed the Astor Club. In New York journalese Harry was described as the Astor's 'Prexy', its President, a term he might not have been familiar with but one which would have surely flattered his ego. Meanwhile the Lansdowne was closing for refurbishment and would be renamed the Colony Restaurant on reopening.

The current Astor, in Park Lane, had started in the '30s and operated throughout the war. Sid Phillips' band had played there. At the end of the '40s Jack Wallace and his band were residents but Paul Adam took over in May 1949. Harry would have known about, and probably patronised, the club as his flat was just along the road.

My hunch is that the Astor's lease was running out and Harry pounced on the name. The story planted in *Billboard* was typical of the way in which he operated – the 1949 equivalent of clickbait – offering titbits and working angles to make a deal happen. In this case it was particularly egregious, even in an industry known for its hyperbole, because the names he was bandying about were stars.

Paul Adam was a passable violinist but a much more successful band leader. His easy manner and good looks had made him a housewife's choice, he was married to the film actress Zena Marshall and his celebrated dance band was known for songs like 'Ain't Nobody Here But Us Chickens' and the era-appropriate 'Smoke! Smoke! Smoke (That Cigarette)'.

If anything, the flamboyant vocalist and percussionist. Edmundo Ros's Latin American Orchestra had an even higher profile. His gently rhythmic style was very popular, even with royalty – he had played to George VI at Windsor – and his number 'The Wedding Samba' had sold heavily that year.

A second announcement a couple of months later allowed Harry to clarify his starting lineup.[34] Edmundo Ros had decided to keep a spot at the Bagatelle Restaurant, which I doubt he ever had

---

34 1 October 1949, *Billboard*.

any intention of leaving – he would actually buy his own venue, the 'Coconut Grove' on Regent Street the following year. It was to be Santiago Lopez with his somewhat less-vaulted rhumba band who jumped from the Milroy Club to the Astor. I doubt Harry felt any contrition at his earlier misinformation; it had generated the buzz he desired. Besides he had managed to snare Paul Adam, although theirs would be a tempestuous working relationship.

The Colony opened on time in September with more evidence of Harry hustling. He knew the publicity value of dropping large salaries into the entertainment news sections of the papers as a hint to other acts and the punters:

> *SUCCESS story. Nine years ago songstress Marilyn Williams worked for club-boss Harry Morris at the Studio Club for £7 a week. Then ENSA. Then a fabulous American success as Marion Harris, Jr (Marion was her wonderful mum). Tomorrow she opens for Harry at the Colony Club. Salary £100 a week. Success story.*[35]

Since both the Astor and the Colony had relatively small capacities, Harry had to keep them full to cover overheads. Hiring a talent like Marilyn Williams illustrates part of his strategy: building the clubs' reputations as serious music-making cabarets as opposed to hostess-led spots.

In pursuit of headline acts he possessed one distinct advantage: although the Colony was a basement club and the Astor ground floor, below ground, the rears of the two clubs backed onto each other. This made for easy logistics in having bands and performers 'double up' – playing both venues on the same night. The commensurate increase in performance fees was what enabled Harry to entice bigger names than either club could have managed on a stand-alone basis.

---

35 September 4 1949, 'The Bright Lights', *Sunday Pictorial (forerunner of the Sunday Mirror)*.

Harry was not one of those hosts who would indulge himself with a spot up-front every night. In private his one and only 'act' was an impression of Bootsie, the put-upon, mutinous demobbed servicemen from the sitcom, *Bootsie and Snudge*. Frankly, Bootsie wasn't much of a stretch. He was played on television by Alfie Bass who, although about a decade younger than Harry, bore some resemblance and had been brought up in the same part of London. Harry could conjure up the nasal, Cockney vernacular at will. 'Never mind, eh?' he would mimic. This sort of levity was so rare that my mother makes specific mention of Harry's impression in her diary.

If he was not much of a performer himself, he possessed a strong sense of what his clientele liked to see. This was a vital quality in the early days of building the clubs' reputations as they would stand or fall on the success of Harry's bookings. He didn't like the financial and reputational risk entailed in showcasing new talent. His approach was to import little-known but already established acts from America. In pursuing that strategy his timing once again proved impeccable as the rules on non-British performers were just changing to mirror those of the American Guild of Variety Artists. A British house was now permitted to have three foreign acts on an eight-act bill.

Early in 1950, *Billboard* ran a story under the title 'London Field open to Yanks', stating that the first two spots to take advantage of the 'lifting of the curfew' (sic) and restrictions on foreign performers in Britain were the Colony and Astor Clubs.[36] The bookings that *Billboard* reported were the sort of cabaret performers that would go on to be the Colony's staple acts under Harry's management. The Mack Triplets (sisters Eileen, Charlotte and LaVerne) had eight weeks from March 13th. They had released a few records with titles like 'One-zy, Two-zy' on the Deluxe label and were regular performers on a radio show called the *Hour of Charm*. A better-known vocalist, Julie Wilson, would follow on May 6th for six weeks then a song-and-dance

---

36 March 4 1950, *Billboard*.

act, Connie Sawyer, and an ex-child star turned light baritone, Bobby Breen.

The *Billboard* article is Harry in upstart mode trying to steal a march on competition in much more established venues. The Command Performance in front of the King had always been exempt from the embargo on international performers and had hosted big-name American acts each year since the war. Lew Grade of Lew & Leslie was in New York at the same time as Harry to buy for that year's show at the Palladium, Harry Levine was also in town buying for the Bagatelle, and Cal Gibbons, for the Savoy. Like them, Harry would have been a frequent visitor to all the talent agencies in this period.

Harry's clubs were described in Billboard as being under one roof – the Colony, managed by Hoey, was open for dinner and the Astor, managed by Harry, open for supper. That may have been Harry testing out the formula for how the two spots could dovetail; more likely it was an artefact of the licensing laws. The way the liquor licence worked at the time was that alcohol could be sold without food up to 11pm. In order to sell liquor from 11pm to midnight the licensee had to have a supper licence: the client had to eat a meal, although this could be as little as a sandwich so long as there was cutlery on the table. To obtain a late hour extension to 2.30am, in addition to the supper licence, Harry needed a music and dancing licence, which you could only get if you had live music and dancing facilities. In any case it was not long before both the Astor and Colony were operating until 2.30am.

1950 must have been a whirlwind for Harry and Hoey. Another *Billboard* story at the end of the year, 'Yanks Comin' to London in Droves', showed how hard they were still working to seize the initiative from the competition and how Harry's practice of 'doubling up' acts each evening had given the two clubs a clout beyond their individual size. They were reported to have just completed a five week sweep through New York clubs, hiring Dana Leslie (opening December 11th), Mae Barnes and Garland Wilson from January 1951, the Mack Triplets, back by popular demand at the end of February, and Savannah Churchill and the Striders at the end of March. They had also signed some support acts: a swing vocalist called Kitty Kallen and a truly obscure outfit called the Four Heater-tones. Harry and Hoey were described as 'dickering' for much bigger names like Sophie Tucker, Pearl Bailey, Eileen Barton and Georgia Gibbs.[37]

The names he landed were a definite step-up in drawing power. Mae Barnes, originally a dancer credited with bringing the Charleston to Broadway, had developed a career as a sassy singer. Her accompanist, Garland Wilson, was a noted boogie-woogie and stride pianist. They were sure bets to bring in an audience as was the famous Black singer, Leslie 'Hutch' Hutchinson, who was the Astor and Colony's number one cabaret star of 1951.

The bankable 'Hutch' played two sets nightly at Quaglino's in Bury Street. Since he had been playing at that spot on and off since the 1930s, the management was relaxed about his contract. The Colony was close enough for him to play a set in between, which he did frequently and which must have suited all parties as Mum records seeing him in cabaret at the Colony as late as May 1961. Throughout the period he could be relied upon to bring in devoted fans, which included some people who were famous in their own right.

None of these names would have come cheaply, which raises a question about where Harry got the capital to buy, refurbish and stock not one but two nightclubs and then go on a buying spree for US talent. Did Hoey put up the money? His subsequent career would suggest not. Did Harry go all-in, selling the Studio Club and the greengrocery shops to fund the launch? It is very doubtful that would have raised enough for the splash that he made. It is much more likely that his title of Astor 'President' implied he was not the sole owner, that an outside investor – someone who had seen what he had achieved at the Studio Club – was willing to fund him on a larger stage.

The most likely backer is a shady character called Thomas William Parker, a civil engineer and builder who made money in the post-war housing boom. He was a serial entrepreneur and

---

37 11 November 1950, *Billboard*.

a wily businessman. In 1948 he was living in some style, with a staff of at least six, in a large pile in Essex called Debden Hall, so on the face of it would seem to have had the finances to bankroll Harry if he had chosen to.

Parker was no recluse – he was well known in racing circles – but appears to have been content to stay in the shadows when it came to running the business. He may have been the majority owner of the business but he let Harry become the 'face' of the clubs and take all the plaudits for their success.

Parker was outed as the club's owner by Douglas Thompson in *Shadowlands*, his book about gambling and the Mafia. Thompson recounts an incident in April 1951 when Judy Garland came to rehearse at the Colony with her future husband, Sid Luft, before a four-month tour of the country.[38] The catering that day was done by the Tolaini Brothers, who ran the Latin Quarter Restaurant in Soho, itself financed by a man called Benny Huntsman. The paths of all those in attendance that day – Parker, the Tolainis, Huntsman – would converge fourteen years later when the Colony would embark on its short and notorious second life.

The revenues generated by Harry's set-up could not possibly cover the fees demanded by artists of Judy Garland's stature to appear on the bill. Besides, she was not the sort to 'double up'. Harry had found a formula for filling his clubs and did not tinker with it. He reckoned that the elements required for success in cabaret dining were an affordable draw: a good band and good food. Dinner and dance at the Colony was not cheap – it cost 25 shillings and sixpence in 1951 when the average weekly wage was £6 and 16 shillings – but it offered value for money in terms of a memorable night out. He called the Colony 'A Distinguished Rendezvous' in his adverts. The city guides of that year said it was particularly popular with foreign tourists.

Harry might not have been an innovator but he swapped the house bands around after a year. He replaced Paul Adam

---

38 Thompson, Douglas (2011). *Shadowland: How the Mafia Bet Britain in a Global Gamble*, Mainstream, UK, p.78.

with Felix King, whose nine-piece orchestra would be one of the bands in situ for the rest of the decade.

King was an obvious choice for the residency. He was a suave and silky-voiced compère more than capable of setting the light-yet-sophisticated tone Harry sought. He was already relatively well known – he had played in various ensembles in the '30s including the Victor Silvester Ballroom Orchestra before his career was interrupted by six years in the RAF. He had cut some records for Decca and done a series of shows for Radio Luxembourg.

In 1947 he opened at the old Nightingale Club with a sixteen-piece orchestra featuring two pianos. It was there that he had composed the tune that would go on to be his signature, 'The Night and the Nightingale'. And he was well-connected: after the Nightingale he and his orchestra had moved to the Orchid Room, frequented by Princess Margaret.

King carried on his broadcasting career while at the Colony, regularly filling one of the *Music While You Work* slots on the BBC. These were the twice-daily live recordings of popular light music which the BBC had launched during the war. Programmers thought that playing a continuous set of familiar music would boost morale and increase factory worker productivity and didn't change their minds until the 1960s.

The BBC shows were always bookended by the familiar Eric Coates melody, 'Calling All Workers' and then the band played a non-stop medley of even-tempo tunes for half an hour. King often broadcast from the restaurant itself. For instance, the Colony hosted the show on the BBC Home Service at 10.30am on 27th May 1955 and at 1pm on the Light Programme (the forerunner of Radio 2) on 21st January 1959, King and his orchestra being joined on that latter occasion by the singer, Gerry Grant. Harry saw the commercial value in this and readily gave permission.

By all accounts he and King got on well: they shared the same taste in music and both were avid travellers. The relationship only came to an end at the end of the decade when King slimmed down his orchestra to five and made a final move to Quaglino's. From then on he concentrated on broadcasting – not just *Music*

While You Work, (he would eventually record over 100 shows in the format) – but also *Piano Playtime* and *Housewives' Choice*.

Unfortunately Harry's relations with his other house band, led by a returning Paul Adam, would prove to be as strained as they were cordial with King.

Bali

Saturday 9th March

Bali lay two days' steaming directly south of Jesselton. The wind fell astern as *Caronia* skirted the coast of Borneo, and below decks it grew hot and stuffy. Harry was forced out of his cabin in search of fresh air.

From the deck he saw some dolphins. Swallows launched themselves from the lifeboat derricks, sped across the wavetops and then alighted on another part of the ship. He found the sight of the boundless wildlife somehow calming.

Harry braved the deck again in the evening. The sky had cleared. The Pole Star dipped towards the sea, the Southern Cross was bright on the port bow and Orion lay on his side along the horizon, all reflected in the calm sea. Harry looked down on the shoals of flying fish skimming over the bow waves, their silvery fins briefly highlighted as they caught the light from curtainless portholes. He luxuriated in the breeze and the gentle rocking motion of the huge vessel. If the price to pay for recuperation was isolation, he felt he could manage it when the backdrop was this peaceful.

When he returned to his cabin he found his steward had delivered an 'Oceanogram' warning all passengers that they were entering King Neptune's domain. On Saturday, Rex Neptune would induct equatorial novices into the Order of those possessing the 'most noble' distinction of crossing from one hemisphere to another in the 'Crossing of the Line' Ceremony.

On the following day, to cheers from the passengers after a good lunch, Neptune and his court appeared at the aft end of the Promenade Deck. Led by a policeman ready to take 'prisoners' – passengers who were crossing the line for the first time – the entourage paraded forward to the Crew Swimming Pool on the foredeck, done up with bunting and a stage for the occasion.

In the lead were two bewigged Judges of the Court, followed by a clerk in black morning coat and top hat, the King and his consort, Queen Amphitrite (a burly engineer). Neptune's train was long enough to require a bearer. The retinue included Dr Hackem in a sandwich board, ('Physician and Mortician, Teeth and Legs Pulled, Watertight Coffins made to order'), sea-urchins and other macabre characters.

The Captain and Senior Officers were presented to Neptune, who then turned and greeted the assembly. Queen Amphitrite read out a list of novices to be inducted into Neptune's court. One by one they were presented to the Judges who asked the time-honoured question to which the crowd's answer was always 'Very, Very Guilty'. Then the prisoners, passengers and crew alike, were ducked in turn. The 'Pollywog', the most junior crewmember, was the last into the pool. The hapless lad, who had had his face blackened with shoe polish to turn him from a Landlubber into a trusted Shellback, was pushed under the water with some violence.

Harry the extrovert, someone who got energy from revelry like this, should have been in his element. The sun was shining, the grey sea had turned blue, the crowd was excited, but it was all too much. He made his excuses very early and retired to his cabin. He sensed he had crossed a line himself, one that made him want to hide away as he weakened. He seemed capable of only seeing one person at a time, a state of affairs he sincerely hoped was tempo-rary; he couldn't ever hope to return to the limelight on this basis.

*

Harry's original roster of house bands lasted a year. Paul Adam took his troupe to the Milroy Club in Park Lane in 1951 only to be tempted back the following year to replace Santiago Lopez and his Latin American Rhythm.

Paul Adam, tall and good looking, fitted the public perception of how a band leader should act and appear. He freely admitted that he relied more on his charisma than his musicianship to front his players but as a result had a winning rapport with the audience and had built up a loyal following.

Harry could not deny Adam's drawing power so, perhaps against his better judgement, in April 1952 he gave him a twelve-month contract extension at an eye-catching £300 a week. This was not quite as lucrative for Adam as it appears, since Adam had to pay all the members of his band – some £157 and 19 shillings a week – from his own wages. Nevertheless, Harry was paying him the equivalent of at least £5,000 a week in today's terms.

After a few months, Harry decided he wasn't getting his money's worth. He sent Adam a couple of warning letters and then dismissed him at the end of June – all of this coming to light when Adam sued for wrongful dismissal in the High Court.

Harry hired a flamboyant silk, Gilbert Beyfus QC, whose nickname was the 'Old Fox'. Beyfus was an expert in libel and divorce law and, rather like his tailor, Cyril Castle, gave Harry the opportunity to drop the names of famous fellow clients as Beyfus had represented celebrities like Liberace, John Aspinall and Aneurin Bevan. He put on quite a show and the details of the trial were salacious enough to make the pages of the press.

Harry's defence rested on Adam breaching a term of his contract requiring him to conduct the band between 11pm and 4am every night save Sunday. Under cross-examination, Harry had to admit that he had asked his head waiter, Nathalla Manzi, to log the time Adam spent on the bandstand. According to one newspaper, Harry swore that despite Adam's offer to conform to the management's requirements, 'he just went on in his own sweet way'.[39]

Manzi gave evidence that Adam was on the bandstand at 11pm during the first week of his engagement but after that he stopped

---

39 20 January 1954, *Birmingham Gazette*.

arriving with the rest of the band. Adam's barrister said this was accepted practice as his client was better employed to greet and socialise with the diners. His presence was not necessary the whole time because the band, under deputy leader, Norman Fantham, were quite capable of playing without direction. 'I call out the tune, give two beats, and the band starts playing automatically by itself. I rely on my personality,' testified Adam.[40] It was contrary to the club's interest, he argued, for him to come on the stand when the room was almost empty because of the risk guests might waylay him and that he might hurt their feelings if he had to reject their invitation.

Harry countered that Adam had an hour and twenty minutes when he was 'free to do all the hob-nobbing he liked' because it was quite possible to greet guests from the bandstand when the band was playing. I am not sure Harry really thought this but he could still have been a persuasive witness because in his own mind it was at least half-true. The lifelong hawker embodied the adage that the best salesman truly believes his own spiel.

On the second day of the hearing, Adam's QC tried another tack, which probably got closer to the nub of the matter. He claimed that the Astor was saddled with a contract they didn't want as the club was not performing in line with expectations and this dispute was merely a pretext to get rid of his client.

His Lordship – Mr Justice Jones – disagreed. He held that Adam must have known throughout that he was acting in breach of his contract and did not change behaviour even after having received written warnings. In fact Adam's refusal in his own letters to do so amounted to a repudiation of the agreement.

He entered judgement with costs against Adam, although he did award the plaintiff £25 for a separate breach as a run of 6,000 brochures had Adam's name in secondary position to that of an American cabaret singer, Jane Morgan, and his contract had stipulated that he would always receive 'premier publicity'.

A strong clue that Adam was on the right track about the real motivation behind his dismissal came in a footnote to one of the

---

40 16 January 1954, *Yorkshire Post and Leeds Mercury*.

court reports. The case actually took place in 1954, a couple of years after the events described. According to a Mr Aiden Evans, solicitor for the Astor Club, the Astor had become a Members Club and was no longer owned by Harry's company, Astor Enterprises Limited. That ties in with the strange story in the *People* in August 1953 about Harry passing the club to Bertie Green and the journalist's hint about the poor state of business 'around the golden square mile'.[41]

Harry and Parker could well have been forced sellers. At any rate, Bertie Green took over the Astor, Harry took control of the Colony and Hoey left for the Wardroom Restaurant. Hoey would find it difficult to repeat the success of the New Paradise and the early years of the Colony and was eventually declared bankrupt in March 1959.

The *People* article had mentioned a 'bargain' price but as ever with Harry there was more to this transaction than met the eye. He certainly kept some shares in Astor Enterprises Limited, and possibly borrowed against them later, because his will contains both an asset and a liability in that name. It would take another High Court case, this time against the man whose moniker was the 'Nightclub King', to shed some more light on his murky deal with Green.

In the world of 1950s West End nightclubs, it would have been impossible for Harry to avoid the ubiquitous Al Burnett, the self-anointed 'king' of the locale. Their association may have gone back further as Burnett was also part of that generation of Jewish entrepreneurs who, with their work ethic and talent for showmanship, would reign over much of the entertainment industry. It was always a question of when, not if, Burnett would figure in Harry's life story given the similarity in their interests and backgrounds. Physically they even bore something of a resemblance although Burnett, a comedian and actor, possessed a much higher profile in the media.

During the war Burnett compèred his 'Nut House' club and went after the same jazz-loving American market as the Studio Club. He too went to New York to scout for US acts for his

---

41 30 August 1953, the *People*.

'Stork Club' on Swallow Street. He took a slightly different approach from Harry. In league with Bernard Delfont, Lew Grade's brother, Burnett's strategy was to offer the talent less up-front for shorter runs. He tried to attract those performers who backed themselves to make more lucrative deals after they made the trip and were seen by other bookers in London.

By the time of the court action, Burnett owned the 'Pigalle', probably the Colony's most direct competitor in the cabaret-dining arena and, at 196 Piccadilly, certainly one of its closest. It has been reported, mistakenly, that it was Burnett who sold the Astor Club to Bertie Green. The truth, rather, was that Harry sold the Astor to Bertie Green in preference to Burnett and Burnett did not take the setback lying down.

The *Daily Herald*, under a headline of 'A Man and a Nightclub. £5,000 for One He Doesn't Own', reported on Burnett's suit against Harry, which appears to have been presided over by one of those crusty Judges later lampooned so mercilessly by Peter Cook:[42]

> *A comedian who owns three West End nightclubs and restaurants was told yesterday that he is to get £5,000 for one he doesn't own.*
>
> *He is Al (Stork Room) Burnett and he was awarded the money as damages in the High Court against Astor Enterprises Ltd, Eustace Hoey, now of the Wardroom Restaurant, and Harry Morris of the Colony because they changed their minds about selling him Mayfair's Astor Club. Last year a High Court inquiry fixed the amount at £10,000 but Mr Justice Roxburgh ruled yesterday that was too much.*
>
> *He had been told how Mr Hoey and Mr Morris 'unjustifiably' broke the contract under which Mr*

---

42 28 February 1957, *Daily Herald*.

Burnett was to take over the Astoria(sic) for a year at £10,400 with the option of buying the share capital for £22,500.

Discussing the possibilities of making a profit in the nightclub business, the judge said: 'I should have thought all nightclubs were speculative.'

Harry and Hoey had argued that since Burnett had not taken up the option he was entitled to only nominal damages.

The judge disagreed: 'I think morals would be absolutely scandalised. It would be a shocking suggestion if you could keep this man out of possession and then say: Not one penny of damages.'

Burnett was wrongly deprived of having a year's trial at the club before deciding whether to exercise the option. Apparently he was in the US at the time of the judgement but 'a colleague was cabling him the news'. Harry and Hoey did not appeal.

At the very least the case puts some numbers around the 'bargain' price at which Harry and Parker sold the Astor to Green. It had to have been more than £34,000, about a million pounds in today's money.

The newspaper report is corroborated in Al Burnett's self-aggrandising autobiography.[43] According to his account Burnett heard that the Astor was on the market at the same time that he was losing the lease on the premises for the Stork Club elsewhere in Berkeley Square. He wrote that he agreed to take over the Astor lock, stock and barrel for '£30,000' before Harry and Hoey suddenly decided to sell the Astor to 'someone else'. Burnett never mentions Bertie Green by name in his book, a strange omission to make for a career clubland rival unless he

---

43 Burnett, Al (1963). *Knave of Clubs*, Arthur Baker, UK, p.124.

bore a lifelong grudge from the transaction. Burnett related his successful High Court action but neglected to mention the halving of his damages. In any case he bragged that he blew the entire sum at the race track in two weeks.

Harry may have sold to Green because he offered more money, he may have sold to him out of some lingering sense of gratitude as the *People* claimed or because of a calculation that Green could be relied on not to compete for the same market that he was targeting. Whatever the reason, involuntary or not, unloading the Astor freed Harry up for the most successful period of his career.

Monday 11th March

The sun was just emerging over the horizon when *Caronia* arrived in Bali. It was the second occasion Harry had called on the tropical paradise, but this time, there was no flotilla of 'bum boats' racing out from the shore to greet the ship like in 1954, when the occupants of that little armada had tossed up lines attached to woven baskets to trade their crafts for dollars. Now, with the arrival of cruise ships commonplace, the bargaining took place on the quay where the tenders tied up.

Harry remembered the children had dived after quarters in the crystal-clear waters. It was as close to the prized American currency as any of them would get as only the local currency – Rupiahs, worth about ten cents – had been allowed onshore.

He recalled the sense of anticipation because on his previous world cruise, in 1951, the landing had been cancelled at the last minute because of the island's political situation. In '54 they had all been given a strict warning not to take photos of the natives but, in Harry's recollection, there hadn't been much to see anyway. It had all been a bit worthy and heavy on education. They had been taken to a compound which housed multiple generations of the same family. The compound's imposing gates and walls were meant to shut out the evil spirits wandering along the open roads. That had been a cue to see the Household Temple, a shrine to Gods, guardian spirits and ancestors, and to be entertained by Balinese dancing and music. One dance involved a group of men chanting cak-cak to someone in a monkey-face costume: colourful but confusing.

Bob O'Donnell had been in irrepressible good spirits, which as Harry remembered was because it had been St Patrick's Day and a Gala Dinner Dance had been laid on in the evening.

Harry was no mean dancer, maybe not as practised as Lew Grade but skilled in the art of dance floor seduction going all the way back to the People's Palace in Whitechapel. His dance floor prowess contrasted strongly with Bob's static and inebriated celebration of his Irishness. In hindsight Harry thought this was where he first realised his and Vinnie's relationship might extend beyond the cruise. The sunset had been magnificent, although perhaps not on a par with the one later in Manila where they had had their first real romantic tryst on the open deck.

He thought back to the Gala Dinner and Dance on the last night of that cruise as they sailed from Cristóbal to New York. He had fixed the date – April 30th 1954 – as it was the night he knew he had met the woman he wanted to spend the rest of his life with.

Vinnie spent part of that summer in London. They met up again in December that year for *Caronia*'s Christmas cruise around the West Indies and South America, both travelling separately and alone. After disembarking in New York, Harry spent a few days scouting for acts and catching the shows and revues with Vinnie, who was obviously no stranger to the city herself given her wild days there with her sister in the '20s and '30s.

That established a pattern of transatlantic cuckolding for the rest of the decade. Harry did not know whether Bob O'Donnell was aware of the affair but, frankly, didn't care. He had very fond memories of a month he and Vinnie had spent together at the Warwick Hotel in New York in early 1956 and again in January 1958 although that time they extended the stay to Dallas. When Bob had died in November 1959, shortly after being diagnosed with lung cancer, Harry had been at Vinnie's side in Texas within two days. Bob had suffered a very short illness but even so Vinnie was ready: no mourning period for her. She sailed for England within the month and she and Harry went to the French Riviera for some winter sun in January 1960.

It was a pleasant reverie but with a hint of melancholy as Harry felt history was repeating itself. Just as after six years of marriage Bob had been supplanted by a younger, more spirited and energetic man, so Harry feared his relationship with Vinnie was now similarly vulnerable. Vinnie had seen him at his peak, a high benchmark of sociability and fun, which he was currently in no state to emulate.

*

Selling the Astor enabled Harry to concentrate solely on the Colony. Of necessity he had to cooperate with his neighbour in 'doubling up' acts and turning a blind eye to the girls shuffling between the venues via the underground passageway as Bertie Green took the Astor down the hostess route. Harry, meanwhile, bet that coupling sophisticated floor shows with haute cuisine would differentiate his offering from both regular nightclubs and the pure dining establishments of the day like Maison Prunier or the Caprice. From the moment the cabaret started at 11pm the restaurant discreetly turned into a nightclub without hostesses. After the floor show had finished the lights were dimmed and the band played for dancing until 2.30am.

The night's entertainment did not come cheap. In 1959 the Colony's prix fixe three-course dinner and dancing cost 31 shillings and sixpence, which would have been quite a chunk out of the average manual worker's weekly wage, barely £13 at that time. However, Harry could not have asked for a better location in his strategy to take the club upmarket.

Diners entered through double doors on the south side of Berkeley Square and descended a brick-sided spiral staircase to a set of Art Deco-style double doors that led into the vestibule, hat check area and cloakrooms. The restaurant was separated from the vestibule by a third set of double doors. Guests were welcomed into quite an intimate space: a stage area ahead and banquette-style seating arranged in tiers on three sides of the dance floor. The bandstand, so shunned by Paul Adam, was separated from the stage. A reviewer for the *Sketch* described the overall effect: 'one turns in from Berkeley Square and down the winding stairway, its walls hung with a small but remarkable collection of paintings, into an environment of charm.'[44]

The charm was a corollary of Harry's settled team. The kitchen brigade was French, the waiters, Italian. Throughout the decade the Maître Chef de Cuisine was Monsieur Bagole from Pau, the Maître D'hôtel, Joseph Della from Milan. Tall, white-haired, soft-shoed Della, described by the *Tatler* as the 'doyen of such functionaries', was especially loyal: after serving an apprenticeship at the Hotel Cecil, he worked for Harry for twenty years. His grace and his elephantine memory for customer's names were major attributes for the Colony.

The restaurant's signature was the breadth and availability of its offering. The 'Carte des Gourmets' and its central column of fourteen house specialities, 'pour les Gastronomes' – restaurant French was de rigueur in Harry's Colony – was one of the longest in town. Any dish could be chosen at any time for lunch, dinner and supper. In the unlikely event that none of the choices appealed, a cold buffet was also permanently on offer. It doesn't take Freud to draw a link between all this plenty and the paucity and monotony of the meals that Harry experienced as a child.

This all meant that Harry had a much better lunchtime and early evening trade than other clubs with less of a focus on food. Within a couple of years the restaurant was being described as 'the famous Colony', 'a "must" for the discerning', 'smart and fashionable', and 'a true successor to those earlier gastronomic temples of France'. Ivan Bickerstaff of the *Tatler* was a particular fan (or rather fans as it was a pseudonym used by rotating

---

44 31 December 1958, the *Sketch*.

reviewers) – in 1958 he experienced what he called 'an oblivion of care' when dining in the restaurant.

Of course reviews were necessary for business but Harry would only have been human if his ego was not boosted by some of the praise. I think his favourite review would have been a long one by S. Rossitor Shepherd in the *Sketch* on New Year's Eve 1958. The full-page portrait under the headlines 'Profile of a Restaurateur' and 'French Impressions' included a shot of Harry leaning in front of the Colony's bar: suit, satiny tie, triangle-fold handkerchief in his breast pocket and a glass of wine in his hand. The image of bourgeois solidity was the perfect repudiation of his childhood poverty.

'Ross', as he was known, was a well-connected food and travel writer with an imposing bearing but he had no defence to the considerable charm Harry brought to bear in order to create his 'French impression'. After a history lesson on the origins of restaurants and pressing the always quotable Dr Johnson into service – 'there is nothing which has yet been contrived by man, by which so much happiness is produced as by a good tavern or inn' – Ross's prose turned purple:

> *I was torn between Poularde Souvaroff, Ris de Veau Madère and Coq au Vin prepared from a Surrey fowl and cooked with Burgundy. In the end I chose Caneton Lucullus, created by Bagole himself.*

> *This proved to be a young duck roasted whole in the ordinary way and without stuffing, which relied for its particular appeal on its garnish and its sauce; I am sure it would have delighted Lucullus himself.*

> *The garnish consisted for the most part of fat French prunes stuffed with chopped almonds and a touch of chutney; a slice of pineapple, a quartered orange and some black cherries, the whole finished with Curaçao sauce and brandy. After saucing, the bird was lightly*

flecked with some finely shredded peel of the orange which most admirably cut its richness. Although I drank a Richbourg Domaine de la Romanée-Conti, my partner chose a Gewurztraminer '53, which he declared to be fitting for such a dish.

The language hasn't dated well. I don't think a restaurant critic, unless they were aiming for parody, would get away with a phrase like 'lightly flecked with some finely shredded peel of the orange' today. However, the article, part of a thickening portfolio of press cuttings, does make clear what Harry was striving to do with the Colony. He was the 'presiding genius' of the Colony because of the way he was able to balance the food and the floor show. He became something of a fixture of not just restaurant reviews, but also showbiz and gossip columns and music reviews.

Harry's true skill in keeping the Colony at the forefront of London nightspots was the ability he had to put together line-ups for shows which kept the audience coming back.

There was always a steady supply of American performers that Harry had spotted in the course of his many scouting trips. Many, such as Betty O'Neill, a television personality songstress, harmony girls Cindy and Lindy, and conjurors Doodles & Spider made their UK debuts at the Colony.

His non-US-based performers included radio stars Jack and Daphne Barker, the Australian singer Shirley Abicair, and Julia from a well-known Hungarian dance couple Darvas and Julia, who apparently could also sing.

Harry hosted his share of comedians such as Bryan Blackburn and Peter Reeves. He also seems to have had a weakness for crossover stars from West End musicals. Shani Wells, best known for her later role as 'Nancy' in the film version of *Oliver!*, had a run there as did Ron Moody, likewise as 'Fagin'.

The 'Kaye Sisters', Carol, Shirley and Sheila, were regular performers despite not actually being related. They recorded a disc in 1959 called *The Kayes at the Colony* with six tracks including 'Sisters' (inevitably), all backed by Felix King and his

Orchestra. The cover had a picture of the three of them with blond pixie-cut hairstyles, strappy gold sandals and full-skirted yellow dresses: the sort of wholesome yet fun image that Harry was keen to project.

Harry would also sprinkle in the occasional big names alongside his discoveries – Hutch, of course, but also Edmundo Ros or Lance Percival, who made up a comic calypso for Mum and Dad when Harry entertained them on the night of their wedding. That might have partially made up for Harry's 'no-show' during their nuptials.

When he ventured into more avant garde music, he found himself having to defend his choice to the critics. For instance, Rex North railed against French cabaret singer Genevieve in a review typical of the prevailing sexism of the time. 'Should a young woman who hasn't got what makes Diana Dors look so good, take artificial action if she happens to be a singer appearing in public?' he asked rhetorically. While acknowledging that she was a good singer, he went on to say that she was too 'Left Bank', wore a very ordinary dress and sported a coiffure like hair on a shaggy coconut. Harry was quoted as saying the look was, 'Deliberate, of course. I think it is very clever of her. It is really sexy to a lot of people', to which Rex's retorts were 'Really?' and 'Very ordinary. The [dress] I saw did about as much to give her what Diana Dors[45] has got as an empty sack.'[46]

It was much more likely that a guest of the club would see someone like clarinettist and saxophonist, Frank Weir – a star after the release of 'Happy Wanderer' in 1954 – and his band. There is an atmospheric shot of Frank on clarinet and Victor Cheeseman on rhythm guitar at the Colony in January 1961 in the Getty Images archive.

The 'show' included the glitterati in the other seats of course. Harry understood the importance of people-watching in attracting a crowd. The debutante types who persuaded their parents

---

45 British 'Blond Bombshell' movie actress, known for her curvaceous figure.
46 18 September 1955, *Sunday Pictorial*.

to take them to the cabaret, hoping to see some famous faces in the house, were rarely disappointed.

Judging by Harry's boasting, faithfully recorded by Mum in her diaries, there was plenty of stargazing to do. One of the photographs in the thin family archive is of Lauren Bacall and Jason Robards staring intently at a pair of Colony menus, probably taken on a night off filming *North-West Frontier* at Pinewood in 1959. Other personalities Mum recorded have now faded from public memory but would have been familiar names at the time: Charles Clore, Joe Loss, Jack Hylton, Dawn Addams, Milton Shulman and theatrical agent Joe Collins. He also used his Park Lane flat for wining and dining his artistes. Dad remembers bumping into Chubby Checker there one night.

His band leaders had to be draws in their own right, and if they brought a celebrity fan base, so much the better. Inevitably one of the people they drew was Princess Margaret: in her early twenties and already a nightclub veteran. She had danced to Felix King's music in the Orchid Room, and Paul Adams would invite her to play (she was an accomplished pianist) and sing some of her favourite Cole Porter songs at Les Ambassadeurs. Margaret and her set – aristocratic habitués of the gossip columns like Billy Wallace, Johnny Dalkeith, Sunny Blandford and Colin Tennant – were no strangers to the Colony, particularly when Leslie Hutchinson was playing. She would often talk and dance with 'Hutch' after his act.

The Maître D', Joseph Della, was as much of a name-dropper as Harry: 'I suppose I have served most members of European royal families who have come to London … Like the Duke of Windsor – he always called for the finest brandy. Ex-King Umberto of Italy … Prince Rainier and Princess Grace of Monaco liked to dine quietly at a corner table,' he recalled when looking back on his front-of-house career.[47]

Naturally in that milieu, Harry also played host to known gangsters, or at least their acolytes: Lord Boothby and Charlie

47 1 May 1962, *Daily Mirror*.

Kray, elder brother of Reggie and Ronnie.[48] Ruth Ellis, notoriously the last woman to be hanged in Britain, was a friend. Distance has perhaps cast the 1950s and '60s criminal vintage in a rather benign light. The protagonists had undeniable charms – local, self-made men who, false memory would have it, made it safe to leave your door open at night. The sharp suits recalled, the razors suppressed. More tellingly perhaps, they were visible characters, not afraid to flaunt their riches in West End clubs in a way that modern career criminals would shy away from. This is probably why the gangsters of today don't enter the public imagination in the way the Krays and Richardsons did but also why they aren't so easily caught. As a young man Harry stayed clear of the razor-carrying fraternity – they were always easy to spot as they were the ones with the badly gashed faces – but they were an unavoidable hazard once he was working the clubs.

Harry was nothing if not an equal opportunity host. Besides, it was incumbent on any nightclub operator of that era to stay in the good books of both sides of the law, so Chief Superintendent Jack Slipper, 'Slipper of the Yard' dined there as well. The balance worked – the closest Harry came to real violence at the Colony was in 1957 when his doorman, Alec Newland, was beaten up by someone who objected to being refused entry. Newland fractured his skull, and his assailant was charged with manslaughter.

In this period – during Betty's Kentish exile and before Vinnie's arrival – Harry enjoyed all the perquisites club ownership offered, especially when it came to womanising. The chart-topping singer Anne Shelton was typical of his girlfriends, and Harry was just as active on his New York jaunts. On one occasion Harry visited his cousin Rose Tannenbaum, Fannie Marmelstein's daughter, in the Bronx. Rose's own daughter Beth Mazer, a child at the time, remembers the splash he made:

---

48 Harry wasn't the only one of the family with a connection to the Krays. Morris supplied their mother, Violet, to whom the twins were obsessively devoted, with fruit and veg from the Clapton store.

'He was on his way to New York City to meet Elizabeth Taylor and Michael Todd, I believe. I remember he told us how stupid she was. He arrived with two gorgeous women who were clearly escorts. When I asked my grandmother who they were, she told me I shouldn't know from it!'

Singapore

Thursday 14th March

Caronia left Bali in the middle of Monday night to sail the thousand miles north-west to Singapore. It was followed the whole way by a light breeze, a slight sea and fine and clear weather, all of which was wasted on Harry as he didn't leave his cabin for two days.

His room service went largely untouched. Vinnie made a perfunctory house call on Tuesday, which could not end quickly enough for either of them, and she did not repeat the effort. Instead she sent him a careful note, wishing him a speedy recovery and informing him of her plan to leave the ship at Singapore and rejoin it in Thailand, where she trusted she would find him in much better health. If so, she suggested they rendezvous at the Imperial Palace in Bangkok. He accepted its contents numbly.

On Wednesday, *Caronia* recrossed the equator with none of the ceremony of its southwards traverse. Harry lay in bed all day; Vinnie didn't drop by. In the evening, Harry showered, put on his pressed navy double-breasted suit, gathered all his energy and in a pretence of normality went to the showing of *No Man Is an Island*, starring Jeffrey Hunter. He was pretty sure he had seen it earlier on the cruise. Repeat or not, it was still preferable to the 'Merry Widow' concert in the Main Lounge – the connotation with regard to Vinnie was too close to the bone. In any event he fell asleep as soon as the lights went down. Even following a conversation on screen was tiring now.

At a little after six o'clock on Thursday morning, *Caronia* entered the roads and tied up at the Harbour Board's Main Wharf. Vinnie was taking an escorted overland tour by plane and automobile to Bangkok, which left the quay at 9.15am. Harry didn't know with whom and he didn't much care. For her part, Vinnie rationalised that Harry needed as much time as possible without distractions to recover his health. If they did indeed meet at the Imperial Palace in three days' time, that would be a sign she was getting her old flame back.

The ship lay alongside for the whole day but as far as Harry was concerned it could have been a week and he would still not have ventured ashore. He simply didn't have the energy to deal with the constant humidity and a temperature in the 30s. Besides, he was familiar with the city that Sir Stamford Raffles had founded from both the 1951 and 1954 itineraries. He had no interest in yet another tour topped off with a Gala Dinner and entertainment from ronggeng dancers in bajus and sarongs.

In 1954 they had anchored a little way off Collyer Quay and he, Vinnie and Bob had joined a tour that visited the Tiger Balm Gardens to see the life-like animal statues and then taken in a display of Jade collected by some family called Aw, who had made a fortune in herbal pain remedies. They joined the stream of cars and bicycle rickshaws following the one-way streets to Raffles Place and took 'Tiffin' on one of the hotel's sweeping verandas The little museum had pictures of Singapore seen from the roads and vice versa, but in truth there was little to recommend the 'Lion City' to the tourist.

Vinnie had wanted to see the orchids in the Botanical Gardens so they skipped the shops in the hotel's arcade, dropped the tour guide and took a taxi there. Walking around, the majority of the population were speaking Chinese – Harry heard more than one dialect – but also English, Tamil and Malay. The guide's strict injunction to the three that they order the driver to 'piggy kapal *Caronia*' once they had finished their sightseeing was definitely Malay and had stuck in his mind ever since.

*

Singapore was where my ill-fated cruise in Harry's wake was due to have finished. It seems as good a place as any to think about his final days and the impact of his determination to keep his families separate.

He certainly didn't find some poetic closing back in his family's embrace. His parents lie side by side in Edmonton Federation Cemetery less than five miles north of their shop in Clapton. When I went to see their resting place one Spring afternoon, I thought I would have difficulty finding their plots among all the urban crowding and Hebrew masonry. I need not have worried. There may be nearly 40,000 graves on the site but the position of each one is neatly recorded – an index of postmortem care to shame Anglican churchyards. Gone but not forgotten. As many of the stones declare: May their souls be bound up in the Bond of Life.

The freezing and thawing over the years had caused some of the metal letters on Esther's upright headstone to drop onto the horizontal tablet in front, but it was still possible to see that the names on both headstones were Vigoda. Morris's read 'Moshe ben Abram' but it struck me that neither Harry nor Betty was mentioned on his tablet. Harry's absence I could understand – he predeceased Morris – but why was only one daughter-in-law mentioned? That would have been Joyce, Ben's wife.

I don't think the monumental wording is a deliberate snub so much as enduring evidence that Betty and her family simply did not figure in Morris and Esther's lives. Standing in front of their memorials was a salutary experience – it was hard not to feel downcast at the human cost of Harry's familial segregation. Because of Harry's desire to camouflage his tracks, his daughters missed out on so much that makes life worth living – robbed of inner lives that would have been enriched by thousands of years of belonging not to mention all the bonds and memories from the get-togethers, celebrations and gossip that they might otherwise have shared with the Keens and Cohens down the years.

Mum remembered sitting *Shiva* – very briefly – with Harry after Esther died in January 1958. (There is no evidence that after Esther's death Harry kept a copy of his mother's *Yahrzeit*, the calendar of the days when her family were supposed to remember her and, if he did, he certainly didn't share it with his children.) Mum also remembered going to her cousin David's *bar mitzvah* in 1959. Two family gatherings in two decades; the exposure both sides of his family had to each other was rigorously rationed by Harry. Perhaps he was wise to limit fraternisation – the only other time Mum records meeting her cousins was one afternoon in Hendon in the early '60s when she remembers they all had a good laugh at his foibles.

What makes his behaviour even more perplexing is that he kept some form of relationship with his parents and selected siblings. Like the prodigal son, he often returned to the Clapton shop. Ben's daughter, Beverly Danan, remembers the occasions because Uncle Harry always gave her a penny for the bubble-gum machine. Later on, after Esther had died, David Keen remembers Harry coming to visit Morris at his parents' house in Hendon. Harry's celebrity persona, his white Rolls-Bentley and his immaculate tailoring – even his suit buttons were monogrammed – made quite an impact on the young boy.

This was the period when Harry was at the top of his game, leading an impossibly glamorous life of nightclubs, jet-setting and entertaining. Nevertheless, like Mr Rochester visiting his wife in the attic, Harry kept all these visits a secret from his own children, an act that smacks more of emotional deprivation than negligence.

Thus his children never experienced Morris's gentleness and Esther's acuity. Esther particularly was about as far removed from Betty's whimsy as was possible. She ran the household and much of the business despite not being able to read or write English, which would have been her third or fourth language if she had learned it as an adult. Esther's cognitive abilities were not in doubt: she was the one who took all the telephone orders in the shop as she could memorise twenty items at a time.

The girls would probably have found more in common with the gentle, diminutive Morris. He might have been the antithesis of his spendthrift son, but Morris passed on to Harry invaluable lessons on not undervaluing what you possessed. The family story is that the only thing that could ever get Morris upset was money, or rather the perception that money was being wasted. In the shop Morris's practice was not to pay up for premium produce at Spitalfields, but rather to buy barrels of second-grade crops and sort out the best. According to David Keen, Anne argued with her father because she saw the potential to sell the remainder, but he preferred to throw it away rather than sell it below the price he thought it was worth.

Harry's daughters missed out on being bridesmaids at Harry's brother Ben's wedding to the effervescent Joyce Leigh in 1950. Ben took over the fruit and veg business after that and Morris and Esther retired first to Edmonton and then back to a mansion block close to the shop. Being kept in the cold meant Mum and her sisters never met any of their four younger cousins when they were growing up. It did mean, however, that they were spared the full shock of Esther's sudden death from a cerebral haemorrhage. Morris had struggled with chest problems for years because of his heavy smoking but, as is often the way, it was the stronger partner who proved more fragile.

Harry had never got on well with Rose and nor it seemed did the newly bereaved Morris. Father and daughter's experiment in cohabiting in a new flat in Highbury did not survive a year. Morris moved in with Anne and her husband Alec Keen in Hendon where it seems his old traits never entirely disappeared. David Keen remembers Morris giving him and his brother Michael five shillings pocket money a week. Parting with the coins still represented something of a psychological hurdle as David remembers the two half-crowns always being hot to the touch since they had spent so much time beforehand balled up tightly in his grandfather's fists.

Perhaps saddest of all, when Morris's health deteriorated and he went into a Jewish Home for the Blind in Dorking – a lifetime of smoking meant it wasn't trachoma now, it was glau-coma – even though it was a stone's throw from Betty and Harry's daughters living in Westhumble they never had an inkling that he was there.

Harry worked hard to preserve his carefully constructed im-age. He would not risk his children meeting anyone that knew him from a previous life. Even that wouldn't be enough – as his daughters grew into inquisitive young adults themselves he increasingly distanced himself from them as well.

Bangkok

Sunday 17th March

It took *Caronia* a couple of days to steam north from Singapore. There had been no question of Harry attending the St Patrick's Day Ball, held two days early because most passengers would be onshore on the 17th. It was traditionally the most uproarious night of the whole cruise and Harry hadn't even been to dinner for three nights.

His steward had communicated his concern at Harry's decline to the hospital, and Dr Winer paid a house call. The medic could tell immediately from the colour of Harry's skin and the whites of his eyes that he was severely jaundiced, an indication that the lymphoma in his liver was very advanced. He needed a full blood transfusion very quickly, not something that could be done on board, so they agreed that Harry should leave the cruise and fly back to London from Bombay. *Caronia* would not arrive at the port until the 27th and the flight would be exhausting – a Boeing 707 via Delhi, Beirut and Geneva – but it was the fastest way of getting home for treatment.

In the meantime, having discovered that Harry had been taking Librium habitually for its calming effect, but had run out, Winer re-prescribed it and advised a rest-cure. Harry should look to increase his intake of liquids and fruit to build his strength for the trip. He took a cable from Harry to send to Betty advising her of the change in plans.

After Winer left, Harry lay in a fever all day, his mind a kaleidoscope of disjointed images and memories, some morbid.

He had been fortunate: other than his mother and his Colony doorman, Alec Newland, he had never seen a corpse, but lifeless bodies invaded his dreams.

He slept virtually all the time and in his few waking moments he felt nothing but anger: in truth that emotion had never been far away throughout his life. Anger at his parents' mulish passivity, at his siblings' lack of ambition, at the way events had turned out at the Colony, at Betty for only giving him daughters, at the girls themselves for their lack of gratitude, at Vinnie for being healthy, but most of all at his own loss of control.

He had no truck with a higher power. If there was one, He had done nothing for Harry, who took full credit for all he had achieved in his life. He had no reason to feel gratitude to anyone or anything else, not for his parents escaping the Shoah or even for his having been spared for so long.

Caronia arrived at its Bangkok anchorage at three o'clock on Sunday morning. Her deep draught meant she could not pass the sand bar across the Menam River so she heaved to by the lighthouse at the mouth of the delta.

Harry felt utterly delirious and drained but was determined somehow to make the rendezvous with Vinnie. In a supreme effort of will, he rose from his sickbed while it was still dark and boarded the *MS Bhanurangsi*, tied up alongside. Fortunately, given his state, there were two strapping able seamen on the pontoon to help him on board.

Since there were 400 passengers on the tender, he was able to disappear into the crowd. In typical *Caronia* fashion they had stewards, a dining service and as many bottles of spirits as water for the trip. Three musicians kept them entertained. The three-and-a-half-hour journey upstream passed quickly: the delta held plenty of interest. The riverside huts – on stilts to allow for the tides – were hives of activity. All along the banks, fishing nets, projecting into the river, were being set as the ship passed.

They tied up at a modern terminal on the outskirts of Bangkok. Some smaller ships were moored there. From now on, as the cruise notes would have it, he would have to navigate the crossword puzzle of 'Chedi, Prang and Klong': the Chedi being the bell-shaped domes; the prangs, the towers atop the hundreds of Buddhist temples; and the Klongs the equally numerous canals criss-crossing the city.

He headed to the Marble Temple – Wat Benchamabophit – at the end of the green triangle of the Turf Club, opposite the Zoo. The wats – overlapping tiers of steep red roofs above the whitewashed walls, dazzled with gilded scythes but were somehow not garish. Bolt upright lion dogs guarded the main doors. The interior of the shrine itself, despite trees of candles, was gloomy and sombre in contrast to the dazzle outside. At one end of the hall a huge gilt Buddha gazed placidly through the incense smoke. He could hear prayers being chanted somewhere in the shrine.

It felt incongruous to be visiting Buddhist temples on St Patrick's Day but it was also a Sunday, which meant Wat Phra Kaew – next to the Royal Palace – was open to the public. It was here, in the central courtyard dominated by tall prangs and guardian statues, that he and Vinnie fell into each other's arms in a tearful embrace after her overland exertions. Her escort, if she had had one, was nowhere to be seen. Together they climbed the steps, took off their shoes and entered the shrine to see the revered Emerald Buddha. The apple-green chalcedonic figure was surprisingly small – the size of a small child – frozen in a yogic posture and sitting on top of a gilded mountain. Reputedly the security of the whole country rested on the little effigy; Harry in some way felt his own prospects had been assured by seeing the icon.

Afterwards they went arm-in-arm to the porcelain temple, Wat Arun, whose central prang rose hundreds of feet into the blue skies. The bricks had been plastered over with thousands of pieces of broken china making them sparkle in the sunshine. As they walked up the steps, Harry could see that the monkeys holding up the tower with their raised arms were actually made of thousands of vibrantly coloured fragments. It looked like whole dinner services had been smashed to make the patterns.

They got up to the high terrace, drunk with effort and vertigo, but the view was worth it. They looked down on the walls of the Royal Palace, the boats on the river, the sparkling roofs and towers piercing the sky and beyond, the dense green jungle pressing in on the white city.

As they headed back to the river pier, a torrential rainstorm flooded the city. Lightning split the black sky, strong winds swept the water down the streets and flapped the canvas in the tram windows. Half-naked children seemed to emerge from nowhere, dodging the bicycle rickshaws, trams, and taxis and squealing with delight as they were soaked by the spray from their wheels. He was transported to a time in his childhood when he ducked traffic in similar conditions on the Commercial Road.

Harry awoke with a start. The familiar surroundings of his stateroom came into focus. He had been in a delirious fever the whole day and had not moved from his cabin. In one period between sleeping and waking he had distinctly heard monks chanting but in reality the anchorage was too far out. Now that he was fully conscious he made two discoveries: a large green praying mantis on his pyjama top and the fact that he had lost control of both his bladder and his bowel while asleep. The revelations sparked him into deranged action.

Remembering his first voyage as part of the crew, Harry knew that there were still Glory-Hole Stewards on the *Caronia* in 1963. He was determined to seek them out and tell them that he, a First Class guest, had been just like them once. They may be making up bunks, changing bedding and doing the personal laundry of the crew but there was no limit to what they could achieve if they believed in themselves. Likewise, the cooks, pantry men, barbers, cobblers, even tattooists below decks – he needed to tell them all. His example would be an inspiration.

It was dark but he managed to get down the stairs behind the Sandringham Restaurant to B Deck. He was now in the bowels of the ship, which was more than simply a figurative term since B Deck housed the 'Working Alleyway'. This functioned like a sort of alimentary canal for the liner as it was the crew's access to all the frozen, chilled and fruit and vegetable stores consumed on the higher decks. The alley ran down the boat for almost its full length, fifteen-feet wide in some places, and even at this time of night it was bustling with activity. If any of the crew noticed the strange visage of a passenger in disarranged pyjamas, walking with difficulty in a part of *Caronia* where they were normally discouraged from visiting, they were too polite to say so.

Harry stumbled over a watertight door and then forward past some storerooms and crew accommodation – some of the men were doing their dhobi, washing their smalls. A fish preparation pantry was on his right and a bakery inboard was on his left, both positioned next to a companionway leading up to the galley between the two restaurants on the deck above. It was hours to the breakfast service so both were quiet. There was some noise coming from his right as he laboured past the separate messrooms for warrant-officers and stewards and he felt a blast of hot air streaming from the open door at the top of the companionway down to the engine room. He entered a lobby he recognised because it had occasionally been used as access to the shore, and then through another set of watertight doors. Now there was a real gathering – he was looking down the corridor to the Pig & Whistle, the crew pub. This is where he could explain to the workers on the ship that despite his outward appearance he was actually one of them and had been so for nearly 40 years.

A group of men appeared in front of him. If he wasn't so confused he could have sworn that it resembled something like a wedding party. Harry got a fleeting impression of risqué outfits and someone dressed up as a bride. The person directing the ceremony turned round and Harry thought he looked just like the Cruise Director. Then his knees gave way and he lost consciousness.

*

It is the nature of memory that some events will be lost while others will take on an exaggerated significance by their frequent retelling. This can lead to selective recollection but there is enough congruence in the childhood stories of Mum and her sisters to observe the weekly pattern of their lives with their semi-absent father.

Growing up in Laleham, Susan was sent to a boarding school called Maltman's Green near Gerrards Cross, Belinda and Anabel to Danesfield in Walton-on-Thames. On the occasions he did turn up, Harry would descend on Friday evening or Saturday afternoon.

There might be an interesting weekend guest – radio and television personalities Bernard Braden and Barbara Kelly, who had a couple of children the same age, were repeat visitors, as was Olga Green, wife of the Astor Club owner Bertie. If there wasn't a guest, Harry would take the younger girls on outings to Burnham Beeches and Virginia Water but usually he was too tired to do anything more active.

Each weekend the atmosphere in the house would deteriorate towards Sunday lunch, which unfailingly culminated in a row about their collective lack of gratitude, after which he would stalk back to London.

Perhaps if he had had sons he might have been more involved. Unusually for someone who hid so much, he made no secret of his chauvinism. Even in the final letter he wrote to Mum from Hong Kong, he wrote that he hoped his first grandchild would be a boy.

When he returned from one of his cruises he did come bearing gifts for his daughters – Anabel remembers him bringing home Navajo turquoise belts, Didi dolls, real US blue jeans, Bazooka Joe bubble-gum, Japanese parasols, geisha dolls, African carvings and Chinese silk. However, she also recalls that a present to any of them was invariably prefaced with an enquiry regarding the level of their appreciation at their good fortune. Harry identified good parenting with material generosity – being given the things he never had as a child – but only if received with the requisite gratitude.

The three girls were often left in the care of the 'help' as Betty, fey and permissive, was also away a lot – in luckless pursuit of her husband on his latest dalliance – at least until she was encumbered by the hotel.

Daniel Gardner

When Betty moved to Westgate to renovate Rowena Court, she weekly-boarded Belinda and Anabel in a convent school run by French-speaking Benedictine nuns in Birchington-on-Sea. For a couple of atheist parents it was a quirky choice. Almost immediately, the early morning mass, incense and silent meals made refuseniks of both girls and they were sent to join Susan at Maltman's Green. Maltman's Green later decided to turn itself into a prep school so that by 1957 both were back in Birchington, their education hopelessly compromised.

My mother's result in the School Certificate in the summer of 1958 was decidedly modest. She headed for Art School in Margate. Anabel's formal education would end in a secretarial course at Pitman's. Susan had earlier taken herself to London, studying at Central School of Speech and Drama. They were all in their own way victims of Betty and Harry's feckless approach to parenting and Harry's casual sexism. Harry and Betty's inattention did have one big positive as far as Mum was concerned, however – it gave her a licence to roam that would be remarkable even today, let alone in that era.

Mum was quite flush for a teenager; she augmented her monthly allowance from the Colony's office with wages she earned as a chambermaid in the 'bungalow', annexed to the hotel. Her teenage diaries in Westgate speak to a simple focus on having fun. Her pages conjure up an everlasting late-'50s summer of enjoyment – listening to *West Side Story* and records by Dave Brubeck and George Shearing, dyeing sweaters and smoking cigarettes or landing 'buckshee' – free – hairdos. She drank coffee at Pelosi's in Margate, swam in Epple Bay and partied on the beach or at Milly's, St Mildred's, a nightclub in Westgate. She saw skiffle bands at the Cave in the basement of the Granville Hotel in Ramsgate, went to jazz jamborees in Canterbury on the back of Lambrettas and consorted with Yanks from Manston Air Base – she is abashed when they see her in her school uniform. She let some of the boys 'go quite far'. Her autonomy is quite striking.

Harry makes remarkably few appearances in her diaries aside from dutiful descriptions of weekend rows, generally triggered

237

by her habit of staying out late at night. Otherwise, it is the occasional treats he offers that inspire most entries. For instance, a visit to the Planetarium with lunch at 'El Cubano', a coffee bar in Knightsbridge famous at the time for its caged parakeet and uncaged monkey, caused a lot of excitement.

This might have something to do with the amount of time and attention his infatuation with Vinnie O'Donnell was taking up. In 1958, Mum mentions Harry just three times in her diary – taking her to his mother's *Shiva* in January, his going to New York two days later and not coming back until the middle of February, and later when he arranges a job for her looking after the two children of friends of his in Dallas, Texas, (obviously friends of the O'Donnell's) after her School Certificate in July. By August the job is off.

The endless seaside summer came to a halt in 1959: after a decade of losses, even Harry's bottomless support for the white elephant that was the Rowena Court Hotel found its limit. He auctioned the business off at the end of the year. The timing could have had something to do with the prospect of a permanent relationship with Vinnie after Bob's death – and the prospect of keeping her in the style to which she was accustomed. In any case, the hotel was no longer fully occupied even in the holiday season.

It was bought by a Mr Lamb, who had no intention of keeping the business going; he had planning permission for 138 flats. One can imagine how Betty felt to see over a decade of effort amount to nothing. She was out of the building by the middle of February 1960 and the site was demolished within the year. The sale proceeds did not cover the hotel's debts. Rowena Court Hotel Limited was voluntarily wound up by a liquidator on 26th June 1963 – at his death, Harry's shares had a negative net worth of over £10,000.

All the family's Rowena Court furniture was put into storage and they moved into a flat on the Edgware Road in London. It was out of the question that any of them would be offered space in Park Lane. Harry never lived full time under the same roof as my mother and Anabel.

Mum got a job with Moyses Stevens, a florist next door to the Colony. Mum records Harry coming into the shop in February 1960 and he starts to become a slightly more frequent presence in her life that year, as he goes into match-making mode. She mentions attending a lot of dinners at the Colony, meeting the owners of Susan Small (children's dresses) on one occasion and the Newmarks (watchmakers) on another. In June she meets Vinnie for the first time. She finds Harry's girlfriend is nicer than she expected but 'insincere and reactionary'. Afterwards Vinnie returns to the US but is back over for Christmas.

In 1961, Betty and the girls moved into a new home in Westhumble outside Dorking. Mum got a temporary job on the Max Factor Beauty Bar at the Ideal Home Exhibition and then moved to Marshall and Snelgrove on Oxford Street selling Elizabeth Arden. She was sacked for non-attendance in September, which was probably something to do with her having met my father, an event which also terminated Harry's interest in her marriage prospects.

In 1962 she mentions Harry's tour of the Greek Islands by yacht in the second half of May – the origin of the postcard in the archive – but otherwise is as wrapped up in her new husband and flat-making (the weekly rent half-subsidised by Harry) as any newlywed.

My mother did not notice the worsening in Harry's health until November. All through the early part of 1963 she was unaware of the deterioration in her father's condition. March 18th is the first time she expresses any sort of concern about him in her diary: *Mum had a letter from Daddy. He's not at all well and has decided to fly home from Bombay to go into hospital. Hope he's alright. Will be here on the 30th.*

In truth he was an ephemeral presence in her life just as he was to everyone else to whom he was related by blood. Keeping his families at arm's length led to stunted relationships but was a price he was prepared to pay to maintain his self-image and control the narrative of his life.

Colombo

Thursday 21st March

Caronia had left Bangkok early on Monday morning just after Harry's collapse. He had been oblivious to the movement as, heavily sedated, he had been carried by the two hospital attendants to the ship's Male Infirmary. The Infirmaries and Operating Theatre were all located conveniently close by on B Deck as this was effectively the waterline of the ship, so offered maximum stability.

The Infirmary was also suitably secluded, but as it happened on the following morning the ship was as quiet as it had been since leaving New York. This was not out of any exaggerated concern for Harrys' predicament, but because most of the passengers were recovering from all the frantic sightseeing in Bangkok.

Harry's lymphoma had now irreversibly disrupted the balance of salts and chemicals in his bloodstream. His liver and kidneys were barely functioning. The hospital attendants had set up an intravenous drip to counter the high levels of calcium in his blood, which might otherwise have caused him to have a heart attack, but he wasn't aware of it.

The week wore on. The Ninth Grand Oriental Ball came and went. The Gods of the Sea played their part in making Harry's last days comfortable. The light breezes came from the east, generating a slight sea and a low swell. Although he would not have known it inside his windowless room, outside it remained fine and clear.

The Infirmary was dominated by his loud and irregular breathing. His anaemia was making him breathe deeper and faster and fluid was building up in the back of his throat as the muscles relaxed. The attendants helped him clear out the phlegm and gave him oxygen.

He had never trusted the electric clocks on *Caronia*, with good reason. There were 570 of them on board – all Art Deco rectangular and each one, including the silent versions in the bedrooms, a slave. Every clock could be altered by the touch of a button in a master control box in the chartroom, a necessity in advancing or retarding the hour uniformly to suit different time-zones, but one that introduced an unaccountable force into every passenger's life.

While Harry was used to time being elastic on *Caronia* cruises and crossings, the way it seemed to leap during the week as he drifted in and out of consciousness became an obsession. Each time he woke he demanded to know the time with a fierce and lucid determination and, after being told, would accuse the attendants of moving the hands forward to confuse him before lapsing into morphia-raddled incoherence. He could hear people around him and feel their touch, but seemingly could not communicate his wishes to them.

Harry was no longer capable of drinking unaided. The hospital attendants helped him take sips of water and gave him ice cubes to suck. They moistened his cracked lips with a balm and cleaned his eyes of crust. They also closed his eyelids: even though Harry was asleep his eye muscles were so weak he could not close them by himself. At least not being able to eat and drink meant his body had less waste to remove so incontinence was no longer a problem. In any case his kidneys had stopped making urine.

Harry's pain and breathlessness was now extreme. The morphine was increased and Harry fell into a sleep from which he would not awaken.

Vinnie had made a point of not visiting Harry in his sick room. His decline had brought back painful memories of Bob's pain-ravaged demise three years earlier and she had no desire to visit another man on his deathbed. She went to see a travelogue in anticipation of one of their next big ports of call – 'A Royal Tour of India'. She was planning a second, impromptu overland tour from Bombay such was the success of the first one. She felt no compunction about attending the Spring Ball even though she had been told Harry's end was near.

Harry was beyond caring, even about this final rejection. The truth is that there was little reason for Harry to wake up from his coma.

*

It wasn't just his family who Harry neglected when Vinnie became a fixture in London. More damagingly in terms of earnings, his infatuation with her distracted him from the smooth running of the Colony. He lost focus just at the time when it was most needed in the face of disruptive new entrants on the West End restaurant scene.

He was often seen with Vinnie on his arm in the theatre or at gala evenings on working nights. He took her on holiday throughout the year, not just in the low trading period after Christmas. Kitchen standards slipped, the floor show became a bit staler – a serious failing in an industry where a venue lived on its reputation – and unscrupulous employees took advantage of Harry's more frequent absences.

Takings were down and worse, money started to go missing. Over the space of three years one of the bookkeepers in the office embezzled £6,000 (£150,000 in today's money). The irony of a career liar being deceived so cripplingly by a work colleague might have been lost on Harry. Even Torr, Harry's long-serving manservant, did a midnight flit with more of Harry's cash in 1962. Presumably Harry's backer, Parker, didn't see the funny side either. The decline in Harry's work ethic was starting to become a real liability for the business.

Rex North's gossip column in the *Daily Mirror* in May 1962 was ostensibly about the memories of Harry's loyal number one waiter, Joseph Della, who was leaving, but in passing North mentioned that Harry had just sold 60% of his shares. The article concluded with a statement that 'after 20 years with Harry Morris he [Della] is not a poor man. So the business of being out of work for a bit won't worry him much. In show business the rule is: "No play, no pay." And it is accepted. In the restaurant business they are equally philosophical.'[49] Now he was no longer the reliable player he once was, Parker seemed to be applying the same standard to Harry.

Peter Hepple's 'Nightbeat' column picked up on the news a few days later. The story was about the pianist Chester Harriott standing in for an indisposed Jeannie Carson in the Colony's cabaret lineup, but Hepple also wrote that 'a familiar face greeted me at the Colony, that of Peter Gualdi, formerly of the Hungaria. Peter and his brother Remo have taken over control of the restaurant, although Harry Morris remains one of the directors.'[50]

The extent to which Harry participated in the negotiations with the Gualdis is open to question as he was out of town for at least part of the time that the details were being thrashed out. He was in New York on the 3rd of March and the 19th of April, staying both times at the Westbury Hotel on 69th Street. If he were central to the negotiations, why would he have removed himself? It certainly would not have been to scout for new talent so late in his tenure. I think it is more likely that, at Vinnie's urging, Harry went to the US to get a second opinion on his lymphoma. It might have been here that he was first prescribed Librium and told that he would need blood transfusions and possibly surgery. Mum's wedding on 31st March might have been the reason he had to split the trip into two, not the sale of the Colony shares.

The 'Nightbeat' report was for public consumption. Parker had engineered a bloodless change of management. But if Parker felt any euphoria it would prove to be short-lived. For the money

---

49 1 May 1962, *Daily Mirror*.
50 10 May 1962, the *Stage*.

man and his new managers, the upheaval in 1962 would prove to be the start of an era of instability the club would endure after its creator's departure.

Meanwhile, after a decade of presiding over one of London's most successful nightspots, Harry cannot but have felt downcast at the manner of his ejection. To outside parties at least he conveyed the impression that he needed a change of venue and it was all part of a plan. He wasn't ready to hang up his tuxedo quite yet. It may have been fantasy but he convinced his family that he was variously negotiating to buy into two Colony competitors, the Pigalle and the Mirabelle.

Purchasing the Pigalle would have been somewhat implausible given the litigious relationship Harry had with its owner, Al Burnett, but diary entries and letters suggest Harry discussed buying into the venerable Francophile restaurant, the Mirabelle.

Harry would have known the Mirabelle very well as it was just round the corner from the Colony at 56 Curzon Street and the layout would have felt very familiar because, like the Colony, it was in the basement of a mansion block. The Mirabelle catered for a similar crowd to Harry's lunchtime and early evening clients – businessmen and advertising men entertaining clients, a smattering of stage and screen – but was more formal. Diners descended past a ticker-tape machine where they could check their stock prices, and even as late as 1962 a strict dress code applied. Women had to wear hats and gloves.

I am sceptical about the diaries and letters. The Mirabelle had been bought the year before by the DeVere group so it stretches credulity to think they would have been partially selling it so quickly. I think it more likely that Harry was actually talking to two ex-Mirabelle waiters about managing their latest venture: a Mirabelle competitor called Tiberio, due to open in Queen Street at the end of the year. Harry was just indulging in his habitual economy with the truth when it came to communications with his family.

The two owners of Tiberio would have been well aware of Harry's credentials and fitness to run the restaurant as the format they envisaged took a number of leads from the Colony. The plan was for a pianist to accompany the main dinner service and then have a small band, Olaf Vas and his Orchestra, play from 10.30 to closing at 3am. If there was less of an emphasis on the entertainment than Harry's old club there would still be the occasional cabaret show to keep him professionally interested.

The irony is that the two founders of the restaurant were probably responsible for the eventual demise of traditional Mayfair Dinner and Dance places like the Colony. Mario Cassandro and Franco Lagattolla were in the process of revolutionising how people ate in the capital.

They had started with the simple insight, commonplace now, that a restaurant's décor should project an image of the cuisine that guests were going to eat. In the case of their first spot in Soho, La Trattoria Terrazza: modestly priced Neapolitan fare. The designer Enzo Apicella's simple arched ceilings with direct downlighters, rustic chairs, rush seats, exposed bricks, green ceramic floor tiles and sculptured holes in interior walls were all much more novel design elements than they sound now. Unlike the Colony, the 'Trat' had no signature dishes; its waiters swapped black tie for hooped Neapolitan jerseys and most radical of all, did not leave the interaction with the diners to the Maître D'. It was a mile away from Harry's slavish attachment to classic French cuisine and silver service.

Harry and the two would agree that eating out should be an opportunity for exuberant fun but would have disagreed on how to achieve it: Harry believing it was the floor show, Cassandro and Lagattolla insisting it was about interaction with the food. In that sense they were part of the iconoclasm of the '60s, delivering new freedoms to diners. In Tiberio, for the first time in London, customers could watch chefs in the kitchen through a glass window.

The combination of aspirational cooking yet relaxed surroundings made competitors start to look old fashioned. Tail-clad waiters, invariably Italian, serving classic dishes to a formally dressed clientele in a muted atmosphere before the lights dimmed for the show felt backward-looking. The photographers, artists, actors and rock singers, hairdressers and fashion designers that made up '60s 'royalty' objected to having their fun timetabled, and increasingly the dukes and princesses, business leaders and politicians that made up the core of Harry's clientele headed after them to the more informal venues. For the future of the Colony, the writing was on the Trat's rough plaster walls.

In 1962, the *Sketch*, that long-time supporter of the Colony, ran a feature entitled 'Who dines where?' which noted that the guests at La Terrazza on a single evening included Ingrid Bergman, Leslie Caron, Danny Kaye, David Niven, Gregory Peck, Laurence Harvey, Sammy Davis Jr, Michael Caine, Julie Christie, Terence Stamp, Carl Foreman, Pietro Annigoni, and David Bailey with Jean Shrimpton.

This was after Mario and Franco had opened the Positano Room downstairs in the restaurant – a space that remained the hot spot for the glitterati throughout the decade. Even at its peak the Colony could not have crowed about a guest list like that. My bet is that after a couple of conversations, Cassandro and Lagattolla found Harry too fixed in his outlook to be the right partner for them.

Although it might not have felt exactly like it at the time, in hindsight, Harry's pretensions and cultural appropriation were being superseded. After two decades of influencing tastes, his reflexive genuflection to French cuisine had had its day and he was probably saved from commercial failure by the unsentimental actions of Parker.

Maybe in his innermost self he knew he no longer had the physical or mental energy to compete in his cutthroat business. If he had lived and fought on at the Colony, he would have had to have economised drastically and admitted to Vinnie and his family that he could no longer keep them in the manner to which they had become accustomed. I don't think he had the appetite for that fight; his race was run.

Friday 22nd March

So it was that on a calm and clear night with an easterly wind speeding *Caronia* towards Colombo, Harry died in the Infirmary.

Betty called Mum on Friday morning to tell her that he had passed away at around 10.30pm the previous night, UK time, which would have made it about 4.30am on Friday in the Indian Ocean.

The time is roughly corroborated by the latitudinal and longitudinal coordinates of the place of death on his certificate. Latitude 5° 49' North, longitude 85° 56' East lies about 450 nautical miles out from Colombo – a day's steaming – and *Caronia* docked at Colombo at 5.48am on the 23rd.

Harry was not buried at sea immediately. His death was neither suspicious, requiring a postmortem before the doctor could issue a death certificate, nor a surprise, which might have necessitated a delay while on-board mourners were contacted. For some reason, however, his body was kept in the cold room until Colombo or, more likely, Bombay. This may have been because there was some confusion about who exactly was in charge of his remains, Vinnie, or Betty back home. Perhaps it was because Harry himself had given instructions for the disposal of his body on his deathbed. What seems clear is that he was cremated, most probably in Bombay.

Wednesday 3rd April

Ideally the ship's authorities would have committed his ashes discreetly from one of the access hatches on C deck, only a few paces from the cold room where he had been moved to after his death. But Vinnie's presence at the funeral made that impossible so Harry got to make his final exit from one of the decks that wrapped around *Caronia*'s stern.

The service required the ship's engines to be stopped. It was timed for eight o'clock in the morning: there was a concern that the increased roll of the stopped ship might inconvenience passengers during breakfast, but in the event the sea played its part in ensuring a smooth ceremony – Harry was jettisoned into light airs and calm water.

Harry's despatch, like much at sea, was bound by tradition. The small gathering – Vinnie, Harry's bedroom and restaurant stewards, one of the doctors – quietly watched as his urn was placed on a white gloss table at right angles to the ship's side. The Captain and a master-at-arms stood at his head, two seamen either side.

Captain Marr's Yorkshire vowels, suppressed by the long years in the Officers' Wardroom, reappeared at this time of stress. He gave the order to 'stop engines'.

The Captain only felt qualified to follow the Order for the Burial of the Dead from the Book of Common Prayer. The usage wouldn't have stirred Harry such was his indifference to the theology and practice of all faiths. If Harry had been in any position to comment on the language he may have pointed to the brevity of his span, which was not exactly the threescore years and ten promised in the book.

'I am the resurrection and the life, saith the Lord: he that believeth in me, though he were dead, yet shall he live: and whosoever liveth and believeth in me, shall never die…' Marr started. At that familiar passage: 'We brought nothing into this world, and it is certain we can carry nothing out. The Lord gave, and the Lord hath taken away…' the crew members removed their hats.

'Abide with Me' was sung, followed by a desultory blessing and the Lord's Prayer. Marr adjusted the Sentence of Committal for a burial at sea:

'Unto Almighty God we commend the soul of our brother departed, and we commit his body to the deep; in sure and certain hope of the Resurrection unto eternal life, through our Lord Jesus Christ; at whose coming in glorious majesty to judge the world, the sea shall give up her dead…'

With that Harry's mortal remains were scattered overboard, a lost Stern lost astern.

The Captain gave the order 'Full speed ahead', the propellers restarted and the Officer of the Watch recorded the exact time and place of the funeral into the ship's log. Despite the early hour Vinnie, even paler than usual, joined Marr in his cabin for a stiffener.

The medical and funeral expenses incurred by the Cunard Steamship Company came to 257 pounds, 7 shillings and 7 pence. Harry would have been gratified by how much the Captain's simple order to 'stop engines' had cost.

Thus Harry made his entry in the Marine Register, pursuant to the provisions of the Merchant Shipping Act 1894 and the Births and Deaths Registration Act 1953. The cause of death was Hodgkin's Disease. His last place of abode was given as 'Friars' in Pilgrims Way, Westhumble, Surrey, which must have come from the ship's passenger list. Perhaps he planned to relinquish the lease on the apartment at 55 Park Lane.

His occupation was given as Managing Director, his age, 56, enshrining official collusion in his misdirection for all time; for I can tell you when Harry died and even approximately where his ashes were committed to the deep – in an area a bit over a square mile at latitude 16° 27' North and longitude 62° 11' East – but I cannot tell you how old he was, just as I cannot tell you exactly where he was born.

When Harry Morris first opened his eyes he was not called Harry Morris. History does not record his birth name but then history has proved itself imperiously indifferent to the waves of refugees arriving in London's East End. He must have had a birth certificate – there is no evidence of him having to naturalise to obtain his British passport – but it has eluded capture. He is not amongst the 1,700 odd Cohens and Vigodas born in London between 1903 and 1907.

In my fanciful moments I cleave to another reason for why his birth certificate is not extant: one a bit more poetic than a spelling mistake. In an alternative history, Harry was born on the ship bringing Esther to London. Unlikely though this might be, and if it had taken place surely Harry would have mythologised it, I would love to think that it might have happened for the symmetry it would bring to Harry's life – the sea surely the fitting final repository for a water baby.

Romantic notions aside, the continuing ambiguity about the details of his birth feels right. Harry, forced to forfeit so much of a story he might have preferred to remain hidden, gets to take at least one secret to his watery grave.

*

This westward circumnavigation of the world would turn out to be the final one for both man and ship.

Harry's beloved *Caronia* lasted barely ten years longer than he did. At the end of 1965 she was refitted to bring her more into line with '60s cruising tastes. The Main Lounge was extended to the whole width of the ship: wood panelling was out, contemporary soft furnishings in. Outside, at the aft of the ship the Lido Deck was massively extended and enclosed on either side by plastic windscreens. A new bar was built, the swimming pool became kidney-shaped and the outdoor tables were given striped parasols. Cruisers were demanding they spend more time on a trip in the sun so even the dress code was relaxed so, unlike Harry and his cronies, they could get a drink from the bar without having to change out of their bathing costumes.

The result was a somewhat uneasy mixture of the old and new – a dowager having to show a little ankle but not overly happy about it. In reality the old ship had already lost that vital cachet that brought in the big spenders and covered her high operating costs. She made a loss in 1967 and, with her best days behind her, Cunard sold her for $3m to a Greek operator who did a cut-price name conversion: *Caronia* to *Caribia* which only required two letters on the bow and across the stern to be replaced.

It was as though the old girl took umbrage at the affront, however. Her first cruise under new ownership in the Caribbean in 1969 was blighted by problems with the waste system and her second by a fatal explosion in the engine room and a complete loss of power at sea. Perhaps even her loyal fans could not bear to see the faded star, because after she limped back to New York, her crew went on strike and she never made another commercial voyage. She spent a year near the Verrazano-Narrows bridge and then tied up at Pier 84 where, having failed to pay berthing fees, she was sued by the port.

The Port Authority didn't get its money, so in 1974 it held a quayside sale of *Caronia*'s fixtures and fittings. Pier 84 was filled with all that bespoke furniture that made her rooms so covetable in Harry's mind. All the stateroom chairs and cabinets, tables, light fixtures, telephones, signs, pots and pans, even the ladders from the swimming pool – advertised as being part of a 'Classic Art Deco Furniture Sale' – went under the hammer. If they were aware of this last act, one can only feel for all those Glasgow-based fitters and weavers who created something re-markable but were destined to see their craft and industry end up in a gigantic yard sale.

The biggest buyer was an Austrian artist called Kiki Kogeln who was designing the interior of a new restaurant called One-Fifth, named for its location at 1 Fifth Avenue, New York, a venue which happened to be owned by her husband, a Man-hattan doctor called George Schwarz. For a while in the 1970s the zany spirit – the Maître D' wore tails and a monocle – and campy décor attracted the arts and *Saturday Night Live* crowds. Nowadays, after various incarnations, the site is a pizzeria and the fittings are long gone.

Post her disembowelment, the *Caronia* herself was sold for scrap. Even then her humiliation was not finished. En route to a breaker's yard in Taiwan, she was caught in a storm near Guam and the tugboat towing her, the *Hamburg*, had to cut its lines to save itself. The *Caronia* went down in the mouth of Apra Harbour, partially blocking the entrance, and was cut up where she lay.

Harry loved the ship but was not sentimental. As someone in the entertainment business himself, he would have recognised that you had to keep up with fashion or flounder. Nevertheless, it is striking that the most forward-looking ship of her time lasted barely a quarter of a century and had an active service life of only two decades.

The name itself was not quite done. When Carnival bought Cunard from the shipping conglomerate, Kvaerner, it renamed the *Vistafjord*, another single-funnelled cruise ship, the *Caronia* in honour of the line's heritage. Saga bought that vessel in 2004 and operated it as the *Saga Ruby* for a decade. It too has now been scrapped.

Cold comfort perhaps, but at least no operator has a ship called *Caronia* currently. One can imagine the difficulty posed by marketing post-pandemic cruises on a near homophone of Corona.

*

While Harry and *Caronia*'s fates may have been sealed by changing tastes in fashion, what of the rising generation? How was Harry's premature death viewed back home?

His niece, Beverly, has a dim recollection of her father Ben visiting Harry in Park Lane sometime in December 1962. Although she had to wait in the lobby she remembers her father telling her that it was a final goodbye. This may be one of those memories coloured by knowledge of subsequent events: we will never know whether Harry setting off in that cold January recognised in his innermost mind, the one he rarely exposed, that this would be his final voyage.

With his business career and physical resilience at a low ebb, did Harry purposely step aboard his own version of a luxuriously appointed, twentieth-century Viking Burial Ship? Or after a lifetime of self-delusion and flight was he as shocked by the rapid deterioration in his health during the cruise as anyone?

Mum managed to fit a lot of her crabby script into the available space in her oblong Conrad pocket books and they make it clear that, at least to her, Harry's premature death came as a shock.

This is what she wrote in her diary on the day Harry died:

Mummy phoned at 11.30. Told me Daddy had died at sea. I couldn't believe it, I just couldn't believe it. So much more upset than I ever thought I'd be. It was 10.30 our time Thursday night between Colombo and Bombay. And he was flying home to go into hospital. I feel utterly drained. Barry and I went home at lunchtime, he was awfully upset and Mum was in an awful state. His solicitor had been onto her about the body, apparently he is going to be buried at sea. Anabel and I went up to Daddy's flat to see the solicitor and Mr Mesquita. Saw the will, they went thoroughly through the flat. Mum has £10,000 and the house, and Susan, Anabel and I have the rest equally. Also Anabel's and my policies of £1205 are due immediately.

Saw Dr Goode, he said I can expect the baby at any time. Anne, Rose and Ben came over. Daddy left them nothing. I keep crying because it was such a lonely way to die. Apparently his disease was incurable and he was only 56. Two write-ups and a picture in the papers. Barry and I are in a hole because he was paying half our rent, we will have to move at once. We went to London to get the baby's things ready.

Mum had seen the co-executors of Harry's will – his solicitor, Arnold Aaron Finer, and his accountant, I.D. de Mesquita. The £1205 was a life insurance policy; another for £5,000 that Harry had promised Betty turned out to be one more fantasy.

This is Mum's entry for the following Monday, 25th March 1963:

My God, what a weekend. I never want another like it. I feel so depressed. The solicitor has had a cable from Mrs O'Donnell laying claim to the flat! I called up estate agents in Herts. We are going to assign the lease on this flat, put it in the hands of Match (estate agents). I am going to stay with Mum after this weekend till the baby comes, don't want to leave Barry. Three South African boys came to see the flat, if they take it they want the carpet and the fixtures. Mr Mesquita told Mum Daddy's estate is probably worth around £40,000.

That would prove to be a wild overestimate as events unfurled. Judging by her diary entries Harry's parlous finances came as another shock to my mother.

On Wednesday 1st May she wrote:

Daddy had such colossal debts I doubt if we will get much at all. At least the £1205 policy is due this week.

And the next day:

Mr Mesquita called me. Wants me to go to the flat one day next week and choose what I want and witness the opening of his things from the Caronia. Awful shock. Mrs O'Donnell is claiming £15,000 she says Daddy borrowed from her.

Mum did go up to the flat. She managed to get some books and glasses and jazz records but Ben and Joyce were there 'with a list from Mrs O.D.' Her entry for Monday 13th May reads:

His watch and jewellery are all missing from the Caronia.

Mum does not accuse 'Mrs O.D.' directly but it's quite possible Vinnie had Harry's cabin unsealed after his death to collect personal mementos and defray the losses on her loan to him.

This brief record was the last time that my mother ever recorded any of her Jewish relatives' names in print, an estrangement that is easier to understand as the relationship was virtually non-existent to begin with. In that sense Harry achieved one of his strategic aims in keeping his families so detached – the people who knew him best would never gather to conduct a postmortem of his life and character. There would never be any comparison of his stories by their recipients, no dissection of his deceptions: he could rest secure in the knowledge that they had died with him.

Anything my mother thought about the family schism was subsumed by more immediate concerns. Thursday 23rd May's entry reads:

> *Terrible shock. Mr Mesquita says he can't get us a credit from the bank after all, now Barry has got the mortgage settled and everything. Mum has got an appointment with him and Finer on Monday to find out about Mrs O.D.'s claim and everything else.*

And Monday 10th June:

> *…in all, a really ghastly day – Mum had a letter from Mesquita. After Mrs O.D.'s £15,000 and Mum's £10,000, probably nothing left for us at all. She can't lend us the £2,500 for the house as nothing to pay it back with but may buy the house and we will rent it from her. But won't do this until sure of her ten so we're tied with probate.*

The Estate of Harry Morris, deceased, was finally published on 14th January 1966. Mrs Elizabeth Morris did get her £10,000, the freehold to her home in Westhumble and a further 1,948 pounds, 17 shillings and eightpence. Her three daughters each received 586 pounds, two shillings and sevenpence. The estate actually had a high gross value – in excess of £138,000 –

but his liabilities meant the net was barely £20,000. The only business with any net worth at his death was Harry's residual stake in the Colony.

By that stage I was a locomotive two-year-old and Mum was pregnant with my sister, Abigail. In an A frame house on a new estate in Ampthill in Bedfordshire she had created the stable environment and nuclear family that she never had growing up

Betty had moved on from 'Friars', the mock-Tudor house on Box Hill that Harry left her, by the time I knew her. I can remember staying in her flat in Hove. The pillows had 'Sweet Dreams' on them (ours were plain at home) and she had real orange juice. She moved to a bungalow near St Neots and then to a 'Granny Flat' in my aunt's house near Wantage. Even in these reduced circumstances I remember her Mink and her bottles of 'Joy' – or 'Worth' if funds were particularly tight. Although I would not have recognised it at the time, she was still a good-time girl, fun loving and flirtatious. She taught me to play Gin Rummy.

Her life had shrunk to two rooms and she was terminally ill with cancer by this stage but she was never self-pitying. We played cards and laughed and she drank gin and sherry. She refused chemotherapy and died one hot summer's day in 1976. I cannot recall having a single conversation with her about Harry.

*

As for Vinnie, we have already witnessed through my mother's eyes just what a doughty defender of her corner she was.

Harry, as seems common with many charismatic philanderers, somehow retained the love of his discarded inamoratas. Betty was distraught when she learned of his death. Despite all the provocations, she never criticised him in front of the girls, and he repaid the compliment. Such residual loyalty cannot be said to characterise Vinnie's relationship with him, however. She was Harry's largest unsecured creditor at the time of his death; she sued his estate for what she was owed and delayed the publication of his will for almost three years.

She eventually received £10,700 – over £200,000 in today's money – against her loan, perhaps augmented by the unknown value of Harry's trinkets and watches that never made it home from the *Caronia* according to Mum's unsubstantiated suspicions.

Vinnie and Harry had a good run together, both before and after Bob's death, but maybe Harry's greatest bequest to her was a taste in English men of a certain age and manner. Within a year Vinnie married again and this time into English aristocracy. I doubt she still answered to 'Tootsie', but if she did, it would be 'Lady Tootsie' from now on.

Her husband was Sir Eustace Gervais Tennyson-d'Eyncourt, 2nd Baronet. She was 58, he, 62; it was her fourth and his second marriage. His first wife, Pamela Gladstone, a distant relation of the Victorian Prime Minister, had died in 1962 after 36 years and three children together.

Is it beyond the realms of possibility that the clubbable Tennyson-d'Eyncourt was also on the cruise to recover from the death of his first wife? That in consoling Vinnie after Harry's death they developed a bond through shared grief? Sadly the passenger list for the 1963 Great World Cruise has gone astray so my speculation remains just that.

Sir Gervais's selection of such a partner, doubtless viewed as somewhat infra dig by his well-connected family, was unlikely to have been met with universal approbation, not that the showbiz-loving 2nd Baronet seemed to care.

The pair socialised and travelled together for the rest of the decade. Doubtless, Vinnie was more interested in some parts of his life as a committee man than others. Being involved in the Standing Council of the Baronetage, the Royal Society of Arts and the Tennyson Society (naturally) might have been exciting for the girl from Spooner but I am not sure she shared Sir Gervais's passion for fish. He was Prime Warden of the Worshipful Company of Fishmongers, and later President of the Shellfish Association of Great Britain, a position which only came to an end with his death in 1971.

Lady Tennyson-d'Eyncourt outlasted him by almost 30 years but did not quite see the century out. She died in 1999 in Tucson, Arizona, all her siblings having predeceased her, and like her sister, Nina, was laid to rest in the Hillcrest Mausoleum in Dallas.

*

Harry's hold over the Colony had ended by the time he left on his final voyage. He took his leave in two steps. He told his family he had sold 75% of the business in late April 1962 and the 'other half' in early October. The timetable, if not the arithmetic, reconciles with the contemporaneous reports in Rex North's gossip column in the *Daily Mirror* and Peter Hepple's review in the *Stage*.

Hepple introduced Peter and Remo Gualdi as the new controllers of the restaurant. Like Harry, they may have been in charge of all aspects of its day-to-day operation and been its public face, but financial control appears to have stayed with Thomas Parker.

Parker may have felt he was swapping like for like. Similar to Harry, the Gualdis were first-generation immigrants, but Italian this time, born in Kent to a father from Modena. Both men certainly had the résumés to fit the brief – Peter Gualdi managed the Hungaria Restaurant and cabaret club in Lower Regent Street, Remo, the Lo Spiedo Restaurant in Soho. But either through inclination or under pressure from powerful changes in entertainment tastes, the Gualdis challenged Harry's playbook for the Colony pretty quickly. In June 1963, 'Two-Ton' Tessie O'Shea was bringing her down-to-earth Music Hall vulgarity to Colony's set, quite the contrast with Harry's sophisticated floor show. Perhaps the change in style did not work well, as at the start of 1964, Peter moved on to be director of catering at 'Danny La Rue's', a new club launched by the drag artist in what had been Bal Tabarin off Hanover Square.

The Colony may have stumbled on parlaying Harry's legacy of formal dinner cabaret to a dwindling band of devotees, if it hadn't been for two unrelated events that gave the club a notorious second life.

First, in January 1961, gambling in Britain was shaken up by the Betting and Gaming Act. Before then, although widespread, it was underground: bets had to be placed with street bookies, gaming parties only took place in private residences. The Act legalised off-course betting and casinos for the first time and led to a commercial feeding frenzy. Thousands of betting shops were opened that year and the poor drafting of the legislation meant that almost anyone could become a casino operator in the UK. A thousand such joints opened in the first half of the decade, naturally including some with links to organised crime.

Second, in September 1964, Parker was taken to court for tax evasion by the Inland Revenue, and at the Old Bailey in November he pleaded guilty to defrauding the Revenue of £65,000 over twelve years by presenting personal expenses as business ones. He was sentenced to three years' imprisonment and banned from serving as a company director for five years. As a result, through an intermediary called Benny Huntsman, Parker sold the club to another pair of Italian brothers, Silvio and Giovanni Tolaini. He had known this much-liked pair for over ten years. They owned the movie star hangout, the Thatched Barn at Elstree, and had catered on occasion in the Colony's early days.

Meanwhile a man called Dino Cellini, who ran Las Vegas Mafia kingpin Meyer Lansky's operation in the Bahamas, had been given the job of making sure the Mob did not miss out on the jackpot offered by the permissive gambling scene in Britain. Alfred Salkin of Crockford's was Cellini's man on the ground in London. Crockford's tried to open an American-style casino at the Cumberland Hotel at Marble Arch, but it came to nothing. Then Cellini's attention was caught by Parker's setback and the possibility that the Colony could be transformed into a casino. He wasn't the only person whose interest was piqued. Jack Cooper, a Miami 'investor' had been keen on buying it in partnership with a New York gambling promoter called Stephen Tolk, but they deemed the venue too small, leaving the path open for Cellini and Salkin to negotiate with the Tolaini Brothers.

The Colony Sporting Club Company was established in September 1965, Salkin resigned from Crockford's in October and in February 1966 the Tolainis sold out, making a quick turn.

Cellini initially wanted an English front man for the club to deal with the authorities. In casting around they settled on Paul Adam, Princess Margaret's favourite and Harry's erstwhile band leader. If Adam had ended up running his old club, Harry would have been spinning in his grave, underwater or not, but the Americans decided Adam's drinking made him too unreliable so the club opened in February 1966 without a 'face' to differentiate it from all the other casinos attempting to cash in on the laissez-faire regulations.

Despite the money lavished on red velvet and gilt, the club was practically empty for the first three months until, in a masterstroke, Hollywood 'tough guy' actor George Raft was brought in as the ambassador. He agreed to put his name above the door in return for five percent of the company, a Mayfair flat – by coincidence in the same apartment block that Harry had lived in – and a chauffeur-driven Rolls-Royce.

Before long 'George Raft's Colony Club' shone out in Las Vegas-neon over Berkeley Square, and in the second half of the year it became *the* high-end casino to be seen at: jet-set stalwarts like Liz and Richard Burton, Ari and Jackie Onassis, and Charlie Chaplin came to play. Even on a quiet night the louche, high-rolling patrons, evening dress de rigueur, guaranteed a sight that brought in the crowds.

Perhaps competitors blew the whistle on the admittedly pretty overt connections to the Mob, because Roy Jenkins, the Home Secretary, brought the Colony's party to an abrupt halt in January 1967. He simply refused Raft permission to re-enter the UK. Cellini was banned in March. At a stroke the Colony's time passed and the one-time money-spinner would close before the end of the decade.[51]

---

51 Thompson, Douglas (2011). *Shadowlands: How the Mafia bet Britain in a Global Gamble*, Mainstream, UK, pp.204–7, 228–230.

Jenkins was also responsible for a new Gaming Act in 1970, which closed the loopholes of the previous act. All gambling was placed under the control of the Gaming Board which answered directly to the Home Office. Casino gaming was confined to members who had to join 48 hours before playing, and advertising was severely restricted. The impact was dramatic. Casino numbers fell from well over a thousand to 120 licensed casinos within a year. Yet despite having the most restrictive gaming regime in the western world, London remained an important gaming centre. On balance, I think Harry would have approved. Business was business.

Needless to say there is nothing left today to mark either phase of the club's existence. Lansdowne House, otherwise known as 57 Berkeley Square, was redeveloped as offices in the 1980s in a postmodern design. In 2020 planning permission was granted for yet another redevelopment. Rather than a nightclub, its basement will now offer space for commuters' bicycles with associated showers, lockers and changing facilities. How many of those cyclists, changing out of their sweaty Lycra, will have an inkling that they are doing so on a site that once hosted a notorious gaming club?

Daniel Gardner

Epilogue

I am separated from Harry by over half a century. Neither the date of his death nor that of my birth is particularly auspicious in history. Their significance for me lies simply in their juxtaposition and my mother's vague notions about the transmigration of souls. That was enough for me to seek to understand the man and then try to undo some of the damage his repudiation of his birthright has done to his family.

I toyed with the idea of calling Harry's life 'An Imagined Past' as it was a behaviour he clearly indulged in. He fabricated more than his fair share of falsehoods and was not even above a bit of biographical bodysnatching. In camouflaging his culture he created the void I have attempted to fill.

Occasionally, genealogy feels like a legally sanctioned snoop into other people's lives. As a family tree spreads across the screen and the cursor steps up and down a generation at a time, it is hard not to succumb to a simplistic view of the happiness of the lives behind the names based on bald register entries and census returns. A long-lived life or a long-term marriage must have been content; a short span, a residence in a bad neighbourhood or being predeceased by a child can only have been unhappy.

The same mental shortcuts coloured the photographs I sourced: someone caught by the camera smiling and enjoying themselves at some long-ago function must have been fun and vivacious throughout their life. In lockdown I felt a strong connection with some of these pictures of long-lost parties – back in a time when we all had a licence to not just gather and enjoy ourselves but also to be *seen* to be enjoying ourselves. It brought home just how taboo images of conspicuous enjoyment became for a while in the Covid era.

In Harry's case, at times the activity has felt like lepidoptery, pinning the seamy underside of a dead butterfly's wings for all to see. However, if Harry's tale has anything which makes it more than just an enormous exorcism or a rum obsession with a single cruise, it is that it exposes how easy it is to vandalise a family tree.

While there is a danger of judging all someone's actions to be intentional, rather than accidental, I see Harry's life in terms of flight – from poverty, from ill health, from his childhood faith, from his marriage, from both his families, and, in the case of his circumnavigations, from it all. The *Caronia* was the setting that gave him the licence to be the man of his imaginings, but the effects of his habitual absconding have rippled down the generations. This is more than my mum simply not being close to her cousins. Harry disowning his family in pursuit of unchecked autonomy was doubtless what made Mum so eager to bind her own progeny to her tightly. In turn, I have probably been more permissive with my own children and so the cycle goes.

For better or worse, an individual can make a difference to a lot of family trees.

Posterity rightly venerates those individuals who save lives and family lines in times of mortal danger. Oskar Schindler is one such. He was a flawed man who nevertheless was invited to plant a tree on the Avenue of the Righteous at Yad Vashem because of the moral courage he demonstrated in defying the Nazis on behalf of the Jewish workers in his factory.

There is a scene at the end of the movie *Schindler's List* where the director cuts from a monochrome image of the factory-workers to a colour panorama of their descendants, arm-in-arm across the screen. They are queuing to pay their respects on Schindler's monument. The camera pans to the grave – it is a mound of stones and the caption reads: 'There are fewer than four thousand Jews left alive in Poland today' – it was 1991 – and then: 'There are more than six thousand descendants of the Schindler Jews'.

'Britain's Schindler', Nicholas Winton, a similar paradigm because of how he helped Jewish children flee Czechoslovakia before the Nazi occupation, is even closer to home. Like Harry, his parents were Jewish immigrants who changed their surname – from Wertheim to Winton – but even though they rejected their religion he never repudiated his roots in the way Harry did.

Winton was unmasked in an episode of the BBC television programme, *That's Life!* In 1988, he was in the audience when a scrapbook detailing his part in the *Kindertransport* was shown to the camera and the host Esther Rantzen, in her typically forth-right way, asked whether anybody in the audience owed their lives to Winton, and if so, to stand up. More than two-dozen people surrounding Winton rose and applauded. Up to that point, Winton's self-effacement meant that even the children he had saved did not know who he was. Nobody could ever fault Ms Rantzen's timing as she then asked if anyone present was the child or grandchild of one of the children Winton had saved and the rest of the audience stood. It is quite the coup de théâtre.

If a single person can make a positive difference to a multi-tude of lives, a malefactor can do just the opposite. A form of ethnic evasion like Harry's can have a negative impact on families that lasts for generations as well.

My grandfather was a mixture of the deplorable – the amo-rality, the lying, the chauvinism, the philandering – and the admirable – the chutzpah, the elan, the drive, the indefatigabil-ity in the face of a life-shortening diagnosis. While I can revere those characteristics which allowed him to soar away from his roots and become the exception amongst Morris and Esther's children, it is only fair that I acknowledge the very real human cost of his Faustian pact for success.

My mother and her sisters never knew the spread of relations because of Harry's ethnic self-purging. They did not know that Morris left £2,997 in his will, a very similar amount to Esther, (3,097 pounds, 8 shillings and ninepence). Thus neither could show much material reward for their courage and enterprise in leaving their homeland and creating their business. Like millions of other arrivals, their lives went largely unrecorded but they stand for the courage and ambition of migrants everywhere.

Before they died, Morris and Esther would have known about their seven grandchildren. They would not have known any of their great-grandchildren (seventeen), great-great-grandchildren (30) and great-great-great grandchildren (one and counting). If they were granted the awareness now, surely they would see this as their true reward for all the risks they took in leaving home. Worldwide there were nine Sterns in their generation, 34 in the next, 67 in the one below that and over 70 identified in the current one. The fanning out of any family is unstoppable unless it runs into genocide.

My mother and her sisters had no idea that Harry's younger siblings considerably outlived him. Rose and her second husband Hymie were together for a quarter of a century. In the 1980s they lived in the same sheltered accommodation in Golders Green as Anne. Anne passed away in September 1998 on the night of atonement, *Kol Nidre*. Rose died in 1990. Ben's wife, Joyce, died at the deplorably young age of 47 but not before she had given birth to Beverly and Malcolm. Ben himself would live until 2000.

In Hendon, Anne and Alec brought up Michael and David. Michael would go on to have a daughter, Natalie, with Viv. David became a successful jeweller. He married Esta, a neighbour growing up, with whom he would have Richard and Alexandria, and then married Shani. Joyce's premature death was not before she witnessed Beverley's engagement to Daniel Danan. Bev and Danny would go on to have three sons – Jamie, Paul and Josh. Malcolm married Carol and also had two sons, Darren and Richard.

If Mum and her sisters were deprived of the opportunity to keep up with the Keens, Morrises and Danans in Britain, they were doubly disadvantaged outside the country as they had no sense of the legion of Sterns, Marmelsteins, Mazers, Tannenbaums and so on waiting for them in the US.

They would certainly have had no inkling that the last of Harry's cousins to die was Rose Tannenbaum, Fannie Marmelstein's daughter. She lived to be 102, dying in Lexington, Massachusetts in 2016 and so actually outlived both my mum and her sister, Susan.

Family-minded Fannie was the antithesis of Harry. She is interred in Riverside Cemetery in Saddle Brook, New Jersey, not only next to husband, Louis, but also her sons, Leo and Murray, presenting a picture of fraternal closeness that would have left Harry aghast.

In the rolling of time there has even been something of a triumphant return to Poland. In the early 2000s one of Moshe Ber's great-grandchildren, Richard Keen, although unaware of the exact details of the family's origins at the time, had been drawn to the country by the opportunities it offered to foreign capital in the property sector. In the last couple of decades the company he started has developed a chain of regional shopping malls and gyms and employs 700 people. I'm sure the knowledge that one member of their family had been commercially successful in the Old Country would have offered tremendous succour to Morris and Esther, and even Harry might have felt some vicarious pride.

Modern tools like social media, messaging apps and genealogy websites will mean that the connections are preserved. In the marketplace of ideas, the remedy for Harry's misinformation is irrefutable counter-information. His tale has had its effect but now the jest was over. It was time to be undeceived.

In January 2023, Anabel, Harry's last surviving daughter, met her cousins Beverley, Malcolm and David for the first time in 65 years. There were eighteen of us: three generations of the wider Morris family. The reunion sparked joy, of course, and anger on Anabel's part at Harry's withholding of his birth family. Afterwards she told me that she had felt an immediate sense of belonging, a remarkable emotion given the time that had elapsed since their last meeting. This is testimony to Beverley's generosity as a host but also a tantalising glimpse into what Harry's interruption of family relationships cost his children.

Beverley had arranged a table with keepsakes of 'Uncle Harry' and the family he worked so hard to obscure. There were more airmail letters he had written to his brother on his final voyage, photos, paper cuttings of the obituaries after his death. The backdrop was a map of the Indian Ocean supplied by Cunard with a cross marking the spot of his committal. Most revelatory of all, the shipping company or Vinnie had forwarded the pictures of Harry taken on board his final voyage. His face looked pinched and shrunken, a far cry from the showman who had larked in front of the camera on earlier cruises. It made me think that there might have been something in Beverley's memory of that last meeting between Harry and his brother in Park Lane. Just perhaps Harry had confided in his brother about his prognosis even though he kept his own family in the dark until the very end.

During the day I talked about this book and how my research for it had unearthed our Polish roots and endowed a family tree across the globe. Not to be outdone, Beverley's husband, Danny Danan, showed me his family line. The Danans can trace their forebears back to at least the fourteenth century and include such luminaries as the last rabbi of Granada in their ancestry.

While the Stern clan can't boast such eminent members, it is undoubtedly in rude health. What I have discovered in writing this account of Harry's life is that it is possible to put the splintered branches of a family back together even if one is dealing with an ocean-going dissembler of Harry's class. The reunion was proof of that.

In the place of the stunted line I grew up with, pollarded by the wilful act of one person, there is now a family espaliered across the globe. My sincere hope is that all of Moshe Ber's descendants will be able to find their place in, and make their connections under, the canopy of this ceaselessly branching tree.

Acknowledgements

I started this book after my mother died, so it has been a decade in gestation. In fact, I have the Covid pandemic to thank for its completion as it gave me both the time (three hours saved daily in not commuting) and motivation (a way to escape the walls of my home 'office') to complete the task.

Needless to say the book did not emerge fully formed. I had to go back and forth many times, like a shuttle on a loom, before its pattern emerged. In the process I relied on the advice and hard work of others.

Chief among these was Naomi Leon of Research Roots. It was utter serendipity that I found her. When I clicked through on the Association of Genealogists and Researchers in Archives (AGRA) website I had no idea that she was a specialist in Jewish genealogy, and Polish Jewish genealogy at that. I take my coming across Naomi as a cosmic sign that Harry was finally ready to give up his secrets. It was entirely due to her patient and diligent endeavour that we discovered as much as we did about the family's Polish roots and Harry's British relatives.

The on-board scenes would have lacked verisimilitude without the invaluable feedback and advice of Peter 'Steve' Stevens who was a First Class steward on *Caronia*. He is also the webmaster of the *RMS Caronia II* timeline (www.caronia2.info/home. php), an extraordinarily rich and detailed archive of material relating to this fascinating ship. I have spent many happy hours exploring the site for insights into life aboard a luxury liner in the middle of the twentieth century.

I have lent on the memories and advice of Beverley Danan, David Keen, Sheldon Sussman, Paul Holzmann, Viviaen Segal,

Beth Mazer and Michael Marmelstein. I would like to thank Richard Keen for hosting me in Warsaw when I visited the ancestral village. We are second cousins but his welcome and hospitality could not have been any more generous.

I would like to thank Anabel Morris and Marietta, my wife, for reading through early drafts and making such constructive criticisms and corrections. Philippa Donovan (www.smartquilleditorial.co.uk) also provided invaluable editorial advice, not once but twice. Gareth Howard and his team at Authoright (www.authoright.com) were first-class aides in bringing this project to a successful conclusion.

Any mistakes in this finished version are entirely my own but perhaps I can be granted a little more latitude than is conventional for an author since the subject of the book truly lived up to his reputation for slipperiness.

Milton Keynes UK
Ingram Content Group UK Ltd.
UKHW012247260224
438492UK00005B/263

9 781915 785350